Athenian Democracy: A Sourcebook

Bloomsbury Sources in Ancient History

The Bloomsbury Sources in Ancient History series presents a definitive collection of source material in translation, combined with expert contextual commentary and annotation to provide a comprehensive survey of each volume's subject. Material is drawn from literary, as well as epigraphic, legal and religious, sources. Aimed primarily at undergraduate students, the series will also be invaluable for researchers, and faculty devising and teaching courses.

Women in Ancient Rome, by Bonnie MacLachlan
Greek and Roman Sexualities: A Sourcebook, by Jennifer Larson

Athenian Democracy: A Sourcebook

Luca Asmonti

Bloomsbury Sources in Ancient History

BLOOMSBURY

LONDON • NEW DELHI • NEW YORK • SYDNEY

Bloomsbury Academic

An imprint of Bloomsbury Publishing Plc

50 Bedford Square	1385 Broadway
London	New York
WC1B 3DP	NY 10018
UK	USA

www.bloomsbury.com

Bloomsbury is a registered trade mark of Bloomsbury Publishing Plc

First published 2015

© Luca Asmonti 2015

British Library Cataloguing-in-Publication Data
A catalogue record for this book is available from the British Library.

ISBN: PB: 978-1-44111-371-9
HB: 978-0-82642-034-3
ePDF: 978-1-44116-531-2
ePub: 978-1-44114-776-9

Library of Congress Cataloging-in-Publication Data
Asmonti, Luca.
Athenian democracy : a sourcebook / Luca Asmonti.
pages cm.– (Bloomsbury sources in ancient history)
Includes bibliographical references and index.
ISBN 978-0-8264-2034-3 (hardback)– ISBN 978-1-4411-1371-9 (paperback)– ISBN 978-1-4411-6531-2 (ePDF)– ISBN 978-1-4411-4776-9 (ePub) 1. Democracy–Greece–Athens–History. 2. Greece–Politics and government–To 146 B.C. 3. Athens (Greece)–Politics and government. I. Title.
JC75.D36A76 2015
320.938'509014–dc23
2014017405

Typeset by Fakenham Prepress Solutions, Fakenham, Norfolk NR21 8NN
Printed and bound in India

Contents

Preface

The primary scope of this book is to introduce students of ancient history to the world of Athenian democracy and its continuing legacy in the Hellenistic and Roman ages.

The people of classical Athens considered their city to be like no other, and the democratic constitution the most extraordinary product of the uniqueness of the Athenian experience, whether they liked it or not. The Greek noun usually translated as 'constitution' is *politeia*. The term derives from the same stem of *polis*, or – not very appropriately – 'city-state', the most typical form of civic organization of the classical world. *Politeia* generally refers to the form of government of a *polis* and its political institutions, but can also indicate its members, the body of citizens, and the right to be one of its members, citizenship. The fact that the same word signified 'constitution' and 'citizenship' (meant both as civic/political rights and body of citizens) is very important for understanding the political mentality of the Greeks: in a society where political participation was not a universal right, but indeed the privilege of a minority, from which women and foreign residents were excluded, not to mention slaves, the set of rules and institutions that formed the *politeia*-constitution represented a vital element in defining the culture and identity of the *polis* community. This book will analyze Athenian democracy from this wider perspective: it will consider the evidence relating to the political activity within the *polis* as well as the other spheres of life to investigate how the development of a system of government based on public debate and collective decision-making, albeit confined to a tiny minority, contributed to the birth of a new kind of society and, indeed, of a new kind of man. This book will therefore present a very wide range of texts, from administrative documents to private letters, from legal speeches to epic poems.

All the translations are my own; the most common proper names and other words have been transliterated in their Latinized or Anglicized version. All the dates in this book are BC, unless otherwise stated.

This book is dedicated to my sister Silvia.

The University of Queensland, June 2014

Abbreviations

Ancient authors

Aes. — **Aeschines**
Ag. Tim — *Against Timarchus*

Aesch. — **Aeschylus**
Eum. — *Eumenides*
Supp. — *Suppliant Women*

And. — **Andocides**
Ag. Ctes. — *Against Ctesiphon*
Myst. — *On the Mysteries*

App. — **Appian**
Myth. — *The Mythridatic Wars*

Ar. — **Aristophanes**
Lys. — *Lysistrata*

Arist. — **Aristotle**
Ath. Const. — *Constitution of the Athenians*
Pol. — *Politics*

Ath. — **Athenaeus**
Deip. — *Deipnosophistae*

Cic. — **Cicero**
Att. — *Letters to Atticus*

Dem. — **Demosthenes**
Ag. Ev. Mnes. — *Against Evergus and Mnesibulus*
Ag. Lep. — *Against Leptines*
Ag. Nea. — *Against Neaera*
Ag. Tim. — *Against Timotheus*
Alex. — *On the Treaty with Alexander*

Answer Alex.	*Answer to Alexander*
Answer Phil.	*Answer to Philip*
Crown	*On the Crown*
Emb.	*On the False Embassy*
On. Org.	*On Organization*
Phil. III	*Third Philippic*
Rhod.	*For the Liberty of the Rhodians*
Diod.	**Diodorus Siculus**
Dion.	**Dionysius of Halicarnassus**
Hdt.	**Herodotus**
Hist. Aug.	***Historia Augusta***
Hom.	**Homer**
Il.	*Iliad*
Od.	*Odyssey*
Hyp.	**Hyperides**
Ag. Ath.	*Against Athenogenes*
Fun. Speech	*Funerary Speech*
Isoc.	**Isocrates**
Areop.	*Areopagiticus*
Hel.	*Helen*
Peace	*On the Peace*
Lyc.	**Lycurgus**
Ag. Leoc.	*Against Leocrates*
Lys.	**Lysias**
Ag. Nic.	*Against Nicomachus*
Aristoph.	*On the Property of Aristophanes*
Corr.	*Defence against a change of corruption*
Paus.	**Pausanias**
Pl.	**Plato**
Ap. Soc.	*Apology of Socrates*
Gor.	*Gorgias*
Hipp.	*Hipparchus*
Lett.	*Letters*

Plin.	**Pliny the Elder**
Nat. Hist.	*Natural History*
Plut.	**Plutarch**
Arist.	*Life of Aristides*
Demet.	*Life of Demetrius*
Per.	*Life of Pericles*
Sol.	*Life of Solon*
Sull.	*Life of Sulla*
Them.	*Life of Themistocles*
Thes.	*Life of Theseus*
Pol.	**Polybius**
Poll.	**Pollux**
PS. Ap.	**Pseudo-Apollodorus**
Ps. Xen.	**Pseudo Xenophon**
Ath. Const.	*Constitution of the Athenians*
Stob.	**Stobaeus**
Tac.	**Tacitus**
Or.	*Dialogue on Oratory*
Theoph.	**Theophrastus**
Char.	*Characters*
Thuc.	**Thucydides**
Xen.	**Xenophon**
Hell.	*Hellenica*
Sp. Const.	*Constitution of the Spartans*
Symp.	*Symposium*

Modern texts and collections

AAntHung	*Acta Antiqua Academiae Scientiarum Hungaricae*
ABSA	*The Annual of the British School at Athens*
AC	*L'Antiquité classique*

Agora Inv.	*Agora Inventory*
AgoraPicBk	*Excavations of the Athenian Agora Picture Book, Princeton, 1958–*
AH	*Ancient History*
AJA	*American Journal of Archaeology*
AJAH	*American Journal of Ancient History*
AncSoc	*Ancient Society*
AncW	*Ancient World*
APRS	*The American Political Science Review*
ATL	B. D. Meritt, H. T. Wade-Gery, M. F. McGregor, *The Athenian Tribute Lists*, Cambridge (MA) and Princeton, 1939–53
Benjamin	A. S. Benjamin, 'The altars of Hadrian in Athens and Hadrian's Panhellenic program', *Hesperia* 32 (1963), 57–86
Bergk	*Poetae lyrici graeci recensuit Theodorus Bergk*, Lipsiae, 1878–82
BICS	*Bulletin of the Institute of Classical Studies*
BSA	*The Annual of the British School at Athens*
CCC	*Civiltà classica e cristiana*
CIL	*Corpus Inscriptionum Latinarum*, Berlin, 1847–
CJ	*The Classical Journal*
ClAnt	*Classical Antiquity*
CQ	*The Classical Quarterly*
DHA	*Dialogues d'Historie Ancienne*
EMC	*Échos du monde classique*
FGH	F. Jacoby, *Die Fragmente der griechischen Historiker*, Berlin and Leiden, 1923–

Fornara	C. V. Fornara, *Translated Documents of Greece and Rome, Volume 1. Archaic Times to the End of the Peloponnesian War*, Cambridge, 1986
G&R	*Greece and Rome*
GHI	J. Rhodes and R. Osborne, *Greek Historical Inscriptions: 404–323*, Oxford, 2003
GRBS	*Greek Roman and Byzantine Studies*
Hansen	M. H. Hansen, *The Athenian Democracy in the Age of Demosthenes: Structures, Principles and Ideology*, Oxford and Cambridge, MA, 1991
HPTh	*History of Political Thought*
HSCP	*Harvard Studies in Classical Philology*
HT	*History Today*
IDRE	C. C. Petolescu, *Inscriptiones Daciae Romanae. Inscriptiones extra fines Daciae repertae*, Bucharest, 1996
IG	*Inscriptiones Graecae*, Berolini, 1873–
ILS	*Inscriptiones Latinae Selectae*, Berolini, 1892–1916
InscrAtt	*Inscriptiones Atticae*, Chicago, 1976
JHS	*The Journal of Hellenic Studies*
JNS	*Journal of Near Eastern Studies*
JP	*The Journal of Politics*
LexRetCant	*Lexicon Rhetoricum Cantabrigense*
M&L	R. Meiggs and D. Lewis, eds, *A Selection of Greek Historical Inscriptions to the End of the Fifth Century* BC, Oxford, 1969
MedArch	*Mediterranean Archaeology*
MHR	*Mediterranean Historical Review*
PCPhS	*Proceedings of the Cambridge Philological Society*

PRIA	*Proceedings of the Royal Irish Academy*
QUCC	*Quaderni urbinati di cultura classica*
RSQ	*Rhetoric Society Quarterly*
SCI	*Scripta Classica Israelitica*
SEG	*Supplementum Epigraphicum Graecum*
SMEA	*Studi micenei ed egeo-anatolici*
SyllClass	*Syllecta Classica*
TAPhA	*Transactions and Proceedings of the American Philological Association*
Tod I	M. N. Tod, *A Selection of Greek Historical Inscriptions*, vol. I, *To the End of the Fifth Century* BC, Oxford, 1946
Tod II	M. N. Tod, *A Selection of Greek Historical Inscriptions*, vol. II, *From 403 to 323 BC*, Oxford, 1948
YClS	*Yale Classical Studies*
ZPE	*Zeitschrift für Papyrologie und Epigraphik*

Introduction

1. The 'messy realities' of Athenian democracy

This anthology aims to offer an introduction to the culture and practice of democracy in ancient Athens. It is primarily aimed at undergraduate students in classics and ancient history, but will hopefully be useful to anybody interested in the history of democracy. The topic of ancient Athens is one which generally excites wonder and admiration. The mind immediately goes to the beautiful temples of the acropolis, the masterpieces of sculpture and literature, the achievements of science and philosophy. And then of course there was democracy. For Athens is generally hailed as the mother of all democracies, and for this reason it has been put on a kind of a pedestal. This is not the ideal situation to approach the study of Athenian democracy. In fact, it makes our understanding of it much more problematic, and one might even go so far as to say that, so far, we have been studying Athenian democracy for all the wrong reasons. To start with, Athens was not at all the place where democracy began. In fact, assembly-based governments were operating in the city-states of Mesopotamia at least since the third millennium BC. Also, if we were to judge it by modern standards, Athenian democracy could not be judged democratic at all. Full citizenship was confined to the sons of a legitimate Athenian father and mother. At the end of the 4th century the number of these privileged fully-fledged citizens was c. 30,000 out of a total population of 100,000. This figure excludes slaves, who might have been four times as many (Hansen, pp. 90–4). Most economic activities depended on slave labour, and slave trade was a very flourishing business in itself. Women were not entitled to take part in the political life of the city and were generally considered to be inferior, and the greatest honour, as Pericles puts it, came to those women who were the least talked about among men (Thuc. 2.45.2). Foreign residents had to be represented by an Athenian patron for legal purposes, and were required to pay a special tax, called *metoikion*, for the privilege of residing in the city. The Athenians did nothing to promote peace. In fact, they were a rather bellicose lot, constantly engaged in war with one enemy or another. The notion of 'democratic peace', i.e. the idea that democracies do not make war on each other, was totally unknown to them. The Athenians had no particular moral objections to waging war against fellow democracies when their disputes could not be settled in any other manner (Dem. *Rhod.* 17). To some extent, war and empire were necessary to support democracy. Athens reached the peak of its power in the decades between the end of the Persian Wars (490–478) and the outbreak of the fratricidal conflict with Sparta, the so-called Peloponnesian War (431–404). In those years Athens became the leading naval power of Greece, ruling over a web of subject cities and islands scattered all over the Aegean Sea. The Athenians were not enlightened masters, but ruled over their presumed allies like iron-fisted tyrants (Thuc. 2.63). The tribute paid by the allies for defensive purpose was channelled into the Athenian treasury and used to support that extraordinary building programme that gave us the Parthenon and all the other magnificent edifices of the city, and to pay for a quantity of more or less important public offices which were the main source of income for many Athenians. Democracy had quite a few critics in ancient Greece, who did not fail to point out the limits of that regime. To start with, political activity in Athens was incessant and sometimes chaotic. According to the anonymous author known as the Old Oligarch, the political calendar of the city was so dense that sometimes a magistrate could spend a whole year in office without ever being admitted before the assembly or the council ([Ps. Xen.] *Ath. Const.* 3.1). Politically, the behaviour of the Athenians was volatile and capricious, and they were notorious for their habit of taking hasty decisions that they would later deplore, often making individual officers pay for their mistakes. Then there is the matter of size. Athens was nothing but a small city-state covering the territory of Attica, a small peninsula of central-east Greece projecting into the Aegean Sea. Athens was in fact larger than most other Greek city-states. Yet its borders encompassed an area of approximately only 2500 square kilometres (965.3 square miles), roughly the same size as Derbyshire, or Pottawattamie County, Iowa.

A number of questions might arise at this point. What was really democratic about classical Athens, if anything? Why do we still give her a special place in the history of political culture? What, if anything, makes classical Athens different, exceptional and still worth studying? In the last years, scholars have approached the study of ancient Athens much more critically, questioning its towering position in the history of democracy. This debate only in part stems from our growing understanding of earlier civilizations. It is also the result of our changing perception of what democracy stands for in an age of growing uncertainty and epochal transformations, where 'Western culture' is becoming less and less dominant. In a controversial book published in 2004, Luciano Canfora criticized the idea that democracy originated in ancient Greece. The use of a 'Greco-classical stamp' to define the values of democracy was nothing but a 'falsification' (Canfora, pp. 7–20). Even more radically, political scientist John Keane wrote that democracy was in fact an 'import from afar', like gunpowder or print, whose seeds were first sown in the city states of Mesopotamia, around 3000 BC, then travelled east towards India, before landing on Western soil (Keane, pp. xi–xii). If anything, Keane seems to argue that the history of Athenian democracy is interesting exactly because it is very often anything but an edifying tale, because it reveals to us the 'messy realities' of democratization, and fortuitous and less than noble circumstances through which democracy often comes into being (Keane, pp. 4–5).

Keane is certainly right: the history of Athenian democracy has many murky and inglorious pages. What Keane fails to observe is that the ancient Athenians were arguably much more aware of that than we are. This might sound like a kind of paradox, but many of them considered the oligarchic constitution of Sparta to be the most perfect in the world. The Spartan constitution was particularly popular among the intellectuals. One of these pro-Spartan thinkers was Xenophon (431–355), a multi-talented historian, essayist and mercenary captain. Among his many accomplishments, Xenophon was the author of a laudatory *Constitution of the Spartans*, whose opening paragraphs run as follows (Xen. *Sp. Const.* 1.1–2):

> One day it came to my mind that Sparta, albeit one of the least densely populated cities in Greece, was still the most powerful and most renowned. So I began to wonder how this could have been, and once I turned my attention to the customs of the Spartans, I did not wonder any longer. I do marvel at Lycurgus, the man who set the laws by obeying which the Spartans became so prosperous, and I judge him to have been wise to the extreme. For Lycurgus made Sparta the most prosperous state in Greece not by imitating others, but by framing laws that were the opposite of those in place in most cities.

Lycurgus (the 'Wolf-worker') was Sparta's semi-legendary lawgiver. He was celebrated as the author of the so-called *Great Rhetra* ('Sayings'), the code of political, moral and educational norms that made up the constitution (*politeia*) of the Spartans. The bulk of the *Great Rhetra* was put together between the eighth and seventh centuries, at the time of Sparta's expansion into southern Peloponnese (Messenian Wars). This code would remain substantially unaltered at least until the end of the Peloponnesian War (404), when the victorious Spartans began to savour the corrupting power of wealth and imperialism. The fact that the body of the *Great Rhetra* was left untouched for so long was an essential element to its perceived perfection. The image of the Spartan constitution was that of a monolith, the gift of an extraordinary man inspired in his work by the oracle of Delphi. In the light of its divine germination, the *Rhetra* could not be criticized or modified, but just obeyed and worshipped. The *Great Rhetra* appeared to be ideally shaped to the needs of a self-sufficient *polis* community. It was impermeable to the influences of other cultures and to the vicissitudes of history.

The case of the Athenian *politeia* was radically different. Far from remaining unchanged throughout the centuries, the Athenian constitution was a constant work-in-progress. Athenian democracy did not come about overnight, nor was it the idea of one enlightened man, but it was engendered by the travails and the conflicts which made up the history of the city. It was the product of an endless series of changes and transformations, reflecting the dynamic and composite character of the city, and the travails of its history. The author of the *Athenaion Politeia* ('*The Constitution of the Athenians*'), a late fourth-century treatise traditionally attributed to Aristotle, calls these transformations *metabolai*, which means 'changes', 'reforms', or even 'revolutions' ([Arist.] *Ath. Const.* 41). The democratization of ancient Athens was a long and difficult journey, fuelled more by strife and fierce divisions than noble ideals. In fact, the 'leaders of the populace' who made Athens democratic were often moved by petty jealousies and personal rivalries. More often than not they were unable to foresee the long-term repercussions of their actions. Democratic Athens was no place for enlightened Lycurguses.

2. How the Athenian people ruled themselves 'to a bewildering degree'

The long journey to democracy began in the mists of time. Athens was born when Ion, the wandering son of Creusa and Apollo, settled in the territory of the city and divided its population into four tribes (Strabo, 8.7.1). This was the first *metabole* of the city. Back then, Athens was nothing but one of the many villages scattered throughout Attica. The second *metabole* was set in motion by the daring scheme of one man, Theseus, the mythical king of Athens who defied the Minotaur in Crete. Theseus, says Thucydides, had the intuition and authority to abolish all the pre-existing municipalities of Attica and merge them into one political community (Thuc. 2.15.2). This process was known as synoecism (from *syn*, 'together', and *oikos*, 'home': 'to share the same home'): the dwellers of all the villages of Attica were now citizens of Athens; the city had become the administrative and political centre of the new state. The people of classical Athens revered Theseus as the founder of their *polis*, and hence as the man who laid the path to democracy. When Cimon, the hero of the battle of Salamis, recovered the bones of Theseus on the island of Scyros and brought them back to Athens to give them an honourable burial, his grave immediately became a sanctuary for slaves, refugees and all those fleeing from the violence of power (Plut. *Thes.* 36.1–2, Paus. 1.15.4, see *infra*, item 6.c). Theseus' role as the father of democracy was immortalized in Euripides' *Suppliant Women*. Written at the time of the war against Sparta, the play tells the story of the mothers of the seven Argive warriors who had died fighting at the gates of Thebes and were still lying unburied. The scene is set at the temple of Demeter at Eleusis, north-west of Athens, where the Argive women had come as suppliants. Aethra, the mother of Theseus, praying with them. Adrastus, the king of Argos, pleads with Aethra to intercede with Theseus and persuade him to assist the Argives in the recovery of the seven bodies so that they may be buried. At first, the Athenian sovereign is dubious; Aethra tries to persuade him by appealing to the traditional mercy of the Athenians. Then Theseus decides to put the matter to popular vote. As he explains to his mother (ll. 346–53),

> This I'll do: I'll rescue the dead by means of persuasive words, or, failing that, the spear will settle the issue, and the gods won't hold ill-will to me for this. But I also need to obtain the approval of the whole city on the matter. This will be ensured merely by my wishing for it, but if I address the people in a speech I will have them better disposed. For I have made the people [*demos*] sovereign and set the city free by giving all the citizens equal right of vote.

Again, when a Theban messenger comes on stage bringing a message for the 'tyrant' of the city, Theseus makes it immediately clear who is really running it (ll. 403–8).

> Foreigner, you have given a false beginning to your speech by seeking a tyrant here. For this city is not ruled by one man, but is free. The people are sovereign here, ruling in succession year by year. No preference is granted to wealth, but the poor has an equal share with the rich.

The original government of Athens was a monarchy ruled by a *basileus* (king). As time went by, the constitution was turned into an oligarchy. The *basileus* was made to share power with a military magistrate called *polemarch* (literally the 'war-lord') and then with a college of *archontes* ('those who are at the head', 'magistrates'). Originally all these offices were held for life. The tenure was later limited to ten years and, by the early-6th century, to one year only. The big breakthrough of Athenian democracy came in the late 460s, when Ephialtes transferred the political and juridical powers of the college of the former *archontes*, the so-called Areopagus, to the city's assembly (*ekklesia*), the council (*boule*) and to the jury courts (*dikasteria*). Since then, the citizens of Athens governed themselves 'to a now bewildering degree' (Dunn, p. 18). The great experiment of Athenian democracy would be brought to an end only about 140 years after Ephialtes' reforms, when the Macedonian army took over Greece following the battle of Crannon (322). This was a remarkable achievement, particularly if one considers the very young age of most modern democracies, and the instability of many of them.

The Greek word *demokratia* is composed of two nouns, *demos*, which means 'people', and *kratos*, 'power'. *Demokratia* therefore was a regime where power rested with the people. *Demos* is in fact a rather ambiguous word, which might refer either to the whole citizen body of a *polis* or only to a part of it, i.e. the poor majority. According to the Old Oligarch, the whole point of Athenian democracy was to make the base and poor better off than the noble and wealthy (Ps. Xen. *Ath. Const.* 1.1, 4). Aristotle, who was no friend of democracy, had a more articulate view. Democracy is a form of government whose fundamental principle is liberty. By this principle, all citizens are called to govern and to be governed in turn, according to an equalitarian conception of justice based on number (*kat'arithmon*), and not on social worth (*kat'axian*; Arist. *Pol.* VI.1.6). To enforce this principle, it was necessary that the exercise of any magistracy was limited in time. In the course of its long history, the Athenian system of government went through a series of reforms and trans-formations; however, its main tenet remained in place up to the Macedonian occupation of Attica: the *demos* was sovereign and embodied in itself all the functions of legislative, executive and judicial power.

The history of archaic Athens was one of civic strife, parochial rivalries between clans from the different areas of Attica, social tensions between a tiny minority of rich families and a large majority of dispossessed. At the end of the 6th century, Cleisthenes, the scion of the noble family of the Alcmaeonids, became the leader of the popular faction and promoted a thorough reform of the government of the *polis*, which was meant to curtail local rivalries and to promote a common Athenian identity. To attain this Cleisthenes abolished the old four ethnic tribes (*phylai*) of the city, a new system based on residence. The territory of Attica was organized into 139 local districts known as *demes*. Each deme was assigned to one of three regions, the city, the coast and the rural inland. The *demes* of each region were then organized into ten smaller units, or *trittyes*. Each of the thirty *trittyes* was to constitute the 'third part' (hence the name) of the new ten tribes created by Cleisthenes, one from each region selected by lot. The new Cleisthenic *tribe* was the main administrative unit of democratic Athens.

Solon is credited with establishing the *boule*, the city's council, originally composed of four hundred members and then extended to five hundred following Cleisthenes' reforms. The members of the *boule* (*bouleutai*) were selected by lot every year. Each *deme* put forward a number of candidates from the lists of those who had applied to be considered for this service, and each tribe appointed fifty councilmen. Every Athenian citizen could serve on the *boule* twice in his lifetime, but not in consecutive years.

The Athenian calendar was divided into ten *prytaneiai*. Every year the group of councilmen of each tribe were to serve as the executive committee of the *boule* for one *prytaneia*. For this period they were known as *prytaneis*. Every day at sunset a lot was drawn to appoint the president of the *prytaneis* (*epistates ton prytaneon*), who remained in service for one night and one day. The *epistates ton prytaneon* held the seal of the *polis* and the keys to the sanctuaries where the treasuries were held ([Arist.] *Ath. Const.* 44.1). The *prytaneis* had to summon the council every day except on holidays. The main duty of the *boule* was to convene and prepare the *probouleuma*, that is the agenda for the meetings of the assembly. The meetings of the *boule* were held in the *bouleuterion* in the *agora*, while the *prytaneis* were housed in the *tholos*, a small round structure nearby the *bouleuterion*. One third of the *prytaneis* in charge were to be present at the *tholos* at any given time.

The *ekklesia* was the assembly of all citizens, and the sovereign institution of Athenian democracy. Its most important functions were to appoint magistrates, judge some political trials, discuss and pass decrees on matters of internal and foreign policy. All male adult citizens were entitled to attend after registering at the assembly register (*pinax ekklesiastikos*) of their deme. The meetings were usually held at the *pnyx*, a semi-circular rocky slope 400 metres southwest of the acropolis. The assemblymen sat directly on the stone, facing north toward the speaker's podium (*bema*). The *ekklesia* was summoned at least once a month, and meetings lasted from dawn to dusk. Any citizen was formally entitled to propose a decree or address the assembly.

The *dikasterion* was the people's court. It was composed of 6000 jurors selected by lot at the beginning of each year. All citizens over the age of 30 years were eligible to serve. The selected jurors were divided into ten sections composed by groups of 600 jurors from each tribe ([Arist.], *Ath. Const.* 68.1). Once appointed, the jurors had to swear the following oath (*heliastikos horkos*):

> I will cast my vote in accordance with the laws, and with the decrees of the assembly and of the council and if there is no law in accordance to what I consider most just, without sympathy or enmity. I will cast my vote only on the matters brought up in the charge and will listen impartially to the accusers and the defendants.

The resolutions of the courts had a decisive impact on the political life of the city. To start with, it was very common practice amongst Athenian politicians to fight their opponents by means of legal charges. In the second half of the 5th century, the courts were responsible for judging cases of *graphe paranomon* ('indictment for (proposing) illegal measures'). This procedure allowed any citizen to bring suit against a decree which was thought to be illegal or in contrast with the interests of the city. This meant that the court had the authority to overturn a deliberation of the assembly. The courts were also in charge of ascertaining the eligibility of newly appointed magistrates and other officers (*dokimasia* = 'scrutiny') and examining the accounts which they were required to render at the end of their mandate (*euthyna*).

Every year the Athenian *demos* appointed about 1100 magistrates, who dealt with a very wide range of military, religious, financial, administrative and judiciary duties (see Arist. *Pol.* 6.1.6). 30 years was the required age to serve in any of these offices. The Athenian magistrates were generally appointed by lot, but there were some important exceptions. The most important of these was the college of the ten *strategoi* ('generals'), who were the commanders-in-chief of the Athenian army. In the second half of the 5th century Pericles attained a dominant position in the city by serving in the board of *strategoi* almost uninterruptedly from 455 to his death in 429. In the last decades of the 4th century, other magistrates with important financial responsibilities were also elected by show of hands. These were the treasurer of military funds, the controllers of the so-called *theorikon* (a fund established in the mid-fourth century originally to assist poor citizens towards the admission to the theatre festivals of the city and later employed for a much wider range of purposes), and the superintendent of the city's water supply. These magistrates remained in office for a period of four years ([Arist.] *Ath. Const.* 43.1).

3. The limits of Athenian *demokratia*

This is the system through which the citizens of ancient Athens governed themselves 'to a bewildering degree'. The Athenian citizens seem to have applied the principle of equality to a degree unthinkable in our age. In principle, any citizen was entitled to speak before the assembly and to propose legislation on whatever matter, regardless of one's experience and expertise – or lack of it. Athenian democracy knew no formal executive power. There was no prime minister or cabinet. All magistrates and officers were appointed for a limited period of one year. Turnover was obviously very high, and the Athenians as a rule preferred to entrust important responsibilities to a college of magistrates rather than an individual. This also applied to military matters. Just to make one astonishing example, in the days of the campaign of Marathon, all the ten *strategoi* were serving on the field and rotated the command of the forces between them on a daily basis. How could this system work? The Athenian constitution had its fair share of critics both within and outside the city. For many of them the Athenians were simply obsessed with politics. As we have seen, according to the Old Oligarch political activity in Athens was incessant, and as a consequence of that the city was chaotic and unruly. ([Ps. Xen.] *Ath. Const.* 3.1). Athenian democracy was underpinned by contradictions, and the behaviour of the citizens was often volatile and capricious. They seemed to know that individual leadership was to some extent necessary, but at the same time were very wary of it. The most prominent orators of the *pnyx* could see their support quickly evaporate and turn into popular hatred. Generals were at risk of being charged with treason whenever they incurred in defeat. This is what happened to Miltiades, one of the heroes of Marathon. Just a few months after that glorious victory, Miltiades failed to seize the Persian outpost of Paros. A trial ensued at which Miltiades was found guilty of treason and sentenced to death. The great general eventually had his sentence converted to a fine; unfortunately he could not afford to pay it and ingloriously died in prison from the wounds sustained at Paros. In 406, following a victorious engagement with the Spartans at Arginusae, the Athenians sentenced to death the eight *strategoi* in charge of the operation, the cream of the city's military, because a storm had prevented them from recovering the body of the dead and shipwrecked after the battle.

These excesses aside, modern observers have pinpointed some important limits of the Athenian *demokratia*. A first problem is of course size. The Athenian system based on the direct democracy and amateurism could only function within the limited horizons of the *polis*. As brilliantly discussed by R. Dhal, this happened because Greek political culture was very exclusive, both internally and externally. Internally, because political rights were limited to a very small group of male citizens defined by kinship ties. Even in democratic Athens full citizenship was confined to the sons of a legitimate Athenian father and mother. Externally, because political rights were never conceived as a universal claim, but as an attribute of membership in one of these exclusive groups. As far as Athens was concerned, most citizens would have certainly agreed with Pericles that that 'in the settlement of their private disputes all men are equal before the law' (Thuc. 2.37.1), but this principle only applied within the borders of the *polis* (see Dahl, pp. 22–3).

This idea of exclusivity is very important to understanding what the Athenians and the other Greeks meant by *politeia*, the 'constitution' of a city. In the famous funeral speech delivered in honour of the Athenian soldiers fallen in the first year of the war against Sparta (429), Pericles celebrates Athens as the 'school' of Greece, and the democratic constitution as one of the most original achievements of this extraordinary city. The Athenian *politeia*, he says, 'is called democracy (*demokratia*) because power is in the hands of the many, not the few' (Thuc. 2.37). These words are much more ambiguous than they might appear at first reading. This ambiguity in part arises from that of the noun *demos*. Pericles uses the first-person plural to talk about democracy: *our* constitution. At the same time, he does not hide the fact that democracy benefits a part of the city, the many, and not another. As we have said, Pericles also celebrates the uniqueness of the Athenians' *politeia*, which does not imitate those of their neighbours, but is a model for others to follow. Why is this claim to constitutional originality so important? To answer this question, we should consider that the word *politeia* did not simply refer to the institutions, norms and procedures which made up the government system of a *polis*. According to Aristotle, the *polis* is first and foremost a community defined by its *politeia*. If the *politeia* changes, the *polis* inevitably becomes a different *polis* (Arist. *Pol.* 3.1.13). Isocrates goes so far as to say that the *politeia* is the 'soul' of a *polis* (Isoc. *Areop.* 14). To be member in a *polis* community, to hold a share in its *politeia* did not simply imply the exercise of political entitlements. To claim membership in a *politeia* was the mark of a specific cultural and social identity. By celebrating *demokratia*, therefore, Pericles did not intend to celebrate a universal ideal, or the values of liberty and equality which we now associate with democracy, but a uniquely Athenian experience. *Demokratia* was the product of the extraordinary history of this *polis* community. The Athenians were persuaded that their *polis* had stood apart from all the other cities of Greece since its earliest history. Attica was the only region of Greece never to experience immigration and invasions from outside, remaining always inhabited by the same people (*autochthony*, 1.2). Pericles does not fail to point this out in his funeral speech (Thuc. 2.36.1).

4. Why ancient Athens is still relevant: Democracy as a value and a struggle

In 1993/94, a great exhibition was held at the National Archives of Washington DC to celebrate the 2500th anniversary of Cleisthenes' reforms and the birth of Athenian democracy. Since then, many historians have questioned whether Athenian democracy is still something to celebrate. For the close-knit, unequal, exclusive society of ancient Athens cannot represent a model of governance for the diverse societies of today's world. Athenian democracy may not be something to celebrate, but this is exactly what makes it still very relevant: the Athenians were not presented with democracy by some god-inspired lawgiver, but built it through the vicissitudes and travails of their history. If, to the eyes of its admirers, the Spartan constitution was notable for its perfection, the Athenian *demokratia* was eminently imperfect and constantly called into question. A very important episode for understanding the attitude of the Athenian citizens took place in 413. Two years earlier, while the *polis* was still recovering from the first phase of the war against Sparta, the flamboyant Alcibiades persuaded them to embark upon the overambitious and extremely expensive project of a naval expedition to Sicily. Two years later the campaign ended in disaster after Sparta decided to send reinforcements to their Sicilian allies. When the Athenians were informed of the annihilation of their fleet, their first reaction was complete disbelief. Naturally their first reaction was to tear into the politicians, who made the easiest target of all. Then they turned against all the omen-mongers and soothsayers who had bamboozled the populace into voting for the expedition. Finally, scared as they were by the perspective of a combined attack from their enemies in Sicily and Greece, and of an all-out revolt of their allies, the Athenians realized that the time called for wiser decisions and efficient governance, and so they resolved to appoint a committee of ten men to revise the constitution and make it more efficient. This, says Thucydides, is the usual course with democracies (Thuc. 8.1).

Many of the defects of the Athenian demokratia emphasized by modern scholars are often still prevalent in modern democratic governments: women are still struggling for fuller political and social recognition, the growing diversity of our societies has called into question traditional forms of citizen and political involvement. In ancient Athens, like today, democracy was never taken for granted, nor should it be. At its best, it is dynamic and reflects the ever-changing face of society. But it is also constantly imperilled both from inside and outside. This is why in ancient Athens the exercise of democracy required responsible and enlightened citizens, as it still does now. This political conscience could only be acquired by engaging with the other members of the community, and by creating a lively public sphere. This is the other reason why it is still very important to confront ourselves with the history of Athenian democracy. The aim of this anthology is to allow students to gain a hands-on approach to the study of the democratic *politeia* of ancient Athens and to understand the influence of the culture and practice of democracy beyond the political sphere. This book will follow the development of the Athenian constitution from its origins to the Macedonian conquest and will consider the influence of the Athenian democratic legacy in the Hellenistic and Roman world. The first chapter will provide an introduction to this analysis by discussing the origins of the *polis* in archaic Greece and the theoretical discussion of the Greek city-state in Aristotle's *Politics*.

1

What Do We Mean By *Polis*?

1. *Polis*: A definition

In ancient Greece, the *polis* (city-state) was a community, a territory and a
political organization. According to Aristotle the *polis* is first and foremost a
'partnership' (*koinonia*): human beings are social animals, and are naturally
driven to form increasingly complex social groups to satisfy their increasingly
complex needs. The household (*oikia*) is the most elementary form of social
organization and serves the purpose of satisfying the most essential necessities:
to provide for the daily needs of its members and continue the species. The next
stage is for a group of households to form a *choma* ('village', 'settlement'), and
move together beyond daily survival. Freed from the urge to provide for their
elementary necessities, men were naturally driven to seek the means not only to
live, but to live well, and so began to merge groups of *chomai* to create larger and
more complex communities. The *polis* is therefore a community formed from a
group of pre-existing *chomai* with the purpose of improving the life standards
of its members. If all men, as Aristotle famously says, are political animals, the
Greeks have developed the natural instinct to live in society into an elaborate
science, and perhaps an art [a-c]. As the philosopher proudly states, the *polis*
was the quintessentially Greek form of political organization, as well as the most
perfect of them all. Just as the territory of Greece was conveniently located in a
milder, temperate region between Europe and Asia, the Greek nation combined
the sense of liberty of those living north of them and the intellectual disposition
of those living south. The *polis* was the most excellent product of this perfect
blend: a well-organized society where citizens could live in freedom [d].

If the *polis* is a community, the *politeia* is the set of norms regulating the life
of this community. Now, since not all residents of a *polis* are members of it at
the same degree, the most important norms of a *politeia* concern who is entitled
to be a citizen (*polites*) and to partake of the juridical and political functions

provided for by the *politeia* [e]. The study of the various *politeiai* of the Greek city-states was one of the most important activities of the Lyceum, the philosophical school of Aristotle. Unfortunately, the *Constitution of the Athenians* traditionally attributed to him is all that remains of this work. Drawing on this meticulous research, Aristotle devoted the final years of his life to the composition of a great treaty of political science (*Politika*, or *Politics*). Unlike Plato's *Republic*, this work does not set out to describe a utopian state. Instead, it aims to offer a comprehensive analysis of the different kinds of constitution operating in the Greek world. According to Aristotle, a well-organized *polis* should be neither too big nor too small in terms of both population and territory. It should have enough citizens to constitute a self-sufficient political community, and an efficient army. As a norm, the territory of a polis was made up of an urban centre (*asty*) and the depending countryside (*chora*). Ideally the size and morphology of the *polis* territory should make it easy to defend and difficult to attack. The *polis* should have easy access to the sea; the *asty* should be conveniently located to be easily accessible from all its regions and close to the harbour.

[a] Arist. *Pol.* 1.1.1: The *polis* is the supreme community

Every *polis* is a form of community and every community is established to achieve some good, because all men always act to obtain what they consider good. Since all communities aim at some good, it is clear that the community which aims at the supreme good is the one which is supreme and includes all of the others: this is the so-called *polis* or political community.

[b] Arist. *Pol.* 1.1.6–9: From the household to the *polis*; man as a political animal

The household is a partnership that comes together by nature for the satisfaction of daily needs [...]. The first form of community formed by a number of households not for the sake of daily needs is the village. The most natural form of village seems to have been that of a colony from a household, formed, as some people say, by 'sons and grandsons' who were 'suckled with the same milk'. Now, since the constituent parts of a *polis* were ruled by monarchs, the poleis were monarchies in origin, as barbarian nations still are. For the eldest member of a household ruled over it like a monarch, and the same happened in the colonies of the household because the inhabitants came from the same blood. As Homer says of the Cyclops,

Each one gives laws
To his sons and consorts.[1]

For the Cyclops lived dispersedly, as people did in ancient times. Likewise, people say that the gods are ruled by a monarch either because they are still so ruled, or used to be in the past. For people make up the forms of the gods to be like their own, and so do with their lives. The *polis* comes into existence when a number of villages come together in a single community which is completely or nearly self-sufficient. Therefore we might say that the polis originates to satisfy the basic needs of life and exists to achieve the good life. Equally, since the first forms of society exist by nature, so does the *polis*, because the *polis* is the end of all of them, and the nature of something is its end, because we call the end of something the form that it reaches when its development is complete, be it a man, a horse or a household. Furthermore, the final cause and end of each thing is the best, and self-sufficiency is an end and a supreme good. Hence it is clear that the *polis* exists by nature and that man is by nature a political animal. A man who does not belong to any polis by nature and not by an accident is either of inferior rank or in fact above humanity, like the man '*without relations, law or soul*'[2] disparaged by Homer. For the man who by nature does not belong to a polis is also a lover of war, he is like an isolated piece at draughts.

[c] Arist. *Pol.* 7.4.2–6.7: What the ideal *polis* must look like

In order to realize the best constitution it is necessary to provide the best equipment. Therefore we should presuppose the presence of certain ideal conditions, in relation for example to the size of the population and the territory, which however should not be impossible to attain. Just as a weaver or a shipwright, or any other craftsman, needs to be supplied with material in the ideal conditions for their trade (for the better this material has been prepared, the finer the product of their craft will necessarily be), so the statesman and the lawgiver should also be supplied with the material suitably prepared for their trade. The primary material for making a *polis* is population, its quantity and quality. Similarly, as concerns the territory one should consider its size and nature. Most people believe that a prosperous polis is a big one. Now, although this is true, these people ignore what makes a city big or small. For they judge a *polis* to be big in relation to the number of its inhabitants, while what they should really consider is its efficiency, not the size. For a *polis* has a task to perform, and the best *polis* is the one which performs this task best: the fact that someone is taller than Hippocrates does not make him a greater physician. And even assuming that a *polis* should be judged on the size of the population, the esteem should take into account not the undistinguished mass of its inhabitants (for in such a big *polis* there must necessarily be a considerable number of slaves, metics and foreigners), but only those who actually have a share in the *polis*, and are parts of it. A superior number of these men is a sign of the greatness of a *polis*, while a *polis* that fields an army of many petty craftsmen but few hoplites cannot be a great one. For one thing is a great *polis* and another is a crowded *polis*. Experience clearly demonstrates that it is difficult and perhaps impossible for a crowded *polis* to have good laws: if one looks at the cities considered to be well governed, they all have some limit to the size of the population. This is also demonstrated by theoretical evidence. For law is order, and good laws necessarily imply a good order, but what is unlimited and excessive cannot be kept in order if not by the divine power which keeps the universe together. Therefore, the *polis* where magnitude is combined with certain limits, as we have said, is necessarily the most beautiful. Beauty comes along with size and number, but there is a limit to the size of a *polis*, just like anything else, animals, plants, instruments. For all of these maintain their own efficiency when they are not too small or too big, but when they are too small they lose their genuine nature and when they are too big they no longer perform their job. For example, a ship a span long is not a ship at all, nor one which is two stadia long. Then there may be a ship of a certain size which is still a ship, but cannot sail either because it is either too small or too big. The same principle applies to cities. A *polis* with too small a population would not be self-sufficient, and a *polis* is supposed to be self-sufficient. On the other hand, a *polis* composed of too many people would be self-sufficient for its basic needs, but more in the manner of a tribal nation than a proper political community, because it would be impossible to give it a constitutional government: who will be the commander of its oversized army? Who will be the herald, if not someone with the voice of a Stentor?[3] It follows that a *polis* should consist at least of enough men to make it self-sufficient for the purpose of living a good life in compliance with the principles of a constitutional community. As we have said, it is possible also for a *polis* exceeding this limit to be greater, but only up to a limit. What this limit should be can be easily ascertained from experience: the affairs of a city are the affairs of the people who rule and the people who are ruled. The task of those who rule is to administer government and justice, and in order to judge the lawsuits and distribute the magistracies according to merit it is necessary that the citizens know each other. When this does not occur it follows that the administration of justice and the distribution of offices go wrong. To act unadvisedly in both these matters is unjust. This is especially evident in the *poleis* where the population is too large, and foreigners and metics are more likely to usurp the right of citizenship, because the excessive size of the population makes it easier to evade controls. Therefore, it is clear that a *polis* reaches the ideal size when it has the largest population which can be self-sufficient and taken in with one view.

This is what I had to say about the size of a *polis*.

The same considerations apply to its territory. As concerns its quality, everybody would certainly agree in approving of the territory which is most-self sufficing: this will be the one which offers the widest variety of produce, because self-sufficiency means to have everything at hand and to lack nothing. In terms of size and magnitude, a *polis* should be big enough to allow its inhabitants to live a life of liberal and temperate leisure.

The ideal configuration of the territory is easy to describe (but there are certain issues upon which one should consult the expert of military strategy): the territory should be difficult for the enemies to invade and easy for the inhabitants to march from.

What we have said about the size of the population also holds true for the size of the territory: it should be easily taken in with one view, for a city which can be easily seen is a city which can be easily defended.

As for the ideal site of the city, it should be conveniently placed in relation to both the sea and the countryside. One important principle is the one which we mentioned above: the city should be in communication to all the areas of the *polis* for the dispatch of military aid. The other is that the city should be easy to reach for the transport of agricultural produce, timber-wood and any other such goods which the land happens to supply.

It is often asked whether access to the sea is a good thing or not for a well governed *polis*. Some people say that a large presence of foreigners brought up under different laws is detrimental to good order, and so is a large population growing out of maritime trades, which is contrary to sensible government. However, it is not difficult to see that if these excesses are avoided, it is in the interest of security and the supply of the necessary goods that the city and the country have access to the sea. When it comes to war, the defenders of a country who are to be kept safe from the enemy should be easily defended by both land and sea, and even if they cannot attack by land and sea simultaneously, they would still cause damage on either element if they have access to both. Furthermore, a community needs to be able to import those goods which are not available in their territory and to export those of which they have a surplus. A *polis* should practise commerce for its own advantage, not for that of foreigners. There are cities that open up their markets to everybody for the sake of revenue, but a city which does not want to partake of this greed does not need a large commercial harbour. Now we see many countries and cities with a harbour conveniently located in proximity to the city, just outside of it, but not too far off, linked to it by walls and other such fortifications. It is therefore clear that if any benefit results from the connection between town and port, the *polis* will enjoy it. If it is an inconvenience, it will be easy to guard against it by means of laws regulating who should or should not mingle with one another.

On the matter of naval forces, it is obviously a good thing to have a fleet of a certain size, because a *polis* should be fearsome to its citizens as well as some of the neighbours, and capable of defending them by sea as well as by land. As for the number and size of this fleet, it should be commensurate to the way of life of the city. If it is a life of international relations and trades, the fleet should be in scale with this activity. It is however not necessary to increase the size of citizen body by including in it the crowd of the sailors, for these do not need to be citizens, because the marines are free and belong to the infantry, and it is they who take charge of and give orders to the sailors, and wherever there is a mass of villagers and dwellers present, there will always be an abundance of sailors. We can see examples of this still today. The city of Heraclaea for instance is small compared to other *poleis*, but it still able to man many triremes.

[d] Arist. *Pol.* 7.7.1–2 The Greeks and other nations

Having discussed above the right size of population, let us now consider what its character should be. Anybody can understand this by looking at the famous poleis of Greece and considering the distribution of races in the inhabited world. The races living in the cold regions and in Europe are full of spirit, but lacking in theoretical and practical intelligence. For this reason they live in relative freedom, but have no any political organization and so are unable to rule over their neighbours.

The nations of Asia on the other hand are of a speculative and skilful nature, but completely lacking in spirit: for this reason they live in a state of subjugation and slavery. As fort the nation of the Greeks, just as they live between these two, they partake of both their natures and are at the same time intelligent and full of spirit. For this reason, they live in freedom and under the best constitutions, and if the whole world were united under the same government, they would rule over it. Similar differences also exist between the different Greek nations: some of them are one-sided by nature, while others are made of a good blend of intelligence and high spirit. It is clear that the people whom the lawgiver will most easily lead towards virtue are those who are both intelligent and high-spirited.

[e] Arist. *Pol.* 3.1.2: Who is a citizen?

A constitution is a form of organization of the residents of a *polis*. The *polis* is a composite body, like any other thing which consists of a number of parts, and the parts that make up a polis are its citizens. Therefore we should first investigate who is a citizen, who is entitled to the title of citizen and what is the nature of a citizen. There is some discrepancy on this point, because someone who is a citizen in a democracy will often not be a citizen under an oligarchy. In this enquiry, we do not need to consider the number of those who acquire the title of citizen in extraordinary circumstances, like those who become citizens by adoption. Citizenship is not determined by residence in a given place, for metics and slaves also share residence with citizens. Citizenship is not determined by the capacity to sue and be sued under a certain legal system, for this right also belongs to the signatories of a commercial treaty, who are also entitled to bring or defend a legal action. Often metics do not have this entitlement, but are required to have a patron, and therefore do not have a full share in the citizenship. In fact, they are citizens in the same limited way as children who are too young to be enrolled in the draft register, or old men who have been discharged. These are citizens in a way, but not completely, because the former have the added qualification of 'under age', and the latter of 'superannuated', or some other title of that kind. Similar observations might also be raised and solved about citizens who have been disfranchised or exiled, but we have set out to define a citizen in the purest sense without need for any other specific qualifications. Now, a citizen pure and simple is defined by nothing but the right to participate in judicial functions and hold public offices.

2. Origins of *polis*: Homer

The poems which we now read as the *Iliad* and the *Odyssey* were put together in the early decades of the eighth century drawing on a long tradition of oral poetry celebrating the deeds of the mythical heroes who had fought at Troy. The two poems are the most precious source for studying the development of Greece's society and culture during the so-called Greek 'dark age'. This is the name traditionally attributed to the long period of apparent decline and silence in the Greek world between the collapse of the Mycenaean civilization and the earliest signs of Greek archaism (roughly 1100–800). The different uses and meanings of the noun *polis* in the two works reflect their composite and diachronic nature.

The noun *polis* probably stems from the Mycenaean *po-te-ri-jo*, 'stronghold', or 'citadel'. In one passage of the *Odyssey*, the term interestingly refers to the ancient palace-city of Cnossos [a]. The noun is occasionally used as a synonym of 'acropolis', to indicate the highest part of a city, that is the old seat of power, which had lost its social and political functions to become a purely religious space [b]. In the two poems, *polis* therefore indicates an urban space, and the circle of walls surrounding it. Communities and individuals are now identified by reference to their *polis*: Troy is the *polis* of Priamus and of the Trojans; Telemachus visits the courts of Greece in his search for his father Odysseus, and the question that regularly greets him is: 'where is your *polis* and who are your parents?' Nausicaa, as she takes the shipwrecked Odysseus to the palace of her father Alcinous, uses the term *polis* to designate a specific social space, opposed to that of the countryside: first she takes him through the fields, where farmers are working, but as they walk through the gates of the *polis*, a new world opens up before them; the polis is the space of public activities, trades, and the administration of the community [c].

The narrative of the Homeric poems is set in the declining phase of a legendary past, the age of godlike heroes, which only Nestor, the eldest of Agamemnon's companions, witnessed in its full flourishing (Hom., *Il.* 1.259–70). Some of the attributes of the Homeric heroes seem to refer to the Mycenaean world. For instance, Agamemnon, the leader of the Greek expedition, is dubbed *anax* (Hom., *Il.* 1.7), the term which in the Linear B tablets indicates the sovereign. Chariots are used in battle, as they were in the Mycenaean world, but the poet does not seem to know exactly how they were used, and so they are simply employed as a mean of transportation or at least to reach the battlefield. However, the world described by Homer, bears very little resemblance to the society emerging from the Linear B tablets and the archaeological evidence. Who are these 'heroes' then? As Moses Finley noted, in the *Odyssey* the word 'hero' acquires a peculiar social connotation: it indicates the whole aristocracy, and sometimes may also refer to all the free men. Achilles, Odysseus, and Agamemnon are first and foremost emblems of those distinctive virtues and abilities recognized as their own by the aristocratic clans of the various regions of the Greek world in the long centuries following the destruction of the Mycenaean palaces.

The world of Homer is a pre-political environment, still dominated by kinship links and the power of the clan, where authority over a group is not completely formalized and is easily challenged. Achilles calls into question the role of Agamemnon as the leader of the coalition of Greeks chiefs besieging Troy. When Odysseus returns to Ithaca after ten years of travels and troubles, he finds his home occupied by 108 men, the *proci*, who are suitors of his wife Penelope, and claimants to Ithaca's throne.

In Homer we can see an epochal transition take place: power moves from its safe sanctuary on the citadel-acropolis down to the most open and public of spaces: the *agora*, which is becoming the centre of the public life of the community. The city of Alcinous is a good example of this important transformation [d]. In the Homeric poems, kings often summon assemblies of their noble counsellors, or of the people. These assemblies have no formal consultative or deliberative function, if not that of letting the king 'how sentiment lay' regarding a specific matter. Yet, as observed by Moses Finley, the noble advisers of the king and the larger community have a right to be heard (Finley, pp. 78–80).

One of these assemblies is summoned to discuss the return of Odysseus to Ithaca. The proceedings do not appear to follow any formal protocol: in this society there are no written norms, Alcinous leads the community by virtue of his superior wisdom. His power is god-given. In the exercise of power he is assisted by a council of elderly advisers, called *basileis* ('kings'). Authority is in the hands of few, but it is exercised in the most public of spaces, the *agora*.

Two other *polis* scenes dominate the narrative of Book XVIII of the *Iliad*. This is an important turning-point of the poem, because Achilles, devastated by the death of his beloved Patroclus, is about to resume fighting, and his mother Thetis has had a new, stunning armour made for him by the divine Hephaestus.

The shield is a true masterpiece as sturdy in its construction as it is beautifully and ambitiously decorated. Its circular shape and vast dimensions make for a representation of the whole universe, an ideal image of what the Greeks called *kosmos*. At the centre of the scene there are two cities, one in war, besieged by a foreign army, and one in peace. Outside the city at war, the besieging army is holding a sort of war council, while on the walls of the city all those who are not fit to fight – women, children, and the elderly – are following the events. The city at peace is bustling with activity: the works of the fields, a wedding party, and an assembly being held in the *agora*. The council of the elderly has been called up to judge the case of two men, two litigants who are arguing over the compensation for the killing of a man. The elders sit in sacred circle, holding in their hands the stave of the herald as they spring up to give their judgement in turn, with geometrical precision, while the commoners gathered around them in the *agora* shout their support for either of the litigants. Homer calls the people *demos*.

Such involvement of the *demos* makes it necessary for authority to become more clearly identifiable and institutionalized, and to make its voice heard. Between the *demos* and the council thus stand the city's heralds, whose duties are those of maintaining order and passing the staff, symbol of authority, to each councillor as they give their judgment [e].

[a] Hom. *Od.* 19.178–9: Cnossus, *polis* of Minos

Cnossus is one of the cities of the Achaeans, the great city where Minos reigned when he was nine years old.

[b] Hom. *Il.* 4.514–16: *Polis* as acropolis

So spoke the fearsome god from the city, while the daughter of Zeus, the most glorious Athena Tritogeneia, advanced through the crowd of the Achaeans and spurred them to fight wherever she saw them being lukewarm.

[c] Hom. *Od.* 6.255–70: Odysseus and the city of the Phaeacians

Get up, stranger, and let's go to the city. I'll take you to the palace of my wise father. There, I tell you, we'll meet the noblest of the Phaeacians. This must be done, and you don't seem to lack understanding. While we pass through the country and the tilled fields of men, proceed swiftly with my maidens behind the chariot and the mule. I will lead the way. But then we'll come to the city encircled by high walls. A beautiful harbour lies on either side, the entrance to the city is narrow, curved ships are dragged along the road, for everyone there has a shed for his ship. There you'll see the *agora* with the beautiful temple of Poseidon at its centre, paved with enormous stones fitted in the ground. Here, they are busy with the halyards, ropes and sails of the black ships. Here they sharpen the oars.

[d] Hom. *Od.* 8.1 61: The assembly of the Phaeacians

As soon as the child of morning, rosy-fingered Dawn, appeared, the divine and mighty Alcinous rose from his couch, and so did the son of Zeus, Odysseus destroyer of cities. The divine and mighty Alcinous led the way to the assembly square of the Phaeacians, which had been built for them near the ships. When they arrived there, they sat side by side on the polished stones. Pallas Athena, who had taken the form of a herald of the wise Alcinous, went throughout the city, planning a return home for the great-hearted Odysseus. So she came up to each man, and said these words: 'Come hither, all you chiefs and advisers of the Phaeacians, come to the assembly and listen to this foreigner who has arrived at the palace of the wise Alcinous after long wandering about the sea. Indeed he resembles the immortal gods in his aspect.'

By speaking these words she raised the spirit and soul of each man. Immediately the square and the seats were all filled with the assemblymen. Many were astounded at the sight of the wise son of Laertes, for Athena had poured divine grace upon his head and shoulders, and made him taller and stouter to behold, so that he might win the friendship, esteem and reverence of all the Phaeacians, and succeed in the many trials which the Phaeacians had prepared for Odysseus.

When they were all gathered in the assembly square, Alcinous addressed them and said:

'Listen, chiefs and advisers of the Phaeacians, that I might say what my heart orders me to tell you. This stranger, I do not know who he is, has come to my palace, coming either from the men of the East or of the West. He wants an escort to take him home, and implores for a reassurance. Let us then arrange an escort promptly, as we have done in the past; for no man who comes to my house will ever remain long here in sorrow for want of an escort. So, let us draw a black ship into the bright sea, one that has never sailed before, and let us select Fifty-two young men from our people, those known to be the best. Then, when you have all securely fastened the oars each by his own bench, come ashore, proceed to my house and prepare for a banquet: I will attend appropriately to everyone. These are the dispositions which I give to the youth. As for you, sceptred kings, come to my beautiful residence and let us entertain our guest in the palace. Let nobody refuse. Let us go and call Demodocus, the divine bard. For the god has made him skilled in singing above all the others, bringing delight to the hearts whatever his soul prompts him to sing'.

So he spoke. Then he led the way, and the sceptred men followed him, while a herald was sent after the divine minstrel. Fifty-two chosen youths went to the shore of the barren sea according to Alcinous' orders. When they got there, they dragged a black ship into the deep sea, placed the mast and the sails in the black ship, installed the oars in the leather straps and then spread the white sail on the mast. Everything was in order. They moored the ship high in the roadstead, then they went to the vast palace of wise Alcinous. The porticoes, the hedges and the chambers were filled with the men who had gathered there. There were many of them, young and old. Alicinous made a sacrifice for them of twelve sheep and eight white-tusked boars and two oxen with rolling gait. These were flayed and dressed, and made for a magnificent banquet.

[e] Hom. *Il.* 18.478–608: The shield of Achilles

First he made a large and strong shield, and decorated it all over. He placed around it a splendid rim made up of three layers, and the baldric was made of silver. The shield had five layers, and the cunning hand of Hephaestus embellished it with many decorations. On this shield he engraved the earth, the sky, the seas, and the untiring sun. He engraved the full moon, and the constellations crowning the sky: the Pleiades, the Hyades, the strength of Orion, and the Bear, which men also call the Wain, always turning around in one place. The Bear watches Orion, and alone never partakes of the baths in the Ocean.

Hephaestus also engraved two beautiful cities of mortal men. In one city there were weddings and banquets taking place. They were guiding the virgins from their chambers throughout the city by the gleaming light of the torches, while the wedding song rose loud. Dancer boys were whirling at the sound of flutes and lyres, and the women were standing in awe in front of their doors. The people were gathered in the square, where a quarrel had arisen: for two men were arguing about the compensation for the killing of a man: one vowed that he had paid the compensation in full, and declared it to the people. The other said that he had not received anything. Both were eager to win the case on the judgment of a wise man. The people were applauding both, voicing their support for one or the other, while the heralds were keeping them back. The elders were seated on polished stones in a holy circle, holding in their hands the staffs of the loud-voiced heralds. Then they rose, and each in his turn gave their judgement. Two talents of gold were lying at the centre, to be given to the one who would give the fairest judgement

Two armies of men were encamped around the other city. The men gleamed in their armour, but were divided whether they should lay waste that fine city or to take half of the properties which it contained. However, the men of the besieged army were not ready to surrender yet, and were secretly arming themselves for an ambush. Their beloved wives and the speechless children were standing on guard upon the walls, and the men who could not go into the field owing to their old age were with them. The other men were moving forward with Ares and Pallas Athena, both made of gold, wearing golden garments. They were beautiful and majestic in their armours, as befitting two gods, while the men who followed them were smaller. Then they arrived at the place where they would lay the ambush, on a river, a watering-place for all animals. There they sat down, covered in fiery-looking bronze. At a distance from them sat two scouts, waiting till the sheep and the curved cows would appear. These soon arrived, and two shepherds were following them, playing on the flute. They knew nothing of the impending ruse. When the ambushers saw this, they ran upon them, quickly cut off the herds of cows and the beautiful flocks, and then killed the shepherds. The besieged army were sitting at the assembly when they heard noise coming from the cows. So they immediately rushed to their horses and ran after them and at once reached the place of the ambush. Once they got there, the two armies engaged battle by the banks of the river, throwing bronze spears at each other. Strife and Riot were among them. Destructive Death was also there, holding one man who had just been wounded, and another one who was unwounded. Another one, dead, she dragged by the heel through the tumult. The shoulders of her tunic were dark of the blood of mortal men. They joined battle with one another as mortal men, and fought, dragging away one another's dead.

He also engraved a soft, rich field. It was broad and fallow, and had been ploughed three times. There were many ploughmen, who were turning the drive of the yoke here and there. Every time that they reached the headland and turned the plough, a man would come over to offer them a cup of honey-sweet wine. Then they would turn back to the furrows, eager to come again to the headland. The land behind them was dark and really looked like it was being ploughed, because it was made of gold. The sight of it was astonishing indeed.

He also engraved a field of corn, where reapers were mowing, holding sharp sickles in their hands. Handfuls and handfuls of corn were falling upon the ground in rows, and the binders bound them with twisted bands of straw. There were three binders, and behind them young boys were gathering armfuls of corn. They were going to and fro, carrying the corn on their bent arms and bringing it to the binders. The master was standing in silence among them, holding the sceptre, and was glad in his heart. At some distance from them, the servants were preparing the meal under an oak. They had sacrificed an ox and were cutting him up, while the women were preparing the mid-day meal for the reapers: a porridge with plenty of white barley.

He also engraved a golden vineyard. It was beautiful and the vines were laden with grapes. The grapes were black, and the vines were held up by silver poles.

He also drew a dark ditch of cyanus and a fence of tin around it. There was only one path to the vineyard, by which the carriers went to gather the vintage. Maidens and young boys, full of fresh thoughts, were carrying the sweet fruit on twisted baskets. There was a boy among them, who played a sweet music with his lyre and sang the song of Linus with his young voice.

3. Origins of *polis*: The earliest uses of *polis* as 'political community'

The *Iliad* and *Odyssey* were composed in a period of great social and cultural transformations for the Greek world. These transformations were engendered by a general improvement of life conditions, which encouraged the Greeks to travel and engage with other cultures. Archaeological evidence reveals a profound change in the tastes and consumption habits throughout the Greek world, particularly among the elites. Inspired by the artifacts coming form Syria, Egypt and Phoenicia, Greek craftsmen began to develop a new style of pottery decorations. The old geometric motifs became obsolete, and were replaced by new, more vivid and naturalistic themes. Four centuries after the disappearance of the Linear B, the Greeks adopted the Phoenician alphabet and readapted it to the needs of their own language. The Greeks had begun to write again; the 'Dark Ages' were over.

The two cities depicted on the shield of Achilles are a very important document of the crucial transition between the old world of the 'dark ages' and the archaic age. The crowd gathered in the *agora* of the city at peace is not yet one of citizens, active members of the *polis*. They are still spectators of decisions taken by others, a body of superior and wiser men, sitting 'in holy circle' so as to set themselves apart from the rest of the community. Yet the *demos* strive to make their voice heard.

The tumultuous growth of the 8th and 7th centuries would undermine the basis of the established order: the steady increase of the population compelled many to seek for new land overseas; new cities were settled. The authority of the traditional nobility was called into question, and perceived as arbitrary, while the development of hoplite warfare changed the nature of how the Greeks fought: gone were the days when wars were decided by the clash between two super-human warriors, heroes like Hector and Achilles. The burden of fighting was now borne by the phalanx, the tight, disciplined formation of heavily armed soldiers, who wanted their role to be recognized and rewarded. The earliest written law codes were produced as a response to these tensions. Ambitious individuals, posing as advocates of the people, used their popular support to overthrow the established regime and established themselves as tyrants.

The two epigraphic texts which are presented here belong to the earliest group of documents where the word *demos* refers to an active political community, and the *polis* is an eminently political environment. The first document [a] is a decree from the town of Dreros, on the island of Crete. The document is dated to the second half of the seventh century, and contains norms meant to prevent the concentration of power at the hands of a single individual by limiting the tenure of the highest office of the city, that of *kosmos*, to one term every ten years. These restrictive norms were essential to enforce the democratic principle that all citizens have to rule and be ruled in turn, as stated by Aristotle (see *introduction*). The Athenians would take them particularly seriously. As we have seen, the vast majority of political magistracies could be held only once in a lifetime, with the exception of a handful of very important offices such as the *strategia*, while it was possible to serve for two terms in the boule, but not in consecutive years.

The second document [b] is taken from a fourth-century stele containing the text of a much earlier decree establishing the colony of Cyrene, one of the Greek *poleis* of Northern Africa. The colony of Cyrene was founded on the coast of Lybia in 630 by a group of settlers from Thera (modern Santorini). The operation of founding a colony had a strong political character. The colonists act as a political community: they constitute the assembly of the new *polis* and their first act is to define who is entitled to partake of citizenship in the new *polis* and in what terms. The new colony is a community of households, whose members enjoy political rights on an equal footing. This text is particularly interesting for observing the implications of the double meaning of *polis* as a territory and as a political community: the settlers might have fled their native city of Thera, but they are still a polis, and in the new city they will continue to enjoy the entitlements of *politeia* in liberty and equality as they did in Thera. If the expedition does not meet with success, the settlers are allowed to return to Thera, where they would enjoy full political and civic rights as they did before setting sail to Cyrene.

[a] Fornara 11 = M&L 2 = SEG XXVII.620: A decree from Dreros, Crete, 650–600

May the gods be kind. This is what the city has decided: when a man has held the office of *kosmos*, he shall not be *kosmos* again for ten years. If he becomes *kosmos* again, whatever deliberations he takes he shall owe the double, and he shall no longer be eligible for office for as long as he lives. Whatever deliberations he will take as *kosmos*, these will have no validity. The swearers are: the college of the *kosmoi*, the people and the twenty councillors of the city.

[b] SEG XXVIII.1565 = Fornara 18 = M&L 5: The colony of Cyrene

Decree of the Assembly: since Apollo spontaneously ordered Battos and the Therans to settle a colony in Cyrene, the Therans have decided to dispatch Battos to Libya as an archegetes and king, and the Therans to sail with him as his companions. They are to sail on fair and equal terms, arranged by households, one son to be chosen [from each family?] from those who are in the prime of life; and from the rest of Therans the free men [who so wish] may sail. If the settlers establish the colony, any of their kinsmen who sail later to Libya is to share in the citizenship and honours of Cyrene, and to be given a lot of unoccupied land. If they do not establish the settlement, and the Therans are not able to help them, and they are pressed by hardship for five years, let them return from the land without fear to Thera, to their own property and to partake of the citizenship. Any man who has been sent to the city but refuses to sail will be liable to the death penalty, and his property shall be made public; and whoever offers him hiding or protection, whether a father to his son, or a brother to his brother, shall be inflicted the same penalty as the person who is unwilling to sail.

2

The Birth of Athens and the Roots of Democracy

4. Basic elements of democracy

Book VI of Aristotle's *Politics* contains a discussion of the different kinds of oligarchic and popular government. Aristotle's idea of democracy might be seen as antithetical to that of aristocracy. According to the philosopher's definition (Arist. *Pol.* 3.5.2), in an aristocracy (*aristoi* = 'the best'; *kratos* = 'power') power belongs to a group of individuals of superior worth, as defined by birth (*genos*) or personal merit (*arete*), and not by any 'arbitrary standard' (*me pros hypothesin tina*). On the other hand, democracy is a form of government whose fundamental principle (*hypothesis*) is liberty. In a democracy political power is not an exclusive and permanent possession of a small group of citizens, or just one of them. Therefore, by this principle, all citizens are called to govern and to be governed in turn, according to an equalitarian conception of justice based on numbers, not worth. In order to give every citizen the opportunity to hold some measure of political power at some stage, the exercise of power ought to be limited in time and clearly regulated. Aristotle then gives a detailed account of the main features of a democratic *politeia*: the system is apparently designed to limit to the utmost the authority of individual magistrates and give the maximum of power to collegial institutions such as the assembly and the council. In principle, democracy is a constitution where all citizens rule and are ruled in turn, but in practice this principle translates into the rule of the poor (and ignorant) majority. Although Aristotle does not expressly criticize democracy, these pages clearly reveal his disapproval of this form of government.

Arist. *Pol.* 6.1.6-9: Principles and institutions of democracy

Liberty is the founding principle of a democracy: as is generally asserted, democracy is the only kind of constitution where all citizens partake of liberty, because, as they say, liberty is the end of democracy. Now, one of the elements of liberty is to rule and be ruled in turn, for the democratic notion of justice is based on numerical equality, not on merit. Since this is the prevailing notion of justice, it necessarily follows that in a democracy the people are sovereign, and the decisions of the majority are final and constitute justice, because, as they say, every citizen must have an equal share in the government. Consequently, in a democracy the poor are more powerful than the wealthy, because there are more of them, and any decision approved by the majority is sovereign. This is one of the elements of liberty, which democrats set down as an essential principle of this kind of constitution. Another one is that everyone should live as they please. This, as they say, is the objective of democracy, because the man who cannot live as he pleases is a slave. This is the second principle of democracy. Based on this principle there comes the claim that men should be ruled by no one, if possible and, if that is not possible, they should rule and ruled in turn. This is how this second principle contributes to equalitarian liberty.

These are the nature and fundamental principles of democracy. The following institutions of government are democratic in character: magistrates are appointed from all the citizens; all citizens rule over each citizen and each citizen over all in turn; all magistracies, or all which do not require particular experience or skill, are assigned by lot; there is no property qualification to hold public offices, or a very low one; no office can be held twice or more than a few times by the same person, or a limited number of offices with the exclusion of the military ones; offices have a limited tenure, all of them or as many as possible; all citizens exercise judicial power on all matters, or at least the most serious and important, such as the audit of official accounts or constitutional issues or private contract, and judges are selected by lot from all citizens; the assembly is sovereign over all matters, no individual magistrate is sovereign over any matter, or a very limited number; or else there is a council which is sovereign over the most important matters, for in those poleis where funding is insufficient to pay for all magistrates, the council is the most democratic institution, but where there is money to pay for all magistrates, the council is also deprived of its authority, because where there is plenty of pay, the people take all the trials to themselves [...]; also, pay is provided for all public offices, including the assembly, law-courts, and magistracies; if it is not, then for the magistracies, the law-courts, the council and the sovereign assembly, or for those magistracies whose holders are meant to sit at the common table. Furthermore, while oligarchy is defined by birth, wealth and education, democracy seems to be defined by the opposite of all these: low birth, indigence, ignorance. Under a democratic government, no magistracy is to be held for life; if any life magistracy has been left behind from a revolution which took place in ancient times, this is deprived of its power, and election by vote is replaced by lot.

5. Athens before the *polis*

The earliest source to call Athens a *polis* is the 'catalogue of the ships', a long section of the Book II of the *Iliad* (*ll.* 2.494–759) listing all the Greek contingents which had joined Agamemnon in the expedition against Troy. The Athenians are called 'the *demos* of Erechtheus' [a], the legendary sixth king of the city, and a double for Poseidon. Athena and Erechtheus-Poseidon were the central deities of the religion of archaic Athens, and were worshipped at the *kekropion*, a joint temple built on what was believed to be the site of the grave of Cecrops, the mythical founder king of the *polis*. This temple was destroyed in the course of the Persian invasion of Attica of 480, and later replaced by the Erechtheum. In the *Odyssey*, 'house of Erechtheus' is used to indicate the citadel/acropolis of Athens [b]. Cecrops was believed to have introduced civilized life in Attica and established the original twelve tribes of the archaic city. Strabo and the Pseudo Apollodorus give two interesting accounts of the stories surrounding Cepcrops, his settlement in Attica and the foundation of the original 12 tribes of Athens [c–d].

The Athenian contingent at Troy consisted of fifty ships. If we are to use this as a measure of how big Athens was compared to the other *poleis*, we should assume that it was a middle-sized *polis*, still quite smaller than the major centres of Peloponnese. Compared to other parts of Greece, such as Peloponnese, Attica was a scarcely fertile region. This was a problem, but one which, if we are to follow Thucydides, was essential to define the character and identity of the Athenian people. The historian says that in origin the peoples of Greece did not live in settled communities, but migrations were very frequent as each tribe moved where they would expect to find the most fertile land. Given the poverty of its soil, Attica was not subject to migrations from other areas of Greece. For this reason, Attica was the only country of Greece which never went through a change of population [e]. Therefore, he Athenians of the classical age were the direct descendants of the original inhabitants of Attica. In the fifth century the myth of the autochthony of the people of Attica would become an important of Athenian ideology and propaganda. The scarcity of tillable land, paired with the population growth fuelled by immigration from other, less peaceful areas of Greece, compelled many inhabitants of Attica to sail out and settle colonies on the shores of Asia Minor.

Originally the people of Attica lived in scattered, independent villages, whose reciprocal relations were often unfriendly. Athens was the most important of these villages, and enjoyed a sort of informal ascendancy over the others.

As we have seen, Theseus, the mythic tenth king of Athens, was the author of the synoecism of Attica [see 'Introduction'], the process whereby all the villages of Attica merged into one political community [f]. Thucydides says that Theseus' was the first synoecism of Attica. The second took place at the outbreak of the Peloponnesian War, when Pericles persuaded the Athenians who lived in the rural districts of Attica to move into the walls of the city. In fact, the historian seems to portray Theseus as a kind of Pericles *ante-litteram*: a leader who used his superior political and intellectual strength to enforce revolutionary measures which, albeit necessary, were bound to have very traumatic consequences on the lives of the people of Attica.

The synoecism transformed the landscape of Athens, which had to adapt itself to the new role of administrative and political capital of the new-born *polis*; this resulted in the citadel losing its political prerogatives, to become an exclusively religious space. The creation of the *polis* also engendered a new idea of citizenship. Thucydides observes that the synoecism was brought about without any notable movement of population from the *chora* to the *asty*. The people of Attica remained to live in their village, but were now citizens of Athens. Central power was now solid enough to exercise its authority without being immediately visible.

[a] Hom. *Il.* 2.546–56: Athenians at the war of Troy

There were the men who held the well-built citadel of Athens, the people of the great-hearted Erechtheus, who was brought up by Athena, the daughter of Zeus, after he was born of the heart, the giver of life. And the goddess settled him in Athens, her fertile shrine, where every year the Athenian youth offers him bulls and rams. Their commander was Menestheus, son of Petheus, the peerless marshal of chariots and shield-bearing warriors. Only Nestor could rival him, because he was the elder. Fifty black ships were with him.

[b] Hom. *Od.* 7.77–81: The Erechtheum as the citadel of Athens

So spoke gleaming-eyed Athena, and then she departed over the unresting sea, and left lovely Scheria. Then she came to Marathon and broad-walled Athens, and entered the solid house of Erechtheus.

[c] Ps. Ap. 3.14.1–2: Cecrops, first king of Attica, and the original twelve tribes of Athens

Cecrops, born from the earth, whose body was a combination of that of a man and a snake, was the first king of Attica. The original name of the country was Acte, but he renamed it Cecropia after himself. It is said that in those times the gods resolved to take possession of the cities in which each of them would be worshipped. Poseidon was the first to arrive in Attica, and with a strike of his trident in the centre of the acropolis he made appear a sea, which they now call Erechtheis. After Poseidon came Athena. She called on Cecrops to witness how she would claim possession of the city. So she planted an olive tree which can still be seen in the Pandrosium. When the two began to quarrel over the possession of the country, Zeus parted them and appointed judges to solve the matter. These judges were not Cecrops and Cranaus, as some people have said, but the twelve gods, and their verdict was that the land should belong to Athena, because Cecrops himself had witnessed that she was the first to have planted the olive tree. So Athena called the city Athens after herself, and Poseidon, angry in his heart, flooded the Triasian plain and put Attica under water.

Cecrops married Agraulos, the daughter of Actaius, and had a son called Erysichthon, who passed away childless. Cecrops also had three daughters, Agraulos, Herse, and Pandrosus.

[d] Strabo 9.1.18–20: Cecrops settles in Attica

Philochorus says that while Attica was being devastated at the same time by the Carians by sea and by land by the Boeotians, who were still called Aoninas, Cecrops for the first time settled the people of the country in twelve munici-palities, whose names were Cecropia, Tetrapolis, Epacria, Deceleia, Eleusis, Aphidna (also known as Aphidnae, in the plural), Thoricus, Brauron, Cytherus, Sphettus, Cephisia. Later on, as they say, Theseus united these twelve hamlets into one city, which is present-day Athens.

[e] Thuc. 1.2.5–6: Autochthony of the Athenians

Owing to the poverty of its land, Attica has been free form internal strife since the earliest times, and has always been inhabited by the same people, and here is a clear demonstration of what I say: these migrations prevented the other regions of Greece from growing as steadily as Athens. When the most powerful people of the other parts of Greece were driven out of their lands by war or civic strife, they all settled in Athens because they thought that it was a safe place to live. Once they became citizens, from the earliest times they increased the number of inhabitants and thus made Athens bigger. The territory of Attica then became too small to accommodate them all, and so the Athenians began to send out colonies to Ionia.

[f] Thuc. 2.15: Theseus and the synoecism of Attica

At the time of Cecrops and the earliest kings down to the reign of Theseus, Attica was divided in a number of independent townships. Each of these had its own council and magistracies, and as long as they were not exposed to any danger, they would not gather to hold joint councils with the king of Athens, but administered their communities and took their deliberations independently. Sometimes they even waged war against the king, as the Eleusinians did with Eumolpus against Erechtheus. Theseus, however, was a man who had wisdom and power on his side, and when he became king of Athens, he reorganized the territory of Attica in every respect and created the *polis* which exists now by abolishing all the councils and magistracies of the other municipalities. Theseus brought all the people of Attica in union and assigned to them one council and one town hall. While each continued to occupy his own land as before, Theseus compelled them to use Athens as their sole capital city. Athens then became great, because all the people of Attica were now paying their taxes to it. It was this great city that Theseus handed to his successors. From his time down to the present day, the Athenians have celebrated the public festival of *synoikia* in honour of the goddess.

Before the synoecism, the city of Athens consisted of what is now the Acropolis and the area at its foot towards the south. This is the proof: the sanctuaries of Athena and of the other gods are located on the acropolis, and the other sanctuaries which are outside the acropolis are located in that area of the city. These are the temples of Olympian Zeus, Pythian Apollo, Gea and Dionysius in Lymnae, in whose honour the older festival of the Dionysla were celebrated on the twelfth day of the month Anthesterion as the Ionians of Athenian ancestry still celebrate it nowadays. In that area of the city there are other ancient temples. Also, in those days people used to take the water for the most solemn ceremonies from the fountain now known as Enneacrunus, 'Nine Conduits', owing to the fashion given to it by the tyrants, and that in antiquity, when the springs were unearthed, was called Calliroe, because it is located nearby. Even now it is common practice to use the waters of that fountain for the rites preparatory to marriage and other religious rituals. As for the acropolis, the Athenians still refer to it as the *polis*, the 'the city', because in ancient times people used to live there.

6. Theseus the democratic icon

The citizens of classical Athens honoured Theseus as the founder of their nation. He was a national hero, and as such he came to embody the democratic virtues of the *polis*. The figure of Theseus was often used to promote and represent Athens in international contexts, such as the sanctuary of Apollo at Delphi [a]. The most important portrait of Theseus in Athens is that of the *stoa basileios*, the royal portico built in the fifth century on the north-west corner of the *agora*. King Theseus is represented standing alongside the personifications of *demos* and *demokratia* [b].

As the legend goes, Theseus spent his final days on the island of Sciros, where he had sought refuge after falling from grace with the Athenians. Theseus was assassinated by the local king Lycomedes, who threw him off a cliff. The body of Theseus was recovered by Cimon in 475, as Athens was beginning to build its naval empire in the aftermath of the victory against the Persians.

The procession that led the corpse of Theseus back to the heart of Athens became the occasion for celebrating the history of the *polis* and its present successes [c].

The deeds of his wandering and adventurous life, from his travels into the Underworld to the killing of the Minotaur, were reproduced on pottery and paintings, and inspired the work of the three great tragic playwrights of the city, Aeschylus, Sophocles and Euripides. Besides his more institutional image as the founder of the *polis* and, consequently, a forefather of democracy, Theseus was more informally celebrated as a friend of the people and the needy [d]. One of the defining characteristics of democracy was the use of public funds to support the poor, and in Aristophanes' *Frogs*, Heracles credits Theseus for introducing the *obolon*, which in this case is not the token to attend the dramatic festivals, but the coin which the dead carried in their mouth to pay Charon for the crossing of the Ades river [e].

The orators of classical Athens loved to borrow images and characters from the history of the city to give more authority to their arguments, and in their speeches the eulogy of Theseus is a particularly recurrent theme [f]. The most interesting of these eulogies is perhaps the one contained in Isocrates' *Helen*, where the deeds performed by Theseus are measured up against those of Heracles. Isocrates presents Theseus as a quintessentially Athenian hero, and a civilizer of the whole Greek world, who forestalled the later accomplishments of his hometown [g and h]. By turning the scattered villages of Attica into one political community, Theseus created a new civic mentality based on the principle of equality. The Athens of Theseus, however, is a kind of ideal *polis*, where the equalitarian spirit of democracy is tempered by the presence of an enlightened monarch. Under Theseus' leadership, as Isocrates says, the Athenian people became 'master of the constitution'. According to Diodorus, Theseus made the Athenians proud and ambitious, and eager to establish their hegemony over the Greek world [i]. On the other hand, the archetypal authoritarian depicted by Theophrastus criticizes Theseus because, as the man who first began to lay the path to democracy, he was ultimately responsible for the many ills of the city [j].

[a] Paus. 10.11.5–6: Theseus and the treasury of the Athenians at Delphi

The Thebans used the spoils of war to build a treasury at Delphi, and so did the Athenians. I cannot say whether the people of Cnidus built theirs to celebrate a victory or to display their prosperity, but the Theban treasury was built out of the spoils of the battle of Leuctra, and the Athenian treasury out of those taken from the army which landed with Datis at Marathon.

The people of Cleonae were afflicted by the plague, like the Athenians, and in compliance with an oracle from Delphi they sacrificed a male goat to the rising sun. This put an end to their woes, and so they sent a bronze male goat to the sanctuary of Apollo. The Syracusans have a treasury built with the spoils taken in the great Athenian disaster; the people of Potidaea built one in Thrace to show their devotion to the god. The Athenians built a portico out of the booty acquired in the war against the Peloponnesians and the other Greeks who were their allies. They also dedicated the figure-heads of the ships and some bronze shields. The epigram on these objects lists the cities from which the Athenians sent the first-fruits: those of the Elians and of the Spartans, then Sycion and Megara and Pellene in Achaia, Ambracia and Leucas and Corinth itself. The inscription also says that from the spoils taken in those naval battles they presented a sacrifice to Theseus and Poseidon.

[b] Paus. 1.3.3: Theseus, democracy and the people in the *agora* of Athens. Truth or myth?

Behind the statue of Zeus the Liberator there has been built a portico, decorated with paintings of the gods known as 'the Twelve'. On the opposite wall there are pictures of Theseus, Democracy and the People. The scene represents Theseus as the man who gave political equality to the Athenians. In fact, a number of stories had spread among the populace that Theseus was the man who put the people in charge of all matters, and the Athenians continued under democracy from his time until Pisistratus rose up and made himself tyrant. But there are many other false stories which the people hold for true, because they do not know anything about history and consider trustworthy whatever tales they have heard in the tragedies and choruses since childhood. Take Theseus: he was in fact a monarch, and after the death of Melanthus,[1] the descendants of Theseus continued to rule the city up to their fourth generation.

[c] Plut. *Thes.* 35.3–36.2: The death of Theseus. Centuries later, Cimon recovers the bones of Theseus

Theseus was overpowered by the demagogues and political factions. Despairing of the situation, he finally resolved to send his children to Euboea, to Elephenor, the son of Chalcodon. Theseus himself was at Gargettus, where there still is the so-called Araterion, 'the place of cursing', and after having invoked curses on the Athenians, he set sail to the island of Scyros, where, he thought, the people would be friendly to him, and where he had his ancestral home. At that time the king of Scyros was Lycomedes. Theseus therefore went to the king and asked him to be restored to his estates, for he intended to settle in there (some however say that he asked for his aid against the Athenians). But Lycomedes, either because he was afraid of the fame of that man, or to make a favour to Menestheus, took him to the high place of the land, as though he wanted to show him his lands from there, threw him from the cliffs, and killed him. Some however say that Theseus slipped and fell down as he was having a walk after dinner, as he used to do. At the time nobody reported of the death of Theseus. Menestheus, the king of Athens, was accompanying Elephenor in his expedition to Troy. The sons of Theseus had also joined in the campaign as private citizens. After Menestheus died there, they returned to Athens by themselves and recovered their reign.

In later times the Athenians turned to revere Theseus like a demi-god, especially because many of those who had fought at Marathon against the Persians thought they had seen an apparition of Theseus in arms rushing against the barbarians in front of them. After the end of the Persian Wars, under the archonship of Phaidon, the Athenians interrogated the Pyhtia, and were told to recover the bones of Theseus and to give them honourable burial in their city and to guard them there. But it was very difficult to localize his grave and collect the bones, owing to the harsh and hostile nature of the Dolopians, who then lived on the island of Scyros. Cimon, however, seized the island, as I have written in his *Life*, and, driven by the ambition of discovering the site of the grave of Theseus, saw an eagle on a hilly spot. The eagle was pecking, as they say, and tearing open the ground with its talons. Theseus, as though inspired by some divine revelation, began to dig. There he found a coffin containing a body of extraordinary size, a bronze spear lying by his side, and a sword. When Cimon brought the corpse to Athens on his trireme, the Athenians rejoiced and welcomed the spoils with a magnificent procession and offerings, as though Theseus himself was returning to the city. The corpse of Theseus now lies in the heart of the city, next to the gymnasium, and his grave is now a sanctuary for slaves on the run and every sort of disgraced men who are afraid of the powerful, because in the course of his life Theseus had always helped and assisted such people, and listened benevolently to the pleas of the needy.

[d] Plut. *Thes.* 24.1–3: Theseus the people's friend

After the death of Aegeus, Theseus envisioned a great and marvelous plan to unite all the inhabitants of Attica into one city, and make one people of those who had always lived scattered about the region and were difficult to call together for any common purpose. In fact, sometimes they quarrelled and moved war against one another. So Theseus visited every district, every village, and tried to win the people of Attica over his project. The ordinary people and the poor immediately answered his appeal. To the powerful, Theseus promised a constitution without a king and a democratic government where he would have served only as commander-in-chief in case of war and as custodian of the laws, while in all other matters equality would be granted to everyone. Some were easily persuaded, while others were afraid of his power, which was already great, and of his bold nature, and so they preferred to be persuaded than forced to give up to him. Theseus therefore abolished the local councils, assemblies and magistracies, then he established one common city-hall and senate-house for all the citizens in the place where the acropolis now stands, and called the city Athens and instituted the common Panathenaic festival.

[e] Ar. *Frogs* 138–43: Theseus introduced the obol

DIONYSUS: How will I get across?

HERACLES: In a little boat, just this big! A mariner, an old man, will take you over. Oh, and he'll take two obols for your fare.

D.: Gosh, these two obols are really powerful everywhere! How did they get there?

H.: Theseus introduced them. Then you'll see thousands of snakes and terrible beasts.

[f] [Dem.], *Ag. Nea.* 75: Theseus the founder of democracy

When Theseus made the synoecism and established democracy, the city became populous. Nevertheless, the people continued to elect a king, choosing him from a list of men renowned for their virtue.

[g] Isoc. *Hel.* 23–5: Comparison of Theseus and Heracles

This is the most splendid thing which I have to say about Theseus: he was a contemporary of Heracles and established himself a reputation to rival his. Indeed, not only did they wear similar armours: they both followed the same pursuits and performed deeds worthy of their common ancestry. Just as they were born the sons of two brothers, one of Zeus, the other of Poseidon, they also pursued kindred ambitions: they alone of all the men who have lived until these days have made themselves champions of human life. Heracles undertook more laborious deeds, which gained him greater applause, but what Theseus accomplished was more useful and more akin to the nature of the Greek people. For instance, Heracles for instance was ordered by Eurystheus to bring the cattle from Erytheia and to get the apples of the Hesperides, and to lead up Cerberus from Hades, and to perform other such deeds which brought no advantage to mankind, but great risk to himself. Theseus, on the other hand, was his own master, and favoured those enterprises, which would make him a benefactor of all the Greeks in general and his native land in particular. For instance, nobody dared to confront the bull let loose by Poseidon that was ravaging Attica, but Theseus singlehandedly subdued him, and so he freed the people of the city from great fear and despondency.

[h] Isoc. *Hel.* 34–5: Theseus brought order to Attica

What is more ominous than living in constant fear lest any passer-by might kill you, and dreading those who should protect you no less than those who want to harm you? Theseus despised all these men: he thought that these men were not rulers but a curse to their city, and showed how easy it is to have absolute power without being less happy than those who live in a regime of equality. To start with, he turned the scattered villages of Attica into one city, which he made so big that from his time up to the present day it has been the largest of Greece. Thereupon, he created a common fatherland and liberated the minds of his fellow-citizens, making them compete for distinction on a principle of equality. Theseus was confident that he would come out first in any case, whether they exercised their rights or neglected them, because he knew that the honours granted by high-minded people are sweeter than those granted by slaves. Theseus was so far from doing anything against the will of the citizens that he made the people masters of the constitution, and the Athenians not only thought that he should rule alone, but also considered Theseus ruling as a monarch to be more trustworthy and more just than democracy. Unlike all the other autocrats, Theseus did not impose all work upon the others while he alone enjoyed all pleasures, but he made the dangers his own, and the benefits common to all.

[i] Diod., 4.61.8-9: Theseus, democracy and the ambition of the Athenians

When Aegeus died, Theseus succeeded him as king. He ruled the people according to law and took many measures to make the city prosper. The most remarkable of his achievements was the unification of the demes, which were numerous and small, into the city of Athens. Indeed, from that time the Athenians became proud of the importance of their constitution and aimed at the leadership of the Greek world.

[j] Theoph. 26.4–6 (The Authoritarian): An anti-democrat who despises Theseus

At mid-day, the authoritarian leaves the house, his cloak gently thrown over the shoulder, the hair neatly cut, his fingernails impeccably trimmed, and, pompous like an actor of the tragedies, he start talking like this: 'all these sycophants have made life in this city impossible!' Or: 'Ah, the things we have to endure from the bribe-takers in the law courts!' And: 'I can't understand why people insist on meddling with politics', and 'how ungrateful the mob is: always after a hand-out or a bribe'. He gets all outraged when some poor grubby fellow sits next to him at the assembly, and there he goes: 'when, pray, are we going to be released from the lethal burden of the liturgies and trierarchies?' And again: 'Demagogues are a loathsome race!' He also adds that Theseus was the instigator of all the ills of the city, because he brought twelve cities together into one and abolished the monarchy. But in the end, he says, he got what deserved, because he was the first to be killed.

7. A brief history of the Athenian constitution

The *Constitution of the Athenians* attributed to Aristotle is divided into two parts. The first one outlines a history of the constitution from Ion's settlement in Attica down to the restoration of democracy after the overthrow of the Thirty Tyrants (403). In the second part, the author describes the organization of the Athenian government at the time of his writing. The historical section of the treaty concludes with a brief summary of the eleven *metabolai* ('changes', 'trans-formations' or even 'revolutions'), which punctuated the history of the Athenian *politeia*. The synoecism of Attica operated by Theseus is the second of these *metabolai*, marking the passage from tribal, pre-political forms of community, based on the informal ascendancy of local clans, to one based on an embryo of institutional order (*politeias taxin*). This is the moment when the political history of Athens and Attica really began.

[Arist.], *Ath. Const.* 41: A summary of Athenian constitutional history to the fall of the Thirty Tyrants

This was the eleventh reform undergone by the Athenian government. The first was the original division of Attica into four tribes, and the appointment of the first tribal kings, which occurred after Ion and his companions settled in the region. The second reform took place under Theseus: this was the first to imply some form of constitutional organization and modified slightly the monarchic ordainment of the city. Then came the reform of Draco, which gave Athens the first code of written laws. The third reform took place after the civic disturbance which occurred at the time of Solon, and marked the beginning of democracy. The fourth reform was the tyranny of Pisistratus. The fifth one was the constitution of Cleisthenes, which was enforced after the overthrow of the tyrants, and was more democratic than the constitution of Solon. The sixth reform came in the aftermath of the Persian Wars, under the leadership of the council of the Areopagus. After this, the seventh reform was set out by Aristides and brought to completion by Ephialtes with the dissolution of the council of the Areopagus. Under this regime, it so happened that the state committed many mistakes owing to the influence of the demagogues and of the dominion of the sea. The eighth reform was the regime of the Four Hundred, and the restoration of democracy after the fall of the regime was the ninth one. The tenth was the tyranny of the Thirty, then that of the Ten. The eleventh was the constitution established after the return of the men from Phyle and Piraeus. This is the constitution which is still in place. From that moment the power of the masses has constantly increased: the people have become the master of everything, all the decisions are taken by the assembly and the tribunals, where the people are sovereign; even the cases debated before the council have been transferred to the popular assembly. The Athenians seem to have acted wisely in this, because the few are more likely to be corrupted by riches and power than the many. The proposal to introduce a payment for those who attend the assembly was at first rejected, but since attendance at the meetings was low and the pritaneis were always devising tricks to gather the people and make them vote by raising of hands, Agyrrius first introduced a token of one obol, and after him Heracleides of Clazomenae, known as 'the King', raised it to two obols, then Agyrrius raised it again to three.

3

Two Lawgivers: Draco and Solon

8. The Athenian state after the synoecism

Sometime between 640 and 632, Cilon, a flamboyant aristocrat famous for his sporting victories at the Olympic Games, tried to seize the acropolis with the military assistance of his father-in-law Teagene, the tyrant of Megara [a]. This is the earliest recorded event of Athenian history. The rise of 'tyrants' in the *poleis* is one of the most significant traits of Greek history in the archaic age. Originally the term 'tyrant' did not have a pejorative connotation, but simply referred to an individual rising to power by his own means in contrast with the established order. Quite often tyrants gained prominence in periods of political crisis by posing as defenders of the poor and dispossessed among the citizens. Political instability was the inevitable consequence of rising social tensions within the *poleis*. Improving life conditions resulted in a rapid growth of population, and, consequently, in the demand for social and political reforms. The most pressing problem was that of land distribution among the citizens. The situation in Attica was very serious: the Aristotelian *Constitution* describes Athens in the 7th and 6th centuries as a kind of feudal state, where all the land was in the hands of a few families, and the rest of the population farmed it for a rent consisting of five sixths of the produce, keeping one sixth for themselves. For this reason the tenants were called *hectemoroi*, 'those who kept the sixth part [of the produce]'. When the *hectemoroi* were unable to pay their due, their creditors had the power to hold them in a state of self-bondage, and eventually sell them or use them as slaves in their estates.

In the second passage reported below [b], the author of the *Constitution* uses a very interesting expression to describe the political and social despondency of the Athenian poor: they did not partake in anything (*metechein*). They had no share in the management of the *polis*. Just as they were precluded from owning land, the Athenian poor were also barred from political representation:

all major offices were assigned according to birth and wealth, and so the *polis* was in the hands of the members of a very restricted group of noble and wealthy families. These social tensions often led to periods of intense civic strife, which our author calls *stasis*. In fact, sometimes *stasis* was so acute that it prevented the regular appointment of magistrates and officers, dragging the *polis* into anarchy. *Stasis* is one of the overarching themes in Greek history: as we have seen, our sources describe the *polis* as the product of a merger of pre-existing and sometimes conflicting communities. The *polis* therefore was by its own nature a complex and diverse organization, where social and political tensions and differences would inevitably emerge. *Stasis* naturally was a source of division and acrimony within the city, but was also essential for stimulating social reforms and innovative political solutions such as the written codes of law devised by Draco and Solon. However, these did not come about overnight, but were the result of an incessant process of political transformations and reforms which had been going on since the birth of the *polis*.

If we are to follow the *Constitution of the Athenians*, the original form of government of the city was a monarchy. This is also the most elementary form of political order which a community can give to itself. As time went by, the prerogatives of monarchy were progressively eroded, and power was exercised by an ever wider number of officials, and for an ever shorter period of time, until all the major magistracies became annual. Although the Athenian constitution was still very far from being a democracy, the assumption that political power ought to be exercised on a temporary and collegiate basis was an essential premise to the successive developments of the Athenian *politeia*. In the second part of the passage the author gives an outline of the birth and original duties of the nine most important magistracies (*archontai*) of the archaic constitution. The collective name *archontes* referred to the holders of these important offices. The singular *archon* indicated the supreme magistrate. With the transition to democracy, these magistracies were not abolished. However, their role became largely ceremonial as most of their powers were taken over by the assembly, the council and the law-courts, or by other magistrates such as the generals. Every year of the Athenian calendar was called after the *archon* in office.

[a] Hdt. 5.71: Cilon tries to seize the acropolis

There was this man in Athens, called Cilon, who had been winner at Olympia. Now, this Cilon gave himself the airs of one who wanted to become a tyrant. So he gathered a band of men of his own age and tried to seize the acropolis.

Since they could not succeed, Cilon and his men took sanctuary by the statue of Athena. The group of suppliants were then removed from their position by the presidents of the naval board, for they were the rulers of Athens at that time. Cimon and his men were subject to any penalty except death, nevertheless they were slain, and the house of the Alcmaeonids were accused of their death. All these events occurred before the time of Pisistratus.

[b] [Arist.] *Ath. Const.* 2–3: Civic strife in the archaic age, Athenian government before Draco

After these events, the notables and the populace remained at loggerheads for a long time. This happened because the constitution was oligarchic in every respect and the people of the poorer classes, men, women and children, were enslaved to the wealthy. They were called *pelatae* and *hectemoroi* because they cultivated the lands of the rich upon payment of a rent (for all the land belonged to a handful of men), and if the tenants failed to pay the rent, then they and their children with them were liable to arrest. In those times all loans were secured upon the debtor's person, and this would remain common practice up to the time of Solon, who was the first to champion the people. So, the most grievous and intolerable aspect of the constitution of the time for the populace was their state of serfdom, but they were annoyed with everything else as well, because they had no share in anything at all.

This is how the ancient constitution was organized before the reforms of Draco. Magistrates were appointed according to birth and wealth. Originally these magistrates held office for life, and later for a period of ten years. The oldest and most important magistracies were those of the king, the polemarch, and the archon. The office of the king is the oldest, for it was established in ancestral times. The second oldest is the office of the polemearch. This magistracy was established because some of the kings had behaved cowardly in war. In fact, this is the reason why the Athenians called Ion to their aid. The most recent of the three offices is that of the archon. Most authors say that it was introduced under Medon, while others ascribe it to the time of Acastus. As a proof they cite the fact that the nine archons still swear to perform their oaths 'as in the days of Acastus'. Therefore, they say, it was in his time that the house of Codrus withdrew from the kingship in return for the privileges attached to the office of archon. Whichever version is true, it would make little difference for the chronology of events. And here is another proof that the archonship was the last of the three offices to be introduced: the archon, unlike the king and the polemarch, is not in charge of any of the ancestral rites, but only performs duties which were added at a later time. This is also the reason why the archonship became a powerful office only recently, as a consequence of its added responsibilities. The *thesmotetai*, or legislators, were elected many years later, when magistrates were already appointed on a yearly basis. This new office was created to keep public records of the deliberations and to safeguard them for the trial of litigants. For this reason the archonship is the only office which has never been tenable for longer than one year.

This is the order in which the various offices were introduced. The nine archons did not reside together, but the king occupied the place which is now called Bucolium, near the prytaneium, as shown by the fact that the ceremony of the union and marriage of the king's wife and Dionysus still takes place there; the archon had the prytaneium, and the polemarch the Epilyceum (this place used to be called polemarch's house, but since Epilycus refurbished it when he was appointed polemarch, it was renamed after him) and the thesmothetai had the Thesmotheteium. At the time of Solon, however, all these magistrates assembled at the Thesmotheteium. They also had the authority to give final judgment in lawsuits, and not just to conduct preliminary examinations, as they do now. These were the norms concerning the supreme magistracies. The institutional role of the council of Areopagus was that of preserving the laws, but in fact the council was in charge of the most numerous and most important affairs of the *polis*, and had the authority to inflict penalties and fines upon the offenders without appeal. The archons were elected according to birth and wealth, and the members of the Areopagus were appointed from them. For this reason, this is the only office to have remained tenable for life up to this day.

9. Draco and the Athenian constitution

The period of Greek history between the end of the so-called 'middle ages' and the Persian Wars goes by the name of 'archaic age'. This was a phase of tumultuous growth and radical changes all over the Greek world. Social and political tension in the cities led to the establishment of tyrannies, while the demand for a fairer and more accountable government inspired the creation of the earliest written codes of law. Tightly linked to these social and political innovations was the development of a new form of warfare, based on the deployment of heavy-armed infantrymen fighting in close ranks. The armoury of these infantrymen consisted in a helmet, bronze panoply, a large double-gripped circular shield and long spear. The signature piece of their equipment was the shield (*hoplon*), after which they were called hoplites. The emergence of hoplite warfare is often associated with the development of a new ethics of patriotic sacrifice, discipline and defence of the common good, which would inspire the values of the classical *polis*, and the rise of the 'middling' sections of the citizen body, which would give momentum to the process of social and political reforms.

The archaic age was also a time of travels, encounters and discoveries. Colonists from the most dynamic areas of the Greek world such as Euboea and Peloponnese took to the sea and created new Greek settlements from the Black Sea to the shores of Spain. These colonies were fertile ground for political and cultural experimentation: for instance, the first Greek written law code is said to have been produced by Zaleucus in the Italian city of Locris. According to Aristotle, Zaleucus was a pupil of the philosopher Thales and was himself the teacher of another renowned lawgiver, Charondas of Catana, in Sicily (Arist. *Pol.* 2.9.5–6).

The first written law code of Athens was drawn up in 621 by Draco. Very little is known about him and his legislation. According to the so-called Suda lexicon, a massive encyclopaedia written in Byzantium in the 10th century AD, Draco was a kind of professional travelling lawgiver-poet, who authored the law code of his native Athens as well as that of other cities such as Aegina [a]. As for his laws, all we can say is that they were severe in the extreme. Most of the Draconian legislation was later abolished by Solon, the second great lawgiver of Athens, with the sole exception of the norms concerning murder. These were the first to distinguish between voluntary and involuntary homicide [b]. The content of Draco's laws on homicide is known from a stele dated to the year 409/408. The need to collect and republish Draco's laws, as well as all others then in force, had arisen in 410, following the fall of the oligarchy and the restoration of democracy. To complete this task the Athenians appointed a special commission of *anagrapheis* ('recorders', or 'inscribers'), whose job would come to completion only in 399 [c].

The evidence on the other enactments of Draco is extremely scanty. The author of the *Constitution* says that the laws of Draco were the second *metabole* of the Athenian *politeia*, that is the first important reform after the synoecism of the polis. On the other hand, Aristotle in the *Politics* says that he did little if anything more than ratifying the constitution which was already in place [d]. The author of the *Constitution* also says that, by the time Draco wrote his laws, citizenship had already been extended to all those who 'could afford to bear arms', i.e. to serve as hoplites in the *polis*' army: these citizens had the right to elect the magistrates and could be balloted for one of the four hundred seats of the newly created council (*boule*), or for a number of minor offices. The *politeia* of Draco was timocratic in nature. Access to the most important magistracies was based on income, and the vast majority of citizens were therefore excluded from them [e].

Draco, as Aristotle suggests, might have simply codified a system already in place, but the act of writing down and displaying in public the laws of the city was revolutionary in itself. Political power should not be exercised arbitrarily, but had to comply with a series of norms which were public, clear, objective and, at least in theory, applied indifferently to all the members of the community.

In the absence of other reliable evidence, we cannot tell for certain whether all the reforms which the *Constitution* attributes to Draco were actually carried out by him, or were rather enforced at a later stage. For instance, there are certain aspects of this constitution attributed to Draco which would later become key features of Athenian democracy, such as the assumption that all citizens should rule and be ruled in turn, and the selection by lot of the members of the *boule*. It is however interesting to observe how our author clearly links the emergence of the Athenian hoplite classes (the hoplite body and the citizen body coincide) and the call for a fairer and clearer organization of power.

Following Draco's reforms, Athens remained in the hands of an entrenched minority of noble and wealthy; debt slavery was still in place and the aristocratic council of the Areopagus, held de facto control over the laws of the city. This situation would soon be conducive to another period of *stasis*.

[a] *Suda* 1495: Life and deeds of Draco

Draco, Athenian lawgiver. He travelled to Aegina to establish a code of law for that city. The Aeginetans honoured him in their city's theatre, but threw so many hats, vests and cloaks upon his head that he suffocated and was buried in that very theatre. He lived at the time of the Seven Wise Men, or rather was slightly older. At any rate, in the year of the XXXIX Olympiad, Draco, already an old man, set up the laws of the Athenians. He wrote his *Precepts* in three hundred verses.

[b] Plut. *Sol.* 17: Solon abolishes the laws of Draco

The first act of Solon was to abolish the laws of Draco, except for those concerning homicide, because they were too cruel and their punishments too severe. In fact, the laws of Draco assigned one penalty to almost all crimes: capital punishment, so much so that even those guilty of idleness were sentenced to death, and those who had stolen some vegetables or fruits received the same punishment as the criminals guilty of sacrilege or murder. Later on, Demades gained much credit when he said that Draco's laws were written with blood, not ink. Draco himself, as they say, when he was asked why he had assigned the death penalty for most crimes, answered that capital punishment was in his opinion an adequate penalty for the smaller crimes, but he could not find a heavier punishment for the more serious ones.

[c] IG I³ 104 = Fornara 15b = SEG XXCIII.10, XXIX.15, XXX.15, XXXI.17, XXXII.14, XXXIII.15: Draco's laws on homicide

Secretary: Diognetos of Phrearrhos; archon: Diocles.

Decree of the council and the assembly.

Tribe holding the pritany: Acamantis. Secretary: Diogenetus. President: Euthydicus

Motion proposed by: [?]

The recorders of the laws (*anagrapheis*) jointly with the Secretary of the *boule*, shall have the law of Draco on homicide inscribed on a marble stele, after they received it from the King Archon, and the stele shall be erected in front of the Stoa Basileus. The treasurers shall let the contract according to the law. The money shall be provided by the Hellenotamiai.

First Axon. When someone kills someone even without premeditation, the culprit shall be exiled. The Kings shall judge him guilty of homicide either [*unreadable words*] ... or the man who plotted the death. The Ephetai shall give the verdict.

Pardon may be granted if the father of the victim is alive, or brothers, or sons, by all of them in agreement, but if there is one opposing it his opinion shall prevail. If none of these is alive, then pardon may be granted by the male relatives as far as the degree of cousin or cousin's son, provided that they are all willing to grant pardon. If there is one opposing it his opinion shall prevail. If none of these relatives is alive, and the murder was involuntary, and judgement is passed by the Fifty-One and the Ephetai that it was involuntary homicide, then the man may be readmitted into the country by ten members of his phratry, if they wish. These men will be selected by the Fifty-One according to their rank. Those who have committed homicide prior to this time shall also be bound to this ordinance. The relatives of the victim as far as the degree of cousin's son and cousin will make a proclamation against the homicide in the agora. The man responsible for homicide will be prosecuted jointly by the victim's cousins, [sons of cousins, sons-in-law, fathers-in-law] and members of his phratry.

[…]

And if a man is repelled and killed as he is caught in the act of stealing one's property by force, there shall be no recompense for his death […].

[d] Arist. *Pol.* 2.9.9: Draco and the existing constitution

Draco laid down his laws upon a constitution which was already in place, and there is nothing distinct or memorable in them except the severity and harshness of the punishments.

[e] [Arist.] *Ath. Const.* 4: The Athenian constitution at the time of Draco

Some time after these events, in the archonship of Aristaechmus, Draco laid down his laws. The constitution was ordained in the following manner: citizenship had already been extended to those who could afford to bear arms. These elected the nine archons and the treasurers from those who owned unencumbered property worth at least ten minae; the other minor offices from those who bore arms; the generals and masters of the cavalry from those who could prove possession of a property of at least 100 minae and sons of at least ten years of age who were born from a legitimate marriage. Incoming magistrates had to bail the outgoing prytans, generals and masters of the cavalry until the audit upon receipt of four sureties from the same class as the one to which the generals and the masters of cavalry belonged.

There was also a council, consisting of four hundred and one members, drawn by lot from the citizen body. This and other offices were drawn by lot from the citizens over thirty years of age. No citizen could hold office twice before all the others got their turn to serve, at which point lots were to be cast again afresh. The council of the Areopagus was guardian of the laws and ensured that magistrates acted in compliance with the laws. Anyone who had been unjustly treated had the right to submit a complaint to the council of the Areopagus, provided he was able to state according to which he had been injured. Loans were guaranteed on the person, as we have said, and all the land belonged to a few men.

10. Solon's reforms: Blueprint to democracy

Draco's reforms might have contributed to giving a more institutional structure to the Athenian *politeia*, but they failed to give political and social stability to the city.

Debt slavery and the unequal distribution of land were still a cause of serious social tensions; the city was still marred by *stasis*. The process of integration of the districts of Attica was faltering; the polis was divided between local clans contending for power: the *diakroi*, the inhabitants of the hilly inland of Attica, supported radical policies; the *pedieis*, the men of the lowlands, favoured oligarchy, and the *paralioi*, the citizens of the shore districts, wanted a mixed form of constitution.

This was the climate in the city when, in 594 or 591, the Athenians elected Solon to the archonship. Solon was the scion of an impoverished house of the Athenian nobility, whom the citizens knew for his morality and patriotism. He first rose to prominence as a young man, when he led a campaign to recover the island of Salamis from the Megarians. At a time of deep divide and factional strife, Solon stood out as an unbiased and respected personality, who had not been involved in the party strife [a]. The new archon had ambitious plans. Solon saw himself as an impartial umpire whose task was to restore *dike*, justice among the Athenians [b-e]. *Dike* was to be restored by means of a comprehensive revision of the *politeia*. Solon called the inspiring principle of this work *eunomia*, 'good government' (*eu* 'well', *nomos* 'law').

If the *polis* aimed to be a thriving community of hoplite-landowners, the most urgent reforms were the abolition of debt slavery and a fairer distribution of land.

Solon, as we have seen, abolished all the laws of Draco, with the exception of those on homicide. The content of Solon's legislation is known only superficially, but what we know for certain is that he wanted to give them the highest degree of publicity. The new norms were inscribed on revolving wooden panels, the so-called *kyrbeis*, and displayed in the *stoa basileos*, the 'royal portico', in the north-western corner of the *agora*. The new laws were to remain in force for a period of one hundred years [f].

The most important reform attributed to Solon is a reorganization of the traditional property classes. His aim was to increase participation in the political life of the city. The Athenian citizenry were divided into four classes according to wealth as measured in cereal production: the wealthiest group was that of the *pentakosiomedimnoi* (citizens whose estate produced at least 500 measures of grain); the second was that of *hippeis*, or 'knights' (300 to 500 measures); then came the *zeugitai*, i.e. those who could afford a *zeukos*, a 'yoke' of oxen (200 to 300 measures); the fourth and poorest class was that of the *thetes* (less than 200 measures). The *thetes* were obviously the largest class; in general they had no property, and worked the land of others

Under the Solonian constitution, magistracies were assigned by lot from a shortlist of candidates. Only the members of the first two classes were eligible for the most important magistracies, such as the archonship. The *thetes* were not eligible for any magistracy, but they had the right to seat at the *ekklesia*, the city's assembly, and to serve as jurors in the law-courts. Some sources also ascribe to Solon the introduction of the *boule*, the council of the four hundred, one hundred members for each of the four tribes of archaic Athens. The aristocratic Arepoagus maintained overall control over the laws, thus remaining the most influential body in Athenian politics.

Just like his predecessor Draco, Solon was hardly a revolutionary. In fact, Solon wanted to be a reformer, he did not want to break radically with the established social and political order, but to make it stronger and more stable, and to bring social peace to his city. Later authors, however, identified him as one of the fathers of Athenian democracy. In Aristotle's *Politics*, the Solonian regime is described as a form of mixed constitution. In this system the tribunals, now open to all citizens, represented the democratic element [g]. Solon therefore expanded political participation beyond the confines of those able 'to bear arms'; the poorest citizens had acquired a share in the *politeia*, however small.

Solon wanted to restore social justice in Athens. A peaceful *polis*, however, was not supposed to be one where political debate was silenced or suppressed. Political engagement was a right as much as a duty, and those who did not take sides with a faction in the event of *stasis*, were to be declared *atimoi*, i.e. deprived of their status (*time*) as citizens: there could be no *polis* without a degree of division and confrontation.

At the end of his term as archon, Solon left Athens and visited some of the most important centres of the Mediterranean world, from Egypt, the cradle of all civilization, to the vibrant court of Sardis. Solon thus became part of an international political and intellectual network [h, i], and under his guidance, Athens too began to gain a certain international role as an important hub for naval trades: wealthy foreigners were encouraged to settle in the city and In some cases were granted Athenian citizenship The reform of weights and measures and the adoption of the Aeginetan standard also contributed to encouraging economic relations with other Greek cities.

If Theseus was hailed as a father of democracy because he gave a common citizen identity to the various peoples of Attica through the sinoecism, Solon began to create a civic identity which was quintessentially Athenian: the city of the *ekklesia* and of the Piraeus. The future of the city lay on the sea. Solon in a way was a precursor of Themistocles, Ephialtes and Pericles [j–p].

[a] Plut. *Sol.* 14.1-2: Solon, an impartial arbiter

At this conjuncture, the most reasonable men among the Athenians cast their eyes on Solon as the only man who was not implicated in the of errors of the time, for he was neither associated with the arrogance of the wealthy, nor was he held fast to the constraints of the poor. Therefore they implored him to come forward publicly and put an end to the strife. Phanias of Lesbos writes that Solon deliberately deceived the two contending factions in order to save the city. For he secretly promised the poor that he would redistribute the land, as they desired, and to the rich that he would confirm their securities. Solon, however, said he was reluctant to enter politics, fearing the greed of one faction and the disdain of the other. At any rate Solon was appointed to succeed Philombrotus as archon. The Athenians made him arbiter and lawgiver to bring an end to the crisis. The wealthy were happy with this choice because he was also well off, the poor because he was a good man. Before being elected, they say, Solon said that 'equality never provokes war'. These words pleased both the wealthy and the poor, the former expecting that equality would be measured in relation to worth and virtue, the latter in relation to proportion and numbers.

[b] [Arist.] *Ath. Const.* 5.1–6.2: Solon freed the people

Since the party strife had been going on for quite a long time and was growing violent, they agreed to appoint Solon as arbiter and archon and committed the constitution to him. Solon was the author of an elegy which begins:

> *I know, and my heart is filled with pain when I see the eldest land of Ionia laying slain…*[1]

In this poem Solon fights on behalf of each party against the other, and acts as a mediator between the two factions. He urges them to come together and stop the quarrel existing between them. He was one of the foremost citizens, both by birth and reputation, but belonged to the middle class in terms of rank and wealth, as other authors have observed. Solon himself acknowledges that in this poem where he urges the wealthy not to be contemptuous:

> *You, who are plunged with so many goods, calm down the strong passions of your heart and put a limit to your vast ambition; we won't bow down, nor will you have everything at your will.*[2]

Solon always blamed civil disturbance on the wealthy. For this reason, at the beginning of this elegy he says he fears

> *Greed and excessive pride,*[3]

as though these were the causes of the hatred that prevailed in the city.

Once he became master of the situation, Solon set the people free for the present and for the future, and banned the loans guaranteed on the debtor's person, and established laws and ratified cancellations of public and private debts. These measures were called *seisactheia*, or 'shaking-off of burdens', for the people had shaken off a heavy load from their shoulders.

[c] [Arist.] *Ath. Const.* 12.1 = Plut. *Sol.* 18.5 = Solon, fragment 5 Bergk: Solon as an arbiter between the rich and the poor

I have given the people as much power as was sufficient; I have not deprived them of their dignity nor given too much. Those who had power and splendid wealth, I made sure that they would not suffer harm either. I stood up between them, holding a mighty shield, and let neither party triumph unjustly.

[d] [Arist.] *Ath. Const.* 12.2 = Solon, fragment 4 Bergk

In this way the people will pursue the best under the guidance of their leaders, and discipline will be neither too lax nor tight. Satiety breeds impudence when people of unsound mind become wealthy.

[e] [Arist.] *Ath. Const.* 12.4 = Solon, fragment 31 (Bergk): Solon on his archonship, successes and failures

Of all the aims for which I united the people, what have I left unachieved? The Black Earth, the almighty mother of the Olympian gods will best bear witness before the tribunal of Time: I have removed many a boundary-marks which had been planted on her. She was a slave then, and now she's free. Many who had been sold off as slaves, some justly, some unjustly, I have brought them back to god-built Attica, their fatherland. I set free those whom dire necessity had made exiles and were wandering so far from home that they could not use their Attic tongue anymore, and those who had endured dire slavery here, and were trembling before their masters.

I made these principles prevail by balancing might and justice, and I have achieved what I promised. I have written laws that apply equally to the commoners and the well-born, fitting justice into each case. If another man, foolish and ravenous, had taken the ox-goad instead of me, he would have been unable to hold back the people. If I had been obliged to the interests of one faction, and then to any countermeasure of the other, the city would have been bereaved of many men. For this reason I have stood on guard on every side, like a wolf surrounded by a pack of hounds.

[f] [Arist.] *Ath. Const.* 7–10: A summary of Solon's constitution

Solon established a constitution and passed other laws; so the Athenians abolished the laws of Draco except those on homicide. They wrote up the new laws on wooden boards called 'kurbeis' and placed them in the royal portico, and they all had to swear to obey them. The nine archons used to swear under oath at the Stone that if they would contravene any of the laws, they would dedicate a life-size statue of a man in gold. For this reason they are still sworn in with this oath. Solon fixed the laws for a period of one hundred years and arranged the constitution of the *polis* as follows: the citizens were divided into four classes, based on income, as they had been divided before: the pentacosiomedimni, or owners of 500 grain measures, the knights, the zeugites, or owners of a yoke of oxen, and the thetes, or labourers. Solon distributed all the other magistracies between the pentacosiomedimni, knights and zeugites — the nine archons, the treasurers, the sellers, the eleven and paymasters — assigning them to each class in accordance with their income. Those who belonged to the class of thetes he only entitled to serve in the juries and to sit at the assembly. The property qualification to be ranked with pentacosiomedimni was a produce of 500 dry or liquid measures,[4] counted together, three hundred measures for the knight, or, as they say, to be able to keep a horse: this they say is demonstrated by the name of the class and the offerings that the knights used to present in ancient times. For instance, there is a statue of Diphilus in the acropolis, whose inscription reads as follows:

Anthemion, son of Diphilus, dedicated this statue to the gods, [...], having exchanged the rank of zeugite for that of knight.

And a horse stands at his side, proving that 'knight' meant 'able to keep a horse'. At any rate, it is more plausible that the knights were classified in accordance to produce, as the pentacosiomedimni were.

Men with a revenue of 200 measures of dry and liquid produce combined were ranked with the zeugites; all the others belonged to the thetes, and were not entitled to hold any office. Hence it still happens that when a candidate for a magistracy is asked which class he belongs to before the drawing of lots, nobody would think of saying that he belongs to the thetes. Solon established that all public magistrates were to be appointed by lot from a shortlist of candidates chosen by the tribes. For the election of the nine archons each tribe had to submit a shortlist of ten candidates and a lot would be cast from these. Hence, the tribes have maintained a system whereby each of them chooses by lot ten candidates from whom the magistrates are drawn by lot. A proof that Solon made magistrates eligible by lot on the basis of income is the law on the treasurers which is still in place. For this law requires the treasurers to be drawn by lot from the pentacosiomedimni.

This is the system created by Solon for the appointment of the nine archons. Under the previous arrangement, it was the council of the Areopagus that summoned and chose those whom they considered suitable for each magistracy, and dispatched them to hold office for one year. Under the Solonian constitution there were four tribes and four tribal kings as before. Each tribe was divided into three trytties, or 'third parts'. Each tribe had twelve naurcraries, or 'ship-boards', and each naucrary had a board of commissioners, who were in charge of levies and expenditures. Solon also created a council of four hundred members, one hundred from each tribe, and made the council of the Areopagus guardian of the laws, just as in earlier times it had served as the custodian of the constitution. The Areopagus was in control of the majority of public matters, and of the most important of them; it had the power to inflict penalties and other punishments for the correction of offenders. Also, the members of the Areopagus were entitled to claim returns for their expenditures to the Acropolis without providing a justification of their claims; they were in charge of the trials for conspiracy against the democratic regime in accordance with the impeachment procedure established by Solon. Seeing that the state was often in a state of civic discord, Solon laid down a law to deal with such situations, stating that any private citizen who did not join either party when the city was in strife was to be deprived of political rights and should no longer be held as a member of the city community.

This was the nature of Solon's measures concerning the magistracies of the state. The following seem to have been the three most democratic measures taken by Solon: the first and most remarkable was the ban on loans granted upon the person; the second was the right for all to seek compensation on behalf of offended parties; the third was the right to appeal to the jury-courts. This measure, as they say, was essential to give power to the populace, because the people, having become master of the vote, also became master of the constitution. Furthermore, the law-courts became the arbiter of all matters, public and private, because the laws had not been written in a clear and straightforward manner, but like those concerning inheritances and heiresses, and this resulted in a quantity of legal disputes.

Some people believe that Solon deliberately made the laws unclear and ambiguous, so that the people could be sovereign, but this seems unlikely. In fact, this probably happened because Solon was unable to achieve perfection when framing the general principles of his laws. For it would be unfair to judge Solon on the basis of the present situation without taking into consideration the wider outlook of his constitution.

These seem to have been the democratic principles of Solon's laws. Before passing this legislation, Solon had already passed the cancellation of the debts and after it he raised the standards of currency, measure and weight. For it was under Solon that the measures were made larger than those of Pheidon, and the weight of the mina was increased from 70 to 100 drachmae. In previous times, the standard coin was the two-drachma piece. Solon also established weights corresponding to the currency: the 63 minae talent, and the odd three minae were added to the stater and the other weights.

[g] Arist. *Pol.* 2.9.2-4: An appraisal of Solon, precursor of radical democracy

Some people consider Solon to have been an excellent lawgiver because he brought oligarchy to an end once it had lost all its authoritativeness; he released the people from slavery and restored the ancestral form of democracy by skilfully blending different kinds of constitution: the council of Areopagus was the oligarchic part, the elective magistracies the aristocratic, and the law-courts the democratic. In fact, Solon seems to have simply restrained from dismantling institutions which were already in place, such as the Areopagus and the elective magistracies, and to have established democracy by instituting the law-courts drawn from all citizens. For this reason, some accuse him of having destroyed the other institutions by having given sovereignty to a body drawn by lot from all the citizens such as the law-courts. For once the law-courts were gaining power, politicians began to court the favour of the populace, as they would have done with a tyrant, and this contributed to transforming the constitution into the type of democracy which is now in place. Ephialtes and Pericles curtailed the authority of the Areopagus; the latter also instituted payment for serving in the law-courts, and in this way, each of the successive popular leaders increased the power of the populace, until the constitution became the democracy which it is now. This however happened more by chance than according to a precise plan of Solon: for it so happened that at the time of the Persian invasion, having been the cause of the naval victories against the barbarians, the populace became bold, and began to choose despicable individuals as their leaders, while the wiser men were opposing their policies. As for Solon himself, he seems to have given the people just as much power as was necessary, allowing them to elect the magistrates, and by requiring the magistrates to give account for their office (even if they were not under control of the people). Still he chose all the magistrates from the notable and the well-off, the pentakosiomedimni, and the zeugitai and a third class called the knights, while the fourth class, the thetes, were not admitted to any office.

[h] Hdt. 1.29–30.1: Solon the traveller, from Egypt to Sardis

At that time Sardis was at the peak of its wealth and all the wise men of that age would travel there from all over the Greek world. Solon the Athenian was one of them. After establishing new laws for the citizens at their request, he spent ten years travelling abroad, admittedly because he wanted to see the world, but in fact because he did not want to be forced to revoke any of his laws, since the Athenians themselves could not do that, as they had solemnly sworn they would obey for ten years whatever laws Solon should make. For these reasons, as well as to see the world, Solon visited Amasis in Egypt and Croesus in Sardis. Once he came there, Solon was entertained by Croesus in his palace. On the third or fourth day, Croesus told his attendants to show Solon around his treasures, and they pointed out everything that was great and splendid.

[i] Hdt.2.177: Solon in Egypt

Under the reign of Amasis, as they say, Egypt reached the height of its prosperity, owing to what the river did to the land, and the land to the people: the number of the inhabited cities in the territory was twenty thousand. Amasis also enacted a law whereby all the Egyptians had to declare all their substances to the governor of their province every year. Those who failed to do so or to show evidence of a legitimate source of income were subject to capital punishment. Solon imported this law from Egypt and established it in Athens. May the Athenians maintain this perfect law forever!

[j] Paus. 1.16.1: The statue of Solon in the agora

In front of the Portico there stands a bronze statue of Solon, who wrote the laws for the Athenians.

[k] Paus. 1.18.1: The Pritanaeum and the laws of Solon

Nearby is the Pritanaeum, where the laws of Solon are inscribed.

[l] Ar. *Clouds* 1177–1200: Solon on stage, the friend of the people

PHIDIPPIDES: What are you afraid of?

STREPSIADES: Of the Old and New.

PHID: Why? Is there any day both old and new?

STREP: Of course. That's the day when they said they would make their deposits against me.

PHID: Well, in that case they'll lose them, because one day can't be two days at the same time.

STREP: Can't it?

PHID: Of course it can't, unless the same woman can be old and young at the same time.

STREP: What about the law then?

PHID: Well, I think they don't understand the meaning of the law.

STREP: What does the law mean?

PHID: Our ancient Solon was by nature a friend of the people.

STREP: But this has nothing to do with old and new!

PHID: That man also established the summons in two days, the old and the new, so that meetings could take place on the day of the new moon.

STREP: So, why did he establish the old day as well?

PHID: My dear, so that the defendants could appear one day early, and settle out of court. And if they did not, they'll get there on the morning of the new moon.

STREP: So, how come the magistrates do not accept guarantees on the day of
the new moon, but only on the old day or the new day?

PHID: I think they do what the food inspectors do before a festival: they want
to cheat on the guarantees, and so they have a taste of them one day early.

[m] Lys. *Ag. Nic.* 2: Republishing Solon's laws [I]

When Nicomachus was made commissioner for the transcription of the laws,
he perpetrated outrages against the city which are well known to everyone. For
while he had been instructed to publish the laws of Solon within four months,
he usurped the title of lawgiver from Solon, and kept his office for six years
instead of four months, and every day he took bribes to insert some laws and
rub out others.

[n] Lys. *Ag. Nic.* 27–8: Republishing Solon's laws [II]

Nicomachus was a slave and now he has become a citizen, he was poor and now
he is wealthy, he was a simple under-clerk, and now has become a lawgiver!
Some might blame this on you, because your ancestors chose as their lawgivers
the likes of Solon, Themistocles and Pericles, confident as they were that the
laws would mirror the spirit of their architects. And you? You have chosen
Teisamenus, Mechanion and Nichomacus, who were under-clerks.

[o] Dem. *Crown* 5–7: Solon, a lawgiver and a democrat

Athenians: I believe you should all agree that I am just as much concerned in
this trial as Ctesiphon, and that I should give it no less consideration than he
does. In fact, any loss arising from a private quarrel is painful and hard to bear,
but nothing compares to the loss of your favour and benevolence, which are
the most precious possessions of all, and this is exactly what this trial is about.
Therefore, I pray and urge you all to listen to my defence against these accusations with a fair mind, as the laws prescribe you to do. Solon, the man who first
established them, was a friend of the people and a genuine democrat: he thought
that the laws should be sovereign because they were written and because the
jurors had to swear on them. For Solon, I think, trusted you, but he was also
aware that no defendant could possibly prevail against the charges and false
accusations which a prosecutor puts forward as he speaks first unless you jurors
keep to your vow of piety to the gods and lend a favourable ear to the arguments

of the second speaker, reaching no final conclusion on the whole matter without having listened to both parties with a fair and impartial mind.

[p] Hyp. *Ag. Ath.* 21–2: Solon, a most democratic man

I think that you are all liable. However, if we don't agree on this point, let the law be our judge, I mean the law established not by some lovers or by people craving for someone else's possessions, but by Solon, that most democratic man. For Solon saw that many sales were taking place in the city and so he passed a law, which we all consider just, stating that all the offences or crimes perpetrated by slaves should be considered the responsibility of the masters who currently own them. This is just reasonable, because whenever a slave does well in anything, or brings in a profit, it is the owner who enjoys the benefit.

4

Pisistratus: Tyranny as a Pathway to Democracy

11. Archaic tyrannies

According to Thucydides, the emergence of tyrannies in the Greek cities was an inevitable consequence of the tumultuous growth of the archaic age. In fact, these ambitious individuals seem to capture very well the dynamic spirit and the anxieties of the time, although the unsettled nature of their power and the necessity to defend it from internal and outside threats kept them from looking beyond the small confines of their cities. The world of the Greek *poleis* was fragmented and divided, and would remain so until the time of the great campaigns against the Persians. The city of Corinth, located on the isthmus between Attica and Peloponnese, is perhaps the best example of the dynamism of archaic Greece. Between the seventh and sixth centuries, under the enlightened tyrannies of the Cypselids and the Bacchiads, the city became arguably became the foremost center of the Greek world. The flamboyant Corinthian pottery, rich in oriental influences, became very popular throughout the Mediterranean and gave an important contribution to the shaping of a distinctively Greek taste [a–b].

Aristotle in the *Politics* describes tyranny in rather negative terms as a corrupted form of monarchy, which shares the worst features of oligarchy and democracy. His judgement however seems to have been more influenced by certain fifth- and fourth-century regimes, such as the tyrannies of Syracuse, than those of the archaic age. Tyranny appears as the least constitutional and least political of all the forms of government. The tyrant is essentially an individual who seizes power in the *polis* exclusively to advance his own interests and those of his family. Tyrants are by nature greedy and arrogant; they attract the hatred of their fellow-citizens and their power was inevitably unstable. Tyrants being tyrants, they lacked the political vision necessary to develop any ambitious plans for their cities [c–e]. This, as we shall see, was not the case of

Athens, where the tyranny of Pisistratus and his heirs gave a vital contribution to the development of the identity of the Athenian citizen.

[a] Thuc. 1.13.1–3: Wealth and tyranny in archaic Greece, the case of Corinth

As Greece was becoming more powerful and wealthy than before, and revenues were also increasing, tyrannies were set up in the cities (previously they had hereditary monarchies based on certain prerogatives). Also, the Greeks began to fit out fleets and apply themselves more assiduously to navigation. The Corinthians are said to have been the first to practise the modern techniques of ship-building. In fact, Corinth is said to have been the first Greek city where triremes were built.

[b] Thuc. 1.17: The limits of archaic tyrannies

Tyrants, wherever there were tyrants in the cities of the Greeks, were only concerned about their personal interests, that is to say their personal safety and the aggrandizement of their houses. For this reason they always kept their cities as peaceful as possible, and so they failed to achieve anything memorable, except for some minor conflicts against their neighbours. So Greece for a long time was kept from undertaking any notable common enterprise, and its individual cities were incapable of any bold action.

[c] Arist. *Pol.* 3.5.4: Tyranny and other constitutional deviations

These are the deviations from the kinds of constitutions which have been taken into consideration: tyranny is a deviation from monarchy, oligarchy from aristocracy, and democracy from constitutional government. For tyranny is a form of monarchy where power is exercised in the interest of the monarch, oligarchy in the interest of the rich, and democracy in the interest of the poor.

[d] Arist. *Pol.* 4.2.2: Tyranny as a corrupted form of monarchy

The deviation from what is best and most divine is necessarily the worst form of deviation. Kingship therefore must necessarily either be kingship by name only, without really being kingship, or be based on the outstanding virtue of the man who exercises power. For this reason tyranny is by necessity the worst kind of regime and the one farthest away from legitimate constitutional government.

[e] Arist. *Pol.* 5.8.3–4: Tyranny drawing on the worst elements of oligarchy and democracy

Royal rule is related to aristocracy, whereas tyranny is a combination of the basest form of oligarchy and democracy. For this reason, tyranny is the most detrimental form of regime for its subjects, for it is a combination of two bad things, which bears the deviations and faults of these two kinds of constitution. These two kinds of monarchies stem from two different sources, which are the exact contrary of one another. The first kind is royalty, which comes into existence to assist the upper classes in the struggle against the commons, when a king is ordained from the upper classes on account of his superior virtue, or of those deeds which stem from virtue, or in reason of his noble birth. On the other hand, a tyrant rises to power from the struggle of the commons against the upper classes, to prevent the people from being abused by them. This is demonstrated by the events of history, for in most cases tyrants rose to power from the ranks of the demagogues, having obtained the trust of the populace by discrediting the notables. Tyrannies of this kind were established when the cities had already become powerful. On the other hand, the older tyrannies originated either from kings who deviated from the ancestral customs and aspired to a more despotic kind of power, or from men who had been appointed to the highest offices of the state (for in ancient times the peoples used to appoint magistrates and the sacred ambassadors for long terms of office), or from oligarchies where a man had been appointed to the highest magistracies. All the tyrants who rose to power in this manner could easily bring about their plans, if only they wished, because they already held royal power in the former case, or a honourable magistracy in the latter: Pheidon of Argos, for instance, and others became tyrants when they already held royal powers; the Ionian tyrants and Phalaris when they held high magistracies; Panaetius of Leontini, Cypselus of Corinth and Pisistratus of Athens and others became tyrants in the same manner, from the position of demagogues.

12. Athenian politics after Solon

Solon's reforms did not give durable social peace to the Athenians. Regular political activity was frequently disrupted by factional strife, so much so that in two occasions it proved impossible to proceed with the election of the archon: Athens found itself in a state of actual anarchy, perpetual *stasis* deprived the *polis* of legitimate political leadership, as embodied by the city's chief magistrate (*an-arche*) [a]. Political divisions were a symptom of the incomplete unification of the various districts of Attica. Political power was still contested by three local factions, the shore, the hills, and the plain, guided by aristocratic leaders, just as at the time of Solon's archonship. Pisistratus was the head of the faction of the hill and a clever politician, who had the qualities and ambition to expand his ascendancy and become the leader of the Athenian populace [b, c].

[a] [Arist.], *Ath. Const.* 13: Political turbulence after Solon's archonship

The city remained at peace for four years while Solon was abroad, although disturbance did not stop completely. On the fifth year since the archonship of Solon, the Athenians were unable to elect the archon owing to the political divisions. Four years later, the Athenians did not appoint the archon for the same reason. After these events, the same period of time having elapsed, Damasias was elected archon and held the post for two years and two months, until he was removed from office by force. After this, owing to the civic strife, the Athenians decided to elect ten archons, five from the well-born, three from the farmers and two from the artisans. These held office for the year following Damasias' archonship. It is clear from this that in those times the archonship was the most powerful magistracy, since political strife seems to have always concerned this office. In short, the Athenians were in a state of perpetual strife: for some of them the main reason for discontent was the cancellation of debts, which they claimed had reduced them to poverty; others were dissatisfied with the present state of the constitution, because it had been sensibly modified; for some, the only reason was mutual rivalry.

There were the three factions: the party of the coastmen, led by Megacles son of Alcmaeon, and they seemed to aim at a moderate form of constitution. The second faction was the party of the Men of the Plain, who favoured the oligarchy, and their leader was Lycurgus. The third party was that of the Hillmen, who had chosen as their head Pisistratus, because he was thought to be the most democratic of all. With this party were also aligned those who had been deprived of the debts due to them, owing to their poverty, and those who were not of pure citizen descent, owing to their fear. This is demonstrated by the fact that after the overthrow of the tyrants the Athenians carried out a revision of the citizen roll, because many people shared the citizenship without being entitled to it. The different factions derived their names from the places where their estates were located.

[c] Plut. *Sol.* 29.1–3: Solon and Pisistratus

While Solon was abroad, civic strife broke out again in the city. The faction of the plain was headed by Lycurgus, that of the shore by Megacles, son of Alcmaeon, and that of the hills by Pisistratus. In this party there were the mass of thetes, who were bitterly at loggerheads with the wealthy. As a result, although the city was still observing the new laws, there was a general expectation and desire for a revolution and a change of government, not because they wanted to achieve equality, but because each party thought that the change would strengthen their position, and give them complete power over their enemies.

This was the state of affairs when Solon returned to Athens. He was respected and honoured by everyone, but owing to his old age he was no longer able, or willing, to speak in public and be actively engaged in politics as he was before. However, he did have private meetings with the leaders of the factions, in an attempt to reconcile them and bring civic strife to an end. Pisistratus seemed particularly attached to him. In fact, there was a flattering and agreeable manner in his conversation; he was always willing to assist the poor, and was reasonable and moderate towards his adversaries. As for those qualities which were not natural in him, Pisistratus dissimulated them so cleverly that they won him more trust than those which he actually possessed. So he was considered to be a prudent and decent man, who loved equality above everything else, and would disapprove of anyone trying to disturb the established order or yearning for change. In all this he managed to hoodwink most people, but not Solon, who quickly discovered his real nature and was the first to see through his plans. Solon, however, never hated him, but tried to soften his nature by giving him direction. For instance, he told him, as he did with others, that, if only the eagerness for power was removed from his soul, and his passion for tyranny could be cured, there would be no other man more naturally inclined to virtue, or who could make a better citizen.

13. Tyranny in Athens

In 561/560, 31 years after Solon's reforms, Pisistratus became master of Athens. He attained power in perfectly tyrannical fashion, by resorting to ruse and violence [a]. In spite of these less than promising beginnings, all our sources describe Pisistratus as an enlightened and compassionate ruler. Pisistratus was a peculiar kind of tyrant, who does not seem to fit in the typical portrait of the tyrant drawn by Arsitotle and Thucydides. Whereas Solon had begun his reforming activity by dismantling the laws of Draco, Pisistratus maintained and observed the laws of Solon. He wanted to give a legitimate and stable base to his power, and rule in the defence of the common interest, and not in opposition to it [b–c].

Under Pisistratus Athens and the Athenians became considerably wealthier. The *Constitution of the Athenians* lists a number of social and economic reforms which resulted in an expansion of the cultivated land in Attica, and consequently of the class of small landowners. A new tax of 5 per cent or 10 per cent on agricultural produce brought an unprecedented quantity of money into the Athenian treasury. If the state of permanent civic strife between the factions of the various areas of Attica was a sign of the incomplete synoecism of Attica, Pisistratus instituted the local tribunals to make the presence of the central institutions of the *polis* felt in the rural districts of Attica [d]. The foreign policy pursued by Pisistratus and his descendants was dynamic and ambitious: the tyrant was twice forced into exile by his political enemies, but the experience helped him to establish important diplomatic relations with foreign powers such as Sparta, Macedon and Argos. Important Athenian settlements were established in the area of the Chersonese, the gateway to the grain of the Black Sea [e–g].

Pisistratus died in 528/527, passing over his power to his sons Hippias and Hipparchus, who followed on their father's brand of enlightened tyranny [h]. Under the Pisistratids, Athens seems to have lived a first golden age: Hippias and Hipparchus promoted the arts and the letters [i, j]; they embarked upon an ambitious building programme, including a new temple to Athens on the Acropolis, the *Olympieon* temple in honour of Zeus, the so-called fountain of the nine mouths, and the Royal Portico in the agora. The promotion of the main civic-religious festivals of the *polis*, like the Great Dyonisia and the Panathenaia, gave an essential contribution to the emergence of a common Athenian identity [k–o].

[a] Hdt. 1.59.3–4: Pisistratus rises to power

When civic strife broke out between the factions of the Athenians of the coast, led by Megacles, son of Alcmaeon, and those of the plain, led by Lycurgus, son of Aristolaides, Pisistratus, who aimed at the tyranny, formed a third faction. Pisistratus collected a group of supporters, under the pretence of championing the hillmen, and then set off the following plan. Having wounded himself and his mules, Pisistratus drove his carriage into the agora, as though he was escaping from his enemies, who, as he said, had tried to kill him as he was driving into the countryside. So he begged the people to give him a bodyguard. Pisistratus had become popular at the time of his command in the war against Megara, when he seized Nisaea and accomplished many other remarkable deeds. Having been deceived by Pisistratus, the Athenian people gave him a guard of chosen men from the city. More than spearmen, these were Pisistratus' clubmen, because these men who followed him used to carry wooden clubs. Pisistratus and his men rose to the acropolis and seized it. So Pisistratus ruled the Athenians without altering the existing magistracies or changing the laws; he led the city as a fair and decent ruler, in compliance with the established laws.

[b] [Arist.] *Ath. Const.* 14.3: Pisistratus and the common interest

Once he attained power, Pisisiratus pursued the common interest more in the manner of a legitimate statesman than a tyrant.

[c] Plut. *Sol.* 31.2: Pisistratus and the laws of the city

Pisistratus retained most of Solon's laws; he was the first to observe them and compelled his friends to do so. For example, once he was summoned before the tribunal of the Areopagus on a charge of murder when he was already tyrant, and he duly turned up to defend himself, whereas his accuser did not show up. He also wrote new laws, one of which prescribes that those who are mutilated in war should be maintained at public expense.

[d] [Arist.] *Ath. Const.* 16.1–5, 7: Pisistratus the compassionate tyrant, his most significant measures

The administration of Pisistratus was moderate and more constitutional than tyrannical. He was compassionate and gentle in every respect, and was indulgent towards the wrong-doers. He advanced money to the poor for their enterprises, so that they could support their families by working the land. He had two goals in doing this: firstly, that they might live scattered in the countryside, and not waste time in the city; secondly, that they might prosper and look after their private interests, so that they would not have time for attending to public affairs, or be interested in them. At the same time, the expansion of the cultivated land increased his profits, because he had levied a tithe on the produce. For this reason he also created the local justices, and often he would go to the country in person to carry out inspections and to settle disputes, so that the people would not have to go to the city and neglect their work.

[...]

The rule of Pisistratus was never a burden on the people. He always strove for peace and preserved tranquillity. For this reason, one could often hear people say that the tyranny of Pisistratus was the Golden Age of Chronos. In fact, as it happened later, when power was passed on to the sons of Pisistratus, the regime became considerably harsher.

[e] Hdt. 5.63.1: Sparta against the Pisistratids

The Alcmaeonids, as the Athenians say, sat at Delphi and bribed the Pythia with money to tell any Spartan who would come there to interrogate her on private or public matters to go to Athens and set the city free. When the Spartans were informed of this oracle, they sent Anchimaolius, the son of Aster, who was a respected man among the citizens, to drive the Pisistratids out of Athens with an army, even if they were their guests, because they considered the words of the god more venerable than those of men. They sent this contingent by sea on ships. Anchimolius landed at Cape Phalerum and disembarked his army. The Pisistratids however had already learnt about this plan, and so they had sent to the Thessalians to ask for help, since they had an alliance with them. The Thessalians joined together at their appeal and sent their King Cineas of Conium, at the head of 1,000 horsemen. Once they got these allies, the Pisistratids devised the following plan: they laid waste the plain of Phalerum, so that it could be ridden over, and then launched their cavalry against the enemy. The horsemen charged and slaughtered many of the Spartans, including Anchimolius himself, while those who survived withdrew to the ships.

[f] Hdt. 7.6: Ambassadors at the court of Xerxes, the Pisistratids and the Thessalians

There came ambassadors from Thessaly, from the house of the Aleuadae, who invited with all eagerness the king to come to Greece. The Aleuadae were the royal house of Thessaly. Then envoys of the Pisistratids also came to Susa and made the same plea as the Aleuadae, but they offered the King something more than they had. In fact, they had come with Onomacritus, an Athenian omen-monger, who had put in order the oracles of Musaeus [...]. Whenever he came in sight of the sovereign, the Pisistratidae would start speaking about him in glowing terms, as he pronounced his oracles. Of those foreseeing losses for the Persians, he would make no mention. For he would choose and reveal only the most favourable prophecies, telling how the two shores of the Hellespont would be yoked up by a Persian man as he described their expedition. So, while the Pisistratids and the Aleuadae were exposing their thoughts, Onomacritus offered his oracles.

[g] Hdt. 6.34–6: Pisistratus, Miltiades and the Athenian interests in the Chersonese

The Phoenicians had seized all the cities in the Chersonese except Cardia. Miltiades son of Cimon son of Stesagoras was tyrant of that city. This is how, in earlier times, Miltiades son of Cypselus had gained power there: this part of Chersonese used to belong to the Thracian Dolonci, but when they were defeated in war by the Apsinthians, they dispatched their kings to Delphi to ask what they should do about the war. The Pythia answered that they should bring to their nation as founder the first man who would offer them hospitality after they left the sanctuary. Now, nobody offered them hospitality as they travelled through Phocis and Boeotia, going along the Sacred Way, and so they diverted towards Athens.

At that time Pisistratus held all power in Athens, although Miltiades son of Cypselus also had great influence. In fact, his household was so rich that they could support a team of four horses. Miltiades traced the origins of his family to Aeacus and Aegina; his later ancestry however was Athenian. Philaeus son of Ajax was the first Athenian member of that house.

Now, Miltiades was sitting on his porch when he saw the Dolonci walk by in their foreign attire and with their spears, so he called them to him and when they came over he offered them restoration and hospitality. The Dolonci accepted and once they had received Militiades' hospitality they told him about the oracle and asked him to obey the god. Upon hearing their words Miltiades was immediately persuaded, for he could not endure the rule of Pisistratus any more, and wanted to get away from it. So Militiades set out for Delphi at once to ask the oracle whether he should do what the Dolonci were asking from him.

[h] [Arist.] *Ath. Const.* 18.1: Hippias and Hipparchus, successors of Pisistratus

Hippias and Hipparchus were in control of affairs owing to their rank and age. Hippias, the elder, was a wise fellow and a natural-born statesman, and was actually in charge of the government of the city. Hipparchus on the other hand was fond of amusement. He engaged in amorous affairs and was fond of the arts: it was he who invited to Athens the likes of Anacreon and Simonides, as well as other poets.

[i] [Pl.] *Hipp.* 228b–229c: The many accomplishments of Hipparchus

Hipparchus, the son of Pisistratus of the Philaidae tribe, a fellow-citizen of mine and yours, was the eldest and wisest of Pisistratus' sons. He gave many and splendid proofs of his wisdom: for instance, he was the first to bring the poems of Homer into this land of ours, and required the rhapsodes at the Panathenaic festival to sing them in relay, one following on another, as they still do today. Furthermore, he sent a 50-oared ship to collect Anacreon of Teos and bring him to our city. He had Simonides of Ceos always at his side, having won him over with magnificent emoluments and gifts. Hipparchus did all this because he wanted to educate the citizens, so that he might rule over subjects of the highest quality. For he was a good and noble man, and thought that nobody should be excluded from knowledge. Once the people of the city had been educated by him and were admiring him for his wisdom, Hipparchus, now wishing to educate those who lived in the countryside, took to placing images of Hermes along the roads in the centre of the town and in all the demes, and having made a selection of the wisest sayings of Hermes, either learnt from others or discovered by himself, he translated them into elegiac poetry, as though they had been written by himself. These verses he inscribed on the images of Hermes as examples of his own wisdom, so that the citizens, before admiring those wise Delphic proverbs, I mean the 'Know yourself' and 'Nothing overmuch' and all the other such sayings, would first think of the wise words of Hipparchus, and then, having grown acquainted with and developed a taste for his wisdom, they would move from the countryside to complete their education.

These inscriptions are of two kinds: the one on the left side of each Hermes, in which the Hermes says that it has been erected in the centre of the city or of the deme, and the other on the right side, which says:

Monument of Hipparchus; walk with just intentions in mind.

There are many other fine inscriptions from his poems on other statues of Hermes; for example, there is the one on the Steiria road, where he says:

Monument of Hipparchus; never deceive a friend.

Therefore, I would never dare to deceive you, my friend, or disobey a man like Hipparchus. After his death, the Athenians remained under the tyranny of his brother Hippias for three years, and you might have heard all the people of the old generation say that it was only in those years that the Athenians experienced tyranny, otherwise, they lived as in the age of Chronos.

[j] Arist. *Pol.* 5.9.4: The Pisistratids build a temple of Zeus. A political ruse?

It is typical of tyrants to keep their subjects poor, so that they may not need to maintain a garrison, and the people, being busy with their daily affairs, would not have time to plot a conspiracy. Examples of this are the pyramids in Egypt, the votive offerings of the Cypselids, the building of the temple of Olympian Zeus by the Pisistratids, and the temples at Samos, built by Polycrates: all these projects have been undertaken with the same aim: to keep the people constantly occupied and poor.

[k] Thuc. 2.15.5: The Pisistratids and water supply, I

In this quarter of the city there is also the fountain which has been known as Enneacrounos, or Nine Pipes, since it was refurbished under the tyrants, but its original name, the one it was given when the spring was open, was Callirhoe, or Fairwater. In those days the fountain was used for the most important ceremonies, since it was so close to the temples.

[l] Paus. 1.14.1: The Pisistratids and water supply, II

Of all the objects you see upon entering the Odeion at Athens there is a figure of Dionysus, which is particularly noteworthy. Also nearby is a spring called Enneacrunos, or 'Nine Pipes', which was embellished in its present form by Pisistratus. Water cisterns are located all over the city, but this is the only fountain. Two temples are located above the spring, one dedicated to Demeter and the Maid, and the other to Triptolemus, where there is also a statue of him.

[m] *FGH* 3 F2: The creation of the Panathenaic festival

Hippocleides: the Great Panathenaia were established under his archonship.[1]

[n] *Suda* s.v. Thespis, the Pisistratids and the earliest dramatic festivals

Thespis. From Ikarion, a municipality of Attica. Tragic poet, 16th after the first author of tragedies, Epigenes of Sicyon, but according to some the second after Epigenes; others say that he was the first tragediographer. At first he used to perform with lead rubbed on his face, then he covered his face with purslane in his performances. After that, he also introduced the use of masks made of linen only. He produced his plays in the year of the 61st Olympiad.[2] He is remembered for his tragedies *The Funeral Games of Pelias* or *The Phorbas*, *The Priests*, *The Youths*, *Pentheus*.

14. The overthrowing of a tyranny

Thucydides praised the Pisistratids as moderate and compassionate leaders [a]. Certainly they were tyrants, and like every tyrant they wanted to keep all the positions of power within their inner circle of friends and close associates, but this, as far as we can judge from our sources, seems to have been the only genuinely despotic trait of their rule. The Pisistratids in sum treated power as a personal belonging of theirs, which they had to defend from their internal enemies. Their foreign policy also seems to have been based on a network of personal relations with other influential houses in the cities of Greece.

The Pisistratids had occupied power, but the initiatives that they took in order to maintain it gave a vital contribution to strengthening the common identity of the Athenians. The *asty*, the urban heart of the *polis*, with all its new buildings, became the place where this identity was shaped and celebrated. At the great religious festivals in honour of Athena and Dionysus, the Athenians gathered to celebrate themselves as members of one community. Thucydides also gives a detailed account of the assassination of Hipparchus at the hand of Harmodius, a beautiful Athenian youth, and his lover Aristogiton, after which the rule of Hippias became harsher, which somehow affected his posthumous image [b]. The rule of the Pisistratids was finally brought to an end by the intervention of the Spartans

The tyranny was finally overthrown by the Spartan king Cleomenes, and by the exiled members of the noble house of the Alcmaeonids, who were the main opponents of the Pisistratids in Athens. Later on, democratic propaganda would celebrate Harmodius and Aristogiton as true national heroes. Soon after the reforms of Cleisthenes, statues were erected in their honour at public expenses (see, *infra* item 16), and their descendants were granted exemption from duties and other hereditary privileges [c–f].

[a] Thuc. 6.53.3–59.4: The two tyrannicides, myths and realities

The people of Athens had heard how harsh the tyranny of Pisistratus and his sons had become when it was brought to an end. Also, they had heard that the tyranny had been overthrown not by the people themselves and Harmodius, but by the Spartans. For this reason, they were always in fear and suspicious about everything. In fact, the truth is that Harmodius and Aristogiton undertook their daring enterprise because of a love affair. Giving a detailed account of this episode, I will demonstrate that the Athenians have no better knowledge than the others of the vicissitudes of their tyrants and the events of their past.

Pisistratus died an old man, while he was still in possession of the tyranny. He was succeeded by Hippias, his eldest son, and not by Hipparchus, as many believe. In those days Harmodius was then a youth in the flower of his beauty; Aristogiton, a citizen of middle rank, was his lover and held him fast to himself. Now, Harmodius was being pursued by Hipparchus, son of Pisistratus. Harmodius however was not won over, and told everything to Aristogiton. Seized by jealousy, and fearing lest Hippias might use his power to take Harmodius by force, Aristogiton immediately devised a plan to overthrown the tyranny, commensurate with his social standing.

In the meantime, following another unsuccessful proposition to Harmodius, Hipparchus, unwilling to resort to violence, embarked on a scheme to insult him in a more covert manner. In general, the regime was not a burden on the people, and power was exercised in an irreproachable manner; the tyrants practised virtue and conscience to the highest degree, they imposed a modest levy of five per cent on the incomes of the Athenians, and still managed to embellish their town, and wage wars and make offerings to the temples. In all other matters, the city continued to observe the established laws. Only, the tyrants took care that the magistracies were always in the hands of someone from their family. One of the men who held the yearly archonship was Pisistratus, the son of the tyrant Hippias, named after his grandfather. During his term in office, this Pisistratus dedicated the altar to the Twelve Gods in the agora, and that of Apollo in the precinct of Apollo the Pythian. The Athenians later built on and expanded the altar in the agora and removed the inscription, but the one on the altar of the Pythian is still visible, although it is faded, and says:

> Pisistratus, son of Hippias set up this memorial to his archonship in the precinct of Apollo the Pythian.

I know for sure and have stronger evidence than others that Hippias, the eldest son of Pisistatus, succeeded him in the government. This can also be ascertained from this: Hippias alone of the legitimate brothers appears to have had children, as shown by the altar as well as the pillar in the acropolis of Athens, which commemorates the injustice of the tyrants. The inscription on the pillar does not mention any children of Thessalus or Hipparchus, but only the five, whom Hippias had from Myrrhine, daughter of Callias, son of Hyperechides, and it is likely that the eldest son was also the first to contract marriage. Furthermore, the name of Hippias is listed first in the inscription after his father's. This is not strange, since he was the eldest after him, and had been tyrant. Nor would Hippias have obtained the tyranny so easily, as I think, if Hipparchus had been in power when he was assassinated, and he had had to set himself up in power on the same day. The truth is that the citizens had already grown afraid of him, and the mercenaries were well accustomed to obey him: this is why Hippias could prevail without any trouble, and without having to face the difficulties of a younger brother who is not acquainted with the arts of power. Hipparchus, as it happened, became famous owing to the misery of his fate, and posterity gave him the name of tyrant.

So, once Harmodius refused the suit of Hipparchus, the latter insulted him, as he intended to do: he invited a sister of Harmodius to serve as a basket-carrier in a certain procession, but then they rejected her. In fact, they said that they had not invited her at all because she was not worthy. Harmodius was outraged, and Aristogiton was even more so owing to his lover's wrath.

Harmodius and Aristogiton had arranged all the details of the enterprise with their associates, and were now waiting for the day of the Great Panathenaea, because that was the only occasion when the citizens joining in the procession could gather together in arms without arousing suspicion. Harmodius and Aristogiton were to strike the first blow, and then their accomplices would join them immediately and repel the bodyguard of Hipparchus. The conspirators were not many, as security demanded. However, they hoped that those who were not involved in the plot would be inspired by their bravery and use the arms that they were carrying to recover their freedom.

When the day of the festival arrived, Hippias was outside the city with his bodyguard, in the area of the so-called Ceramicus, marshalling the various sections of the procession. Harmodius and Aristogiton had already their daggers in hand and were ready to spring into action when they saw one of their accomplices talking in familiar terms with Hippias, who was a man affable with all. The pair took fright; they thought that they had been betrayed and were about to be arrested. Nevertheless, they were eager to take revenge, if possible, upon the man who had vexed them and for whom they were running all those risks. So they rushed within the gates, as they were, and when they ran into Hipparchus by the so-called Leocorium, they furiously assaulted him at once, one moved by anger, and the other by love, and killed him. Aristogiton immediately escaped from the guards, as the crowd was running up, but was later captured and mercilessly dealt with. Harmodius on the other hand was killed on the spot.

When news of what happened reached Hippias at the Ceramicus, he did not rush at once to the scene of the murder. Instead, he went to the men who were carrying arms in the procession before they might know anything, because they were still some distance away. Having composed his expression for the occasion as not to betray himself, he indicated a certain spot, and ordered them to move there without arms. Accordingly, the men withdrew there, in the belief that he wanted to address them. At this point, he ordered the mercenaries to remove their arms, and immediately picked out those whom he believed guilty, and they were all found carrying daggers, whereas the weapons usually carried in the procession were shield and spear.

This is how an outraged love set in motion the plot of Armodius and Haristogiton, and the fear of the moment drove them to hasten their action. Following this episode, the tyranny became more burdensome for the Athenians. Hippias put to death many citizens owing to his growing fear, and at the same time he began to look abroad to see if he could find a place of refuge in case a revolution took place. So, although he was Athenian, he gave his daughter Archedice to Aentides of Lampsacus, the son of the city's tyrant, since he knew that they had great influence with King Darius. Her grave is in Lampsacus and bears the following inscription:

> This dust covers Archedice, daughter of Hippias,
> Her father, brother, husband and children were all tyrants,
> But her soul was never lifted up to arrogance.

Hippias ruled over Athens for three years, and in the fourth the Spartans and the exiled Alcmaeonids deposed him. Hippias was granted a safe conduct and went to Sigeum, to Aeantides at Lampsacus. Thence he went to King Darius. He left his court twenty years later, as an old man, and came with the Persians to Marathon.

[b] Ar. *Wasps* 488–502: Hippias, the Athenians' obsession with tyranny

> BDELYCLEON: Tyranny nowadays is all around us, large or small. I haven't heard the word once in fifty years, but it is more common than salt-fish, it whirls around in the market-place: if you want to buy gurnards, but don't want anchovies, the anchovy seller next door immediately starts shouting: 'that's the chap whose kitchen smells of tyranny!' If you ask for onions to season your fish, the woman selling vegetables winks one eye and asks, 'Tell me: you want onions? Do you want to be a tyrant, or do you think that the Athenians should pay for your seasonings?'
>
> XANTIHAS: Yesterday I visited a whore; it was about noon. I asked her to get on top and she went completely ballistic. She said that I wanted to restore the tyranny of Hippias.

[c] Plin. *Nat. Hist.* 34.17: The overthrow of the Athenian tyrants and the kings of Rome

I do not know whether the Athenians were the first to erect statues at public expense in honour of Harmodius and Aristogiton, the men who killed the tyrant in the same year when the kings were expelled from Rome.[3]

[d] Plin. *Nat. Hist.* 34.70: The statues of Harmodius and Aristogiton by Praxiteles

Praxiteles also executed statues of Stephanusa, Spilumene, Oenophorus, and two figures of Harmodius and Aristogiton, the tyrannicides. These were taken away by Xerxes and later restored to the Athenians by Alexander the Great, following the conquest of Persia.

[e] Paus. 1.8.5: The statues of Harmodius and Aristogiton in the agora

Nearby are the statues of Harmodius and Aristogiton, the men who killed Hipparchus. The reasons and mode of their act have been related by other authors. Some of the figures were the work of Critius, the old ones were made by Antenor. When Xerxes seized Athens after the Athenians had abandoned the city, he took away these statues with the booty, but afterwards Antiochus returned them to the Athenians.

[f] Dem. *Ag. Lep.* 18: Demosthenes and the honours for the heirs of Harmodius and Aristogiton

Now perhaps Leptines will try to divert you from what I am saying by arguing that under the current system it is the poor who carry the burden of public services, whereas under his law the wealthiest will perform all the liturgies. This may sound reasonable, but if you consider his words more carefully, his lies would emerge immediately. For, as you know, there are some services that are carried out by the metics, others by the citizens, and the exception which Leptines plans to remove would apply to both. But nobody is exempt from the special contributions for war or national security, or from the equipping of triremes, justly and rightly in accordance to the laws of old, not even the descendants of Harmodius and Aristogiton, whom Leptines has specifically mentioned.

5

Cleisthenes and the Birth of Democracy

15. Cleisthenes the aristocratic democrat

The overthrow of the Pisistratids made Athens plunge once again into factional strife. Two parties were contending for power, one supporting the deposed tyrants, whose leader was Isagoras, and one supporting the noble house of the Alcmaeonids, the arch-rivals of the Pisistratids. The head of this faction was Cleisthenes, who had important international connections. Cleisthenes might have been a fully pedigreed nobleman, but he was very popular with the Athenian *demos* owing to his contribution to the demise of the tyrants, while he met with the opposition of the members of the so-called *herairiai*, the aristocratic clubs that controlled Athenian politics [a, b].

Once he became 'leader of the people' (*prostates tou demou*), Cleisthenes carried out a series of reforms of the tribal system and administration of the *polis*. These reforms, as our sources point out, had two tightly intertwined aims: to give more power to the people [c], and to promote a common civic and political identity, which would overcome parochial divisions between the various regions of Attica. As a result of Cleisthenes' reforms the citizen body of Athens was considerably expanded. Citizenship was also granted to a number of foreigners and apparently even slaves who had joined Cleisthenes' faction.

At the heart of Cleisthenes' reforms was the abolition of the four traditional tribes of Attica and the creation of ten new ones, each of which included districts from the different areas of Attica, and was therefore representative of the whole *polis*. Accordingly, the territory of the *polis* was divided into three main regions, the urban centre (*asty*), the midlands (*mesogeia*), and the coast (*paralia*). Each region was divided into ten districts, called tritties, which were to constitute the third part of one tribe. The ten new tribes were created by selecting by lot one tritty from each of the three regions. The Cleisthenic tribes were named after ten heroes of the history of Attica. As the story goes, these names were selected by the oracle of Delphi from a list of one hundred prepared by Cleisthenes. These were the names of the Cleisthenic tribes, as listed in their official order: Erechteis, Aigeis, Pandionis, Leontis, Acamantis, Oineis, Cecropis, Hippothontis, Aiantis, Antiochis.

The new tribes became the basic units for the military, political, and administrative organization of Attica. The tribes, as we have said, were meant to represent the whole city. This was most visible in the reorganization of the council of the *polis*, the *boule*, whose membership was increased from four hundred to five hundred members, fifty councilmen from each tribe. The *bouleutai* did not sit all together, but one tribe at a time, according to a new civic calendar divided into ten *prytanies*. Each tribe was meant to represent the whole of the *polis*, and for one month a year it was in charge of running the affairs of the state on behalf of all the Athenians.

Cleisthenes is one of the most mysterious personalities of Greek history. Although his name is associated to perhaps the most epochal reform in the history of Athenian democracy, no source reports a single word from him, and nothing is known of what he did after he passed his reforms. Cleisthenes, as Herodotus says, gave Athens 'the tribes and democracy', but that is not the name by which he referred to the administrative reform that he had put in place. In fact, he called it *isonomia*, or 'equality before the law'. The transformations brought about by Cleisthenes were political as well as cultural: following the example of his homonymous grandfather, who had been tyrant of Sycione, Cleisthenes wanted to create a civic identity and iconography deliberately alternative to those of the traditional Ionian tribes [d]. Aristotle, who was no friend at all of democracy, is critical of the regime put in place by Cleisthenes, particularly as concerns the creation of new citizens, which is a typical trait of democracy. At the same time, Aristotle seems to praise him for establishing a well-structured regime in which the excesses of popular rule were somehow contained [e, f].

[a] Hdt. 6.130–1: The ancestry of Cleisthenes of Athens; suitors for the hand of the daughter of Cleisthenes of Sycione

Cleisthenes asked for silence and said to them: 'Suitors of my daughters, I express my gratitude to you all, and if it was possible I would gratify you all, without choosing one to lift above the others and rejecting the rest. But since I only have one maiden daughter to marry and cannot please you all, those of you whose suit is rejected will receive a gift of one talent of silver, as a reward for your desire to take a wife from my house and your long stay away from home. As for my daughter Agariste, I give her to Megacles son of Alcmaeon, in accordance with the laws of the Athenians.' Megacles accepted the betrothal, and the marriage was ratified by Cleisthenes.

This is how the suitor was chosen, and so the name of the Alcmaeonids resounded throughout Greece. Cleisthenes, the man who gave Athens the tribes and democracy, was born from this marriage. He was called after his mother's father, a man of Sycione. Cleisthenes and Hippocrates were born to Megacles. Hippocrates was the father of another Megacles and another Agariste; the latter was called after Cleisthenes' daughter, Agariste. She married Xanthippus, the son of Ariphron. During her pregnancy she had a vision in her sleep, whereby she imagined giving birth to a lion. After a few days, she delivered a son to Xanthippus, Pericles.

[b] [Arist.] *Ath. Const.* 20.1–21: Civic strife and reform in Attica

Once the tyranny was put down, civic strife broke out between the faction of Isagoras, son of Teisandros, who was a friend of the tyrants, and Cleisthenes, of the house of the Alcmaeonids. Cleisthenes, finding himself at a disadvantage in the political clubs, brought the populace to his side by giving political rights to the masses. Isagoras was losing power and so he called back Cleomenes, who was bound to him by links of hospitality, and persuaded him to dispel the pollution from Athens, because the Alcmaeonids were supposed to be under the curse of pollution. Clisthenes therefore withdrew from the country, and Cleomenes entered Attica at the head of a small force and drove out the pollution by expelling seven hundred cursed Athenian families. Having attained this, Cleomenes tried to disband the council and make Isagoras and three hundred of his followers rulers of the city.

The council however made a stand, and the populace got together, while Cleomenes, Isagoras and their supporters sought refuge on the acropolis. The people kept them under siege for two days. On the third day, they let Cleomenes and his men go under a truce, and called back Cleisthenes and the other exiles. The people were now in control of the situation, and Cleisthenes was their chief and leader. It is safe to say that the Alcmaeonids had been chiefly instrumental in expelling the tyrants, since they had been fighting them for most of the time.

Caedon had already made an attack against the tyrants before the Alcmaeonids, on which account people sing in his honour:

Fill the cup again for Caedon, boy, don't forget about it, if we have to raise our glasses to the good men.

These are the reasons why the people trusted Cleisthenes. Having become the leader of the people, in the fourth year since the demise of the tyrants, in the archonship of Isagoras, Cleisthenes first divided all the citizens into ten tribes, instead of the traditional four. His aim was to amalgamate them and so to increase the number of those who partook of citizenship, whence the saying 'do not look at the tribe', addressed at those who asked people what was their clan. Next he made the council of five hundred members, instead of 400, 50 from each tribe, whereas under the old system each tribe gave one 100 councilmen. This is why he did not divide the city into 12 tribes, so that he would not have to use the system of tritties which was then in place (the old four tribes had 12 tritties), for if he had maintained the existing division the people would not have amalgamated. Cleisthenes therefore arranged the demes of Attica into 30 parts, ten from the demes of the city, ten from those of the coast and ten from those of the countryside. He called these pools trytties and assigned three of them by lot to each tribe, so that each tribe would include a part of all three districts. Furthermore, he made all the inhabitants of the various demes fellow-demesmen of one another, so that nobody could tell whether someone had just acquired citizenship by addressing people by their father's name, but could all address each other by the name of their deme. This is why the Athenians even in private use the name of their deme as their surname. Also he appointed demarchs whose responsibilities were the same as the former naucraries. As for the names of the demes, he called some of them after the place where they were located and some after the founders, for not all demes now coincided with a locality with a certain name. Cleisthenes maintained the local clans, clubs and priesthoods according to tradition. The tribes were named after ten eponymous heroes, as selected by the Pythian priestess from a list of 100.

[c] Isoc. *Areop.* 16: Cleisthenes restored the Solonian constitution

I find that the only way that we have to prevent future dangers and relieve us from our present ills is to bring back the democratic regime established by Solon, the most democratic men of them all, and then restored by Cleisthenes when he deposed the tyrants and gave power back to the people.

[d] Hdt. 5.66: Cleisthenes and the greatness of Athens

Athens had already been great before, but became even greater after the tyrants were deposed. The two most powerful men of the time were Cleisthenes of the house of the Alcmaeonids, and Isagoras, son of Tisandros. Isagoras also belonged to a noble house. What his lineage is I cannot say, but his kinsfolk offer sacrifices to the Zeus of Caria. These two men were contending for power; Cleisthenes was coming out the loser and so he resolved to take the populace into his faction. Cleisthenes then divided the Athenians into ten tribes, instead of the old four. He removed the old tribal denominations of Iones, Hopletes, Argadeis and Aegicoreis, and introduced new names taken from those of other heroes, who were all native of Attica, except Aiax. The name of Aiax was added because he was a neighbour and an ally, even though he was a stranger

It seems to me that Cleisthenes did all this in imitation of his maternal grandfather, Cleisthenes, the tyrant of Sicyone. In fact, Cleisthenes, after he waged war against the Argives, abolished the rhapsodic contests in Sicyon, because the Homeric poems were all about singing the deeds of the Argives and Argos. Furthermore, he wanted to expel from his land Adrastus, son of Talaus, the hero who had a shrine right in the agora of Sicyon, because he was an Argive. Accordingly, Cleisthenes went to Delphi and asked the Priestess if he should expel Adrastus. The Pythia said that Adrastus was the king of Sicyon, and Cleisthenes nothing but a stone-thrower.

Since the god would not allow him to do as he wished, Cleisthenes returned home and started to consider how he could get rid of Adrastus. When he thought he had a good plan, he sent to Thebes in Beotia to say that he wished to bring Melanippus, son of Astacus to Sycione, and the Thebans handed him over. When Cleisthenes had brought him to Sycione, he built a shrine in his honour in the most secure area of the city's town-hall.

The reason why Cleisthenes brought Melanippus to Sicyon (which I should relate) is that he was the fiercest enemy of Adrastus, because Adrastus had killed his brother Mecisteus and his son-in-law Tydaeus. Once the precinct for Melanippus was ready, Cleisthenes took away all the sacrifices and festivals for Adrastus, and gave them to Melanippus. Now, the Sicyonians had grown accustomed to paying the greatest honours to Adrastus, for Polybius had been the lord of that city, and Adrastus was the son of Polybius' daughter, and since Polybius had no sons when he died, he passed the kingdom to Adrastus.

On top of the other tributes paid by the Sicyonians to Adrastus, they commemorated the vicissitudes of his live by staging tragic choruses in his honour instead of Dionysus. Cleisthenes however returned the choruses to Dionysus and all the other sacrifices to Melanippus.

This is what Cleisthenes did in relation to Adrastus. Also, he changed the names of the tribes of the Dorians, so that the Sicyonians and Argives would not share the same tribe names. Cleisthenes however made the Sicyonians objects of ridicule, because the names that he gave to the tribes were 'swine' and 'donkey' with the addition of an ending. As for the name of his tribe, Cleisthenes called it 'Archelai', or the 'Rulers of the people', as an indication of his own power. The other tribes were called Swinites, Donkeytes and Porkites. These were the names of the tribes of Sicyon when Cleisthenes was in power, and for sixty years after his death. Afterwards however the Sicyonians considered the matter and resolved to rename the tribes Hylleis, Pamphili and Dymanatae. A new tribe was also created and called Aegialeis in honour of Aegialaeus, son of Adrastus.

These were the deeds of Cleisthenes of Sicyone. My impression is that Cleisthenes of Athens followed the example of his homonymous grandfather when he resolved out of hatred for the Ionians that his tribes should not have the same names as those of the Ionians. The people back then had no entitlements whatsoever, and once he had them on his side, Cleisthenes changed the names of the tribes and increased their number and instituted ten chiefs of the tribes instead of four, and assigned ten demes to each tribe. Having obtained the support of the commons, the party of Cleisthenes became much stronger than the opposing faction.

[e] Arist. *Pol.* 3.1.10: Cleisthenes expands the citizen body

Questions arise concerning those who become citizens as a result of a revolution. Take the case of the new citizens created by Cleisthenes after the overthrow of the tyrants, when he enrolled in the tribes many foreign residents who previously had been foreigners or slaves. The point of dispute here is not whether or not they were citizens, but rather if it was right or wrong to give them citizenship.

[f] Arist. *Pol.* 6.2.11: Cleisthenes and other radical democrats

Not every *polis* can endure the extreme form of democracy, because all citizens have an equal share in the government. Nor can any such regime survive easily, unless it rests on good laws and good customs [...]. In order to establish democratic regimes of this kind and give power to the people, popular leaders usually try to put together as many supporters as possible including not only legitimate citizens but also the baseborn and those who are citizens on one side only, I mean to say those of whom only the father or the mother is a citizen. For it is the people of this sort who are more at home in this kind of democracy. Demagogues generally arrange the state in the following manner: the number of citizens is increased up to the point where lower orders outnumber the notables and the middle classes, without crossing that limit. For if they go beyond that point the state becomes unruly, and the notables more hostile towards democracy. This for instance was the cause of the civil unrest in Cyrene. For when the base element is small within a city, it is overlooked, but when it grows bigger it becomes more visible. Any democracy of this kind would find useful the reforms put in place by Cleisthenes to strengthen democracy in Athens.

16. *Isonomia* in practice

What follows is a small selection of sources relating to the practical and cultural effects of Cleisthenes' *isonomia*. Item [a] is an inscription from the *agora* of Athens, engraved on a pillar serving as a gatepost to an area where citizens entered arranged by tribe and tritty. Item [b], dating to the end of the 6th century, is the earliest surviving decree of the assembly. It contains norms concerning the Athenian citizens living on the island of Salamis.

Cleisthenes actively promoted the cult of the tyrannicides (see *supra*, item 14c). Item [c] is a *scholion* ('hymn') of the late fourth century, celebrating Harmodious and Aristogiton as the men who restored *isonomia* in Athens, and made all citizens equal before the law.

Item [d] is a fragment from Cleidemos, a fourth-century writer of local Attic history, discussing the etymology of *pnyx*, the name given to the slope one kilometre west of the acropolis, where the Athenian assembly held its meetings.

[a] IG I³ 1127: A gatepost in the *agora*

This is where the tritty Paianieis ends and the Myrrhinousini begins.

[b] IG I³. 1 = Fornara 44b = M&L 14 = SEG XXVI.39, XXXI.1 = Tod I 11: A decree of the Athenian *ekklesia*

The people decreed: the settlers in Salamis shall live in Salamis […];

They shall pay taxes and give military service […];

They shall not lease their land except to a […];

They shall provide their own arms to the value of thirty drachms, and the Athenian governor will oversee […]

[c] Callistratus' scholion to Harmodius and Aristogiton, translated by Elton (Athenaeus, *Deipnosophistae* 15.69a–b): The tyrannicides gave equality to Athens

In myrtles veil'd will I the falchion wear,
For thus the patriot sword
Harmodius and Aristogiton bare,
When they the tyrant's bosom gored,
And bade the men of Athens be
Regenerate in equality.

Oh! beloved Harmodius! never
Shall death be thine, who liv'st for ever.
Thy shade, as men have told, inherits
The islands of the blessed spirits,
Where deathless live the glorious dead,
Achilles fleet of foot, and Diomed.

In myrtles veil'd will I the falchion wear,
For thus the patriot sword
Harmodius and Aristogiton bare,
When they the tyrant's bosom gored;
When in Minerva's festal rite
They closed Hipparchus' eyes in night.

Harmodius' praise, Aristogiton's name,
Shall bloom on earth with undecaying fame;
Who with the myrtle-wreathed sword
The tyrant's bosom gored,
And bade the men of Athens be
Regenerate in equality.

[d] Cleidemos, FGH 323 F7 = (Harpocration, *Lexicon*, s.v. Pykni): The meaning of the term *pnyx*

Hyperides in his first speech *On behalf of Chairephilus*, says: 'so much of the Pnyx…' Pnyx was the name of the Athenian assembly; there are plenty of references to it in the Attic authors. Cleidemus in the third book of the *Protogonia* says: 'the Athenians used to meet at the pnyx. The name stems from the fact that the assembly was always tightly packed (*pyknoumenen*)'.

The ten Cleisthenian tribes

Tribe	Tritties
1. Erechteis	A: Euonymon
	P: Lamptrai
	M: Cephisia
2. Aigeis	A: Collytus
	P: Halai Araphenides
	M: Epacrias
3. Pandionis	A: Cydathenaium
	P: Myrrhinous
	M: Paiania
4. Leontis	A: Scambonidai
	P: Phrearrioi
	M Eupyridai
5. Acamantis	A: Ceramicus or Cholargus
	P: Thoricus
	M: Sphettus
6. Oineis	A: Lacidai
	P: Thria
	M: Pedias
7. Cecropis	A: Melitas
	P: Aixones
	M: Phyla
8. Hippothontis	A: Piraeus
	P: Eleusis
	M: Decelia
9. Aiantis	A: Phalerum
	P: Tetrapole
	M: Aphidna
10. Antiochis	A: Alopeces
	P: Anaphlystus
	M: Pallenes

A: tritty of the city (*asty*)
P: tritty of the shores (*paralia*)
M: tritty of the midlands (*mesogeia*)

Democracy, Empire and the Persian Wars

17. Democracy and maritime expansion: The effects of Cleisthenes' *isonomia*

The regime of *isonomia* put in place by Clisthenes in 509/508 gave unprecedented momentum to the process of democratization of the Athenian constitution [a]. The institution of the new tribes had important repercussions on the organization of the Athenian military. The army was now divided into ten tribal regiments commanded by a *strategos* ('general'). The original role of a *strategos* was that of leading his tribe's hoplite phalanx on the battlefield. After the Persian War, the development of the naval power of Athens changed radically the military policies of the city and, consequently, the duties and political responsibilities of the *strategoi*. The *strategia* would soon become the most important office of the city, leading to an equally swift decline of the archonship. Unlike the other Athenian magistrates, the *strategoi* were not appointed by lot, but by popular vote. Also, it was possible to be re-elected to the strategia for an unlimited number of times. Pericles, for instance, the greatest leader of classical Athens, was elected to the *strategia* for a record 22 times, and almost uninterruptedly between 448 and 429.

Cleisthenes is also credited with the introduction of ostracism, a curious procedure whereby the Athenians could expel any citizen considered to be politically dangerous for a period of ten years. The first man to be ostracized was Hipparchus, an associate of the Psisitratids, in 487. In the same year, the Athenians changed the procedure for appointing the nine archons from election to lot. This was a clear sign of the declining importance of archonship, which was becoming a largely ceremonial magistracy.

The term *ostrakismos* was derived from the pieces of broken pottery (*ostraka*), where the Athenians wrote down the name of their fellow-citizens whom they wanted to be exiled. A detailed description of how ostracism worked is given in a fragment of the 3rd-century historian Philochorus [b]. According to Aristotle, the presence of such procedures to expel potentially troublesome citizens was a typical feature of democratic regimes [c]. Syracuse for instance had an institution similar to ostracism known as *petalismos*. The name in this case was derived from the olive leaves (*petala*), which the people of Syracuse used to cast their vote. The author of the *Constitution* argues that Cleisthenes devised this procedure in order to get rid of the supporters of the Pisistratids [a]. In 484, Xanthippus, the father of Pericles, was the first Athenian citizen to be ostracized without having been involved in the activities of the tyrants [d]. Two years later, the Athenians ostracized Aristides, a conservative politician, who was opposing the policies of naval expansion promoted by Themistocles [e].

[a] [Arist.] *Ath. Const.* 22.1–6: Cleisthenes made Athens more democratic

Once these reforms were put in place, the constitution became more democratic than that of Solon. For it had so happened that under the tyrants the laws of Solon had disappeared due to disuse, while Cleisthenes created new ones aimed at the people, such as the law on ostracism. In the fifth year after the introduction of these laws, in the archonship of Ermocreon, they instituted the oath for the council of the five hundred, which is still in use. Then they began to appoint the generals by tribe, one from each tribe, while the polemarch was the head of the whole army. In the twelfth year after this, the Athenians won the battle of Marathon; two years after the victory, in the archonship of Phainippus, the emboldened people put into practice for the first time the law on ostracism. This law had been established owing to the mounting suspicion against those in power, because Pisistratus had risen to tyranny from the position of demagogue and general. The first man to be ostracized was one of his relatives, Ipparchus, son of Charmus, of the deme of Collytus. In fact, Cleisthenes had set up the law on ostracism especially to get rid of him. This he did because the Athenians, with their customary mildness, had permitted the friends of the tyrants who had not been directly involved in their crimes during the civic unrest to remain in the city, and Ipparchus was their leader and chief. Straight after that, in the following year, in the archonship of Telesinus, for the first time since the tyrant, the Athenians appointed the nine archons by lot, tribe by tribe, from a preliminary list of five hundred candidates chosen by the demesmen. Previously they used to elect the archons by vote. Also, they ostracized Megacles son of Hippocrates of the deme of Alopeche. For three years they went on ostracizing the friends of the tyrants, in accordance with the original purpose of the law, but in the fourth year, they used it to expel any citizen who appeared to be too powerful. The first man with no link with the tyrants to be ostracized was Xanthippus son of Ariphron.

[b] Philochorus, FGH 328 F30 = *Lexikon rhetoricum Cantabrigense* p. 354.1N; Lexikon to Demosthenes, against Aristocrates (P. Berol. 5008, B27): How ostracism worked

These were the rules of ostracism: before the eighth pritany[1] the people held a preliminary vote to decide whether they should hold an ostracism. If they voted to do so, the agora was fenced in with wooden panels, and ten entrances were opened on these panels, through which the people would enter arranged by tribe to cast their secret ballots. The nine archons and the *boule* were in charge of proceedings. Once they had counted the shards (*ostraka*) to determine who had the most votes, if the total number of votes was no less than 6,000, this person had to settle his affairs within ten days and leave the city for ten years (this term was later reduced to five years). He continued to receive the profits of his estate, provided that he did not get into the territory of Attica past the promontory Gerastaeum on the coast of Euboaea.

Hyperbolus was the only man of no prominence to be ostracized not because he was suspected of aiming at tyranny, but on account of the vulgarity of his character. After the ostracism of Hyperbolus the practice was discontinued. Ostracism had been introduced as part of the reforms of Cleisthenes, when he dissolved the tyranny. His aim was to expel the friends of the tyrants from Athens.

[c] Arist. *Pol.* 3.8.2: Ostracism and democracy

Democratic states have conceived the practice of ostracism because they are meant to pursue equality above all other things; therefore these states used to ostracize the men considered to be excessively powerful in terms of wealth, or popular support or any other form of political ascendancy, and these men they banished from the city for a fixed period of time.

[d] M&L 21: Xanthippus' ostrakon

The cursed Xanthippus, son of Arriphron has done more harm than any other politician.

An ostrakon of Xanthippus from the Agora Museum of Anthens.

[e] Plut. *Arist.* 7.1-4: The ostracisms of Aristides and Hyperbolus

Aristides at first happened to be much loved by the Athenians owing to his surname. Later on however this sentiment turned into hatred and jealousy, especially since Themistocles began to spread stories among the people that Aristides had abolished the law-courts by examining and judging every case himself, and that he had established a monarchy without anybody noticing it, except that he did not have a bodyguard. Furthermore, the people, emboldened by their victory, were now convinced that nothing was too good for them, and therefore hated those who stood above the crowd owing to their fame and name. So, the Athenians gave to their envy for his reputation the name of fear of tyranny, and having gathered from the countryside into the city, ostracized Aristides.

Now, the procedure of ostracism was not a measure to correct one's immorality. Rather, it was considered with some speciousness to be a form of humbling and docking of an individual's prestige and power. In fact, ostracism was a humane way of releasing jealousy, which vented a malignant desire to cause harm without inflicting any irreparable injury, but by imposing a change of residence for a period of ten years. And when the ostracism began to be employed against the low-born scoundrels, then the Athenians ceased to use it. The last ostracism was that of Hyperbolus, and they say that Hyperbolus was ostracized for the following reason: Alcibiades and Nicias were the most powerful politicians of the time, and were at variance with each other, but when the people were about to hold an ostracism, and were clearly going to ostracize either of them, then they mended their differences, brought their factions together, and prepared the ground for the ostracism of Hyperbolus. This outraged the Athenians, who felt that the institution of ostracism had been mistreated and abused, and so they abandoned and put an end to it altogether.

18. Democratic Athens and the other Aegean powers

The cultural and political revolution brought about by Clisthenes' reforms at the end of the 6th century was to have major international repercussions. The democratization of Athens was a cause of great concern among the Spartans. In 506, King Cleomenes launched a campaign to invade Attica, overthrow democracy and install a tyranny under Isagoras. The campaign resulted in a fiasco, and was soon followed by a series of successful Athenian operations in Peloponnesian territory. Democratic Athens was a power on the rise: no longer oppressed by tyranny, the Athenians could now release their energy, ambition and inventiveness to make their city great. Herodotus describes the revolution set in motion by Cleisthenes with one word: *isegoria* (*isos* = 'equal'; *agoreuein* = 'to speak in public'). *Isegoria* did not refer to the natural equality of all citizens before the law. Rather, it implied that all citizens had an equal right to address the assembly. This does not mean that all citizens were expected to address the *ekklesia*, but any Athenian who was willing to contribute to the life of the community was given the opportunity and a suitable platform to do so (see Hansen 83–4) [a]. The emergence of democratic Athens was an unsettling force in the world of the *poleis*, which asked a number of questions of the established powers of Greece, particularly in the Peloponnese. When Cleomenes tried to persuade his Peloponnesian allies to embark upon a new expedition into Attica to restore the tyranny of the Pisistratids, he met with no success. The king was confronted by a Corinthian envoy, who did not hesitate to condemn the evils of tyranny [b].

Athens was not the only city to experiment with popular government. The decades between the sixth and fifth centuries were a time of lively debate on the various forms of constitution. One of the most interesting sources for the study of this debate is the so-called 'dialogue on constitutions' contained in the third book of Herodotus' *Histories*. The dialogue is set in Susa, the capital of the Persian Empire, in September 522. A conspiracy of Persian notables has just deposed and killed Gaumata, a usurper who ruled Persia for a few months after the death of Smerdis, pretending to be the deceased sovereign. Herodotus says that after the assassination of Gaugamata, the leaders of the conspiracy, Otanes, Megabyzus and Darius, met to discuss what constitution should be adopted for the government of the empire. The three eventually chose monarchy, and Darius became king. Otanes, however, delivered a heartfelt celebration of popular rule, which he calls *isonomia*, the same name which Cleisthenes gave to his reforms. In fact, what Otanes proposes is a very Greek kind of popular regime, based on public debate, accountability and the use of lot to assign magistracies. It is extremely unlikely, to say the least, that such debate did take place in the forms and times described by Herodotus, but the dialogue is an important document of the international debate surrounding the new ideas of political equality [c].

[a] Hdt. 5.74–8: The new Athens, liberty and bravery

Cleomenes knew that the Athenians had wantonly insulted him in word and deeds, and so mustered an army from all the parts of Peloponnese. The purpose for collecting this army, although he did not make it public, was to take revenge upon the Athenian people and set up a tyranny under Isagoras, who had fled with him from the acropolis. Accordingly, Cleomenes marched into Eleusis with a large army, while the Boeotians, by a previously concerted plan, seized two villages on the Attic border, Oinos and Ysias, and the Chalcidians broke in from another point and laid waste the territory of Attica. The Athenians, finding themselves attacked from two sides, decided to engage the Spartans at Eleusis first, and confront the Boeotians and Chalcidians at a later time.

The troops were about to engage battle when the Corinthians, thinking that they were acting unjustly, turned back and withdrew. Later Demaratus, son of Ariston, the other Spartan king, did the same, although he had come from Sparta in shared command with Cleomenes and had never had any difference with him in the past. As a result of this dissension, a law was passed in Sparta to the effect that the two kings should not take part in a campaign together. Before then, both kings used to go with the army, whereas now one of the kings and one of the sons of Tyndarus should stay at home. Before then, they both had to offer their services and campaign with the army.

So, now at the Eleusis, when the other allies saw that the Spartan kings were in disagreement and the Corinthians had abandoned the campaign, they also withdrew and went home. This was the fourth time that the Dorians had marched into Attica; they had come twice as an invading force and twice to bring aid to the Athenian people: the first time was when they established a settlement in Megara. This expedition, as might correctly be said, took place under the reign of Codrus. The second and third times were when they moved from Sparta to drive out the Pisistratids. The fourth one was the present campaign, when Cleomenes led the Peloponnesians into Eleusis. This was the fourth Doric invasion of Attica. Once this campaign was so ingloriously aborted, the Athenians set off an army to punish the Chalcidians; the Boeotians came to the Euripus to help the Chalcidians, and as soon as the Athenians saw this Boeotian contingent, they resolved to attack them before the Chalcidians. The Athenians engaged in battle with the Boeotians and obtained a great victory, killing many of them and taking seven hundred prisoners. On the same day the Athenians crossed to Euboea to deal with the Chalcidians. Having achieved another victory, they left four hundred settlers in the territory of the Horse-breeders, for this was the name given to the wealthy among the Chalcidians.

The prisoners taken in this battle and the captured Boeotians were kept in chains. After some time, however, they released them for a ransom of two minae, and the fetters in which the prisoners had been bound were hung up in the acropolis and were still there in my time, hanging from the wall scorched by the Persian fire, opposite the temple facing west. Furthermore, they dedicated the tithe of the ransom, and this money was used to build a four-horse chariot of copper, which stands on the left as one walks into the acropolis. The inscription reads as follows:

> *The sons of Athens, victorious in battle, bound the enemy in iron chains and quenched their pride, and offered these horses from the tenth of the spoils as a gift to Pallas Athena.*[2]

Athens was growing powerful, proving that political equality (*isegoria*) is an excellent thing, not in one single respect but in all of them: for when they were oppressed by tyranny they were not more successful in war than any of their neighbours, but once they were released from their tyrants they became by far the first army of Greece. This demonstrates that as long as they were oppressed, like slaves working for a master, they were cowardly, but once they were set free, each of them was eager to be successful for himself.

This is what the Athenians had achieved. Afterwards, the Thebans, desiring to take revenge on the Athenians, sent to Delphi for advice. The priestess said that this was not possible, and ordered them to disclose the matter to the 'Many-voiced' and seek the aid of the 'nearest'. When the envoys returned, an assembly was summoned and the response of the oracle was revealed to it. When the Thebans heard that they had to seek the aid of the 'nearest', they said: 'If this is what we have to do, the peoples who dwell nearest to us are the Tanagrians, and the Coroneans and the Thespians. They have always been our allies in battle, gallantly bearing the efforts of war with us. Perhaps the oracle is telling us to seek their aid.'

[b] Hdt. 5.91–2: Sparta, Corinth and the emergence of democracy

When the Spartans acquired the oracles and saw that the Athenians were becoming more powerful and had no intention of obeying them, they realized that if the people of Attica remained free they would become as powerful as they were, but if they were held fast under a tyranny, they would be weak and prone to obedience. Sensing all this, the Spartans sent to recall Hippias, son of Pisistratus from Sigeum on the Hellespont, where the Pisistratids had sought refuge. When Hippias arrived, the Spartans sent for envoys from their allies, and addressed them as follows: 'Allies, we recognize that we acted unadvisedly when, misled by false oracles, we drove out of their fatherland men who were our guests and had promised to subjugate Athens to us. Then we handed that city to an ungrateful lot, and as soon as they raised their heads in the liberty that we had given them, they wantonly insulted us and our king, and threw us out of their city. But now Athens has grown so proud and powerful, as their neighbours of Boeotia and Chalcidas have already realized at their cost, and others will soon too. Since we have made this mistake, we now ask for your help to take revenge upon them. On this account we have sent for Hippias and called you from your cities: let us unite our counsels and forces to bring him back to Athens and let us give back to him what we had taken from him.'

This is what the Spartans said, but their speech was not well received by the majority of the allies. While the others were keeping silence, Sosicles of Corinth spoke in the following terms: 'Certainly, heaven will be beneath the earth, and earth above the heaven, and the men will be living in the sea and fishes where men used to live, if you, Spartans, are resolved to destroy regimes based on equality to restore tyranny in their place. Tyranny is the most unjust and murderous thing existing among men. If it seems to you a good thing to have the cities ruled by tyrants, you should set up a tyranny among yourselves first, and then seek to establish tyrants among the others. Coming from people like you, who have no experience of tyranny, and have always taken the utmost care lest Sparta may be subject to one, your request is an insult to your allies. For if you had the same experience of tyrannies as we have, you would be better advised on this matter than you are now.'

[c] Hdt. 3.80–3: A debate on the best form of constitution

Once the disorders had settled down and five days had passed, the insurgents against the Magi held a council to discuss the whole matter. At this meeting, words were spoken which some Greeks would consider incredible, but which were spoken nevertheless. Otanes demanded that power should be turned over to the Persian people: 'It seems to me – he said – that we can no longer endure a single sovereign ruling over us, for this is not pleasant nor good. You have seen how far the arrogance of Cambyses has gone, and now you have experienced the arrogance of the Magus. How could monarchy ever be a convenient thing, since the ruler is allowed to do whatever he pleases without being accountable for anything? Even the best man on earth, once bestowed with that power, would be stirred to bizarre and unwonted thoughts: the good things at his disposal would make him arrogant, while envy is rooted in every man from birth. The man who is both envious and arrogant possesses the fullest form of evil: once his appetites have been satiated, arrogance and envy drive him to commit many wicked deeds. A monarch should be free from envy, because he possesses all good things, yet he behaves in the very opposite way towards his subjects. He is envious of the most notable men who flourish around him, and is fond of the basest among his fellow-citizens and is always glad to listen to slander. He is the most incongruous man of all. For if you admire him moderately, he is grieved because you are not giving him enough attention, but if you give him plenty of attention, he is grieved because you are a flatterer. But I still have worse things to say about him. The sovereign meddles with the ancestral customs of the city, and rapes women, and kills indiscriminately. On the other hand, popular rule has the most beautiful name of all: *isonomia*, equality before the law. Also, popular rule is immune from all the vices typical of monarchy: offices are assigned by lot, magistrates have to give account of their activity, and all decisions are taken through public deliberation. I therefore propose that we abolish monarchy and exalt the masses, for everything is possible for the many.'

This was the advice given by Otanes. But Megabyzus argued for oligarchy. He said: 'I do agree with everything Otanes said about tyranny, but I think he deviates from the best advice when he urges you to give power to the masses. Nothing is more foolish and arrogant than the useless mob. For it cannot be tolerated that men are released from the arrogance of a tyrant to fall victim to the arrogance of the licentious mob. Whatever the tyrant does, he does with knowledge, but knowledge is impossible for the masses. How could they have knowledge those who have not learnt or seen by themselves what is best, but rush into the affairs of the city without thinking, like a flooding river? Let those who wish ill to Persia prefer democracy, but let us select the best men and give power to these. And we shall be among them, for it is among them that the best advice is likely to be found.'

This was the advice of Megabyzus.

Darius was the third to illustrate his opinion: 'It seems to me that Megabyzus has said the right things about popular rule, but not about oligarchy. For if we were to choose, for argument's sake, between the best form of democracy, oligarchy and monarchy, I say that monarchy would be by far the best. Nothing, as it seems, is better than the rule of the best man: using his best judgment, he will direct the populace without reproach, without revealing anything of the plans against enemies. In an oligarchy, there are many who strive to apply their virtue to the affairs of the community, every leading citizen wants to make his advice prevail, and this is the cause of great hatred between them, and this hatred leads to factional strife, and strife to violence, and violence brings about monarchy. This demonstrates how superior monarchy is. Then, when the people are in power, wicked things inevitably occur, and when wicked things against the common interest occur, the wicked are not divided by hatred, but are held together by strong friendships, for those who want to cause harm to the state, they do it together. This goes on until someone from the people rises up to stop these men, and so he gains the admiration of the populace, and being the object of their admiration, he also becomes their sovereign. This also demonstrates that monarchy is the best form of government.

To sum up: where did liberty come to us and from whom? From the people, from an oligarchy, or from a monarchy? Since we have been set free by one man, I think that we should maintain such kind of government. Besides this we should not obliterate the ancestral laws that are still in place: they are good and will not get better.'

The choice was between these three options, and four of the seven men favoured the last one. At this point Otanes, whose proposal of giving equality to the Persians had been defeated, spoke to them in these terms: 'Companions, it is clear that one of us has to become king – either by lot, or by vote of the Persian people, or by some other system. I will not take part in this contest, for I have no desire to rule or be ruled. But I lay forth this condition for the withdrawal of my candidacy to the crown: that neither I nor any of my descendants shall be ruled by any of you.' The others agreed on these terms. Otanes stood aside and did not take part in the contest, and up to this day his house is the only one to remain free, and is ruled only insofar it wants to be ruled, as long as they comply with the Persian laws.

19. Growing democracy, growing Athens: Democracy, naval mastery and urbanization

The campaigns against Cleomenes were the first important test of the new Athenian army. Equality, as observed by the Corinthians, enabled the Athenians to unleash their bravery and ambition, both within and outside the boundaries of continental Greece. In 499, the Athenians sent troops to Asia Minor in support of the anti-Persian revolt of the Greeks of Ionia. Initially the operation met with success. The Greek rebels went so far as to seize and burn the city of Sardis, the capital of the Persian satrapy of Lydia. In 497, however, the Persians went on the counteroffensive and three years later they obtained a decisive victory in a naval battle off the shores of Lade. In 490 the Persian commanders Datis and Artaphernes landed in Attica to punish the Athenians for their involvement in the revolt. The Persians made camp at Marathon, 40 kilometres northeast of the city of Athens, and there they engaged in battle with a greatly inferior contingent of Athenians and Plataeans. In one of the most glorious days of Greek history, the Athenians and their allies pushed back the men of Datis and Artaphernes, who withdrew to their ships. The Athenians had defeated the mighty Persian army and saved Greece from slavery.

The battle of Marathon had been won by the bravery, patriotism and discipline of the Athenian infantrymen, and by the tactical nous of their generals. All the ten *strategoi* were serving on the battlefield, rotating the supreme command of the army between them day by day. Athens acquired new international prestige, in Greece and beyond. The enthusiasm engendered by the victory at Marathon boosted the ambition of the Athenians. That momentous battle was a turning point in the history of Athens: the years immediately after the victory at Marathon were dense with important events, which would transform the face and the destiny of the city forever. Miltiades, one of the heroes of Marathon, was ostracized in 489, and so was, five years later, his political rival Xanthippus.

In 493 a new vein of silver was found in the mines of Laurium. The original intention of the Athenians was to distribute this silver among the citizens, but Themistocles persuaded them to use it to finance the fitting of a new fleet for the war against the island of Aegina. The initiative of Themistocles marked the beginning of a completely new story: Athens was to become a city of sailors, and the face and identity of the city were to change forever.

The Athenians soon became the foremost naval power of Greece. On the eve of the second Persian invasion of Greece, Themistocles persuaded the Athenians to fit out a new fleet and challenge the Persians at sea off Salamis, while others were advising the Athenians to take more literally a response of the priestess of Delphi prophesying that Athens will be saved and build a 'wooden wall' around the acropolis [a]. Two years later, most of these galleys would make the backbone of the allied Greek fleet that defeated the Persians at the battle of Salamis, a small island 16 kilometres west of Attica. The commander-in-chief of the Greek forces was Themistocles himself. As the war against the Persians progressed and moved into the waters of Asia Minor, the role of the Athenians within the Greek coalition would become more and more relevant. The Spartan leadership was no longer undisputed. A turning point came after the naval battle of Mycale. This was another notable Greek naval victory, which brought the second Persian War to an end. This is at least the opinion of the Spartans, who decided to withdraw from the campaign. In fact, the Spartans were now worried by the steady growth of Athens (they did not want any city to have walls), and did not want to be stuck in the Persian Aegean any longer. Urged by the allies of Ionia, the Athenians took over the command of the operations. In the winter of 478 the Greeks seized the city of Sestus, in the Thracian Chersonese, one of the last standing Persian strongholds. The fall of Sestus encouraged the Greek cities of the area to revolt. The Greeks of Ionia and Chersonese who fought at Sestus would become the first nucleus of a new naval alliance led by the Athenians. The military alliance established to deal with the contingencies of the war became a permanent, political institution. All the members were required to contribute to the activities of the League; most of them were unwilling to provide ships and crews and preferred to supply money, which was used by the Athenians to strengthen their fleet and finance the city's democratic apparatus. The treasury of the alliance was located at Delos, the seat of the pan-Ionian sanctuary of Apollo, and for this reason the alliance was known as the Delian League. As time went by, and the need for a permanent anti-Persian mobilization became less urgent, the league would progressively become an Athenian empire [b].

The *Constitution of the Athenians* offers a dense synthesis of the political repercussions of the historical transformations of the early-fifth century [c]. Under the political and military leadership of Themistocles and Aristides, and the moral guidance of the Areopagus, which somewhat tempered the democratic enthusiasm of the Athenians, the city became the greatest naval power of the Greek world. The naval development of Athens was to have deep repercussions on the social and political equilibrium of the *polis*. It would also transform the landscape of Attica and modify the balance between the *asty* and the countryside. The years following the end of the Persian Wars saw a rapid growth of the urban centre of Athens and of the port of the Piraeus; the city and the harbour were becoming more and more relevant to the wealth and power of Athens. Aristides urged his fellow citizens to abandon their farms – and the activities, and culture of the *chora* with them – to embrace the life of the *asty*. The unprecedented wealth stemming from the Aegean empire was essential to finance the new democratic machinery of the city. New offices were established which would provide an important source of income for the less fortunate Athenians.

The new daring and dynamic spirit of Athens was perfectly embodied by Themistocles [d]. The text of the decree proposed by Themistocles and approved by the Athenian assembly on the eve of the second Persian invasion has been preserved on a stele found in 1959 in the Peloponnesian district of Troezen [e].

[a] Hdt. 7.140–4: From the war between Athens and Aegina to the second Persian invasion; the mines of Laurium and the new Athenian fleet

The Athenians sent messengers to Delphi to ask for an oracle. Once they performed all the prescribed rites at the temple, they proceeded into the inner hall and sat there, and the priestess, whose name was Aristonice, gave them the following response:

> *Why are you lying there idle? Flee to the ends of the earth!*
> *Flee from your houses! Flee from the circle of the citadel of Athens!*
> *For the head won't remain in its place, nor will the body, nor the feet beneath, nor*
> *the hands, nor what is in between. Everything is misery,*
> *For fire and the swift Ares, advancing on a Syrian chariot, will bring you down.*
> *He'll destroy many a fine fortress, not yours alone.*
> *He'll consign many shrines of the immortal gods to the raging fire.*
> *They are sweating, as they stand, and quivering for fear of the enemy,*
> *Their roofs are pouring with black blood, foreseeing their misery and pain.*
> *But now go. Leave the sanctuary. Spread courage over your ills.*

The Athenian ambassadors were quite dismayed at the words of the priestess, and gave themselves up, hearing the disgraces that she foretold. At this point Timon, son of Androbolus, one of the most eminent men in Delphi, advised them to take the olive-branch of supplication and approach again the oracle, as suppliants. The Athenians followed his advice and said: 'Lord, have mercy for these symbols of supplication that we bring you, and give us a better response for our fatherland, or we won't leave your shrine, and we'll stay here until we die.'

At this point the priestess gave them this second oracle:

Pallas wants to propitiate Zeus the Olympian, to no avail.
In vain does she pray to him, with many words and cunning wisdom.
But now I'll speak to you again, with unalterable words:
Everything which is kept in the sacred borders of Cecrops will be taken and lost,
And so will the lairs of sacred Cithaeron.
But the far-seeing Zeus will leave a wooden wall to Athena,
This will be an unravaged stronghold for your and your sons.
Don't wait for the host of cavalrymen and infantrymen coming from the continent.
Don't stand still, but turn your back and withdraw from the enemy,
Then one day you'll be face to face against them.
O divine Salamis, you will kill many a woman's son,
When the corn of Demeter is still scattered, or when it is gathered in.

This response seemed to them to be much more propitious than the previous one, and so the ambassadors, having written it down, returned to Athens. Once they left Delphi and revealed the oracle to the people, many different interpretations were proposed. Two in particular were in complete contrast with each other: some of the older men were saying that the god was telling them that the acropolis would be spared, for in ancient times the acropolis was hedged round by a thorn-edge. This fence, according to their reading of the oracle, was the 'wooden wall'. Others on the other hand said that the god was in fact referring to the ships, and that his order was to equip them and forget about the rest. But those who believed that the wooden wall was the ships were baffled by the two final lines of the oracle, '*O divine Salamis, you will kill many a woman's son, When the corn of Demeter is still scattered, or when it is gathered in*'. These words they could not interpret clearly, for the interpreters of oracles assumed that they meant that they would be defeated at Salamis after offering battle there.

Now, there was a man in Athens, Themistocles, son of Neocles, who had recently risen to prominence. This man claimed that the soothsayers had not given the correct interpretation of the oracle, and said that if those verses really referred to the Athenians, then the god would have used less gentle words, calling Salamis 'cruel' instead of 'divine'. So, if interpreted correctly, the oracle was meant to speak not to the Athenians, but to their enemies. His advice therefore was to prepare for a naval battle, and the ships would be their wooden wall. When Themistocles exposed this interpretation, the Athenians judged him to be a better interpreter of oracles than the soothsayers, who would not have let them prepare for the naval battle, or offer any resistance at all, but leave the territory of Attica and settle somewhere else.

The advice of Themistocles had also prevailed on another occasion. The Athenians had a large amount of money in the public treasury owing to the revenues of the mines of Laurium, and each citizen was to take a share of ten drachmae from this money. Themistocles however persuaded them not to distribute the money in this manner, but to use it to build two hundred new galleys for the war against Aegina. The outbreak of this war saved Greece, because it compelled the Athenians to become sailors. In fact, these ships would not be employed for the purpose for which they had been built but would later serve the Greeks in their time of need. These ships had already been built and were ready to be employed. Now the Athenians needed to build others. Upon receiving the oracle, the Athenians resolved, in obedience to the god, to await the attack of the barbarians who had invaded Greece with the whole of their fleet, together with the other Greeks willing to join in the struggle.

[b] [Arist.], *Ath. Const.* 22.7-24.3: Silver, fleet and democracy; Aristides and the birth of the Delian League

In the archonship of Nicomedes, following the discovery of the silver mines at Maronaea, whose working gave the city a profit of 100 talents, some people advised that the money should be distributed among the populace, but Themistocles prevented this. In fact, he did not say how the money should be used, but recommended that the silver should be lent to the 100 wealthiest citizens, giving one talent to each of them, and if they employed it in a manner profitable for the city, the state would make a profit. Otherwise, the borrowers would have to return the money. Having obtained the money on these terms, Themistocles used it to prepare a fleet of one hundred triremes, each of the borrowers building one, and with these ships the Athenians would later fight at Salamis against the barbarians. It was in this period that Aristides son of Lysimachus was ostracized. Three years later in the archonship of Hypsechides, the Athenians allowed all the ostracized citizens to return, owing to the expedition of Xerxes. From that moment on, the Athenians drew a line from Geraestus to Scyllaeum and resolved that the ostracized should not live within this border, under penalty of the permanent loss of citizenship.

This is how the city had progressed so far, growing by little and little as democracy advanced; but after the Persian Wars the council of the Areopagus became powerful again and held the government of the city. Now, the council had not gained the leadership in reason of any public ordinance, but because it had been responsible for the victory at the battle of Salamis. For while the generals were in great doubt about the situation, and publicly commanded that each citizen should look after his own safety, the council made a fund available and gave eight drachmas a head to embark them on the ships. For this reason the council came to surpass the general in the esteem of the citizens, and Athens was well governed at that time. For in those years it so happened that the Athenians gained the respect of the Greeks and obtained the hegemony of the sea against the will of the Spartans by devoting themselves to the exercise of arms. The leaders of the people at that time were Aristides, son of Lysimachus, and Themistocles, son of Neocles. The latter was especially devoted to becoming skilled in the affairs of war, the former in those of politics, and to surpass everybody else in justice: the Athenians therefore employed the one as a general and the other as a counsellor. In spite of their diverging political views, these two men carried out together the rebuilding of the long walls. It was Aristides however who urged the Ionians to secede from the alliance with Sparta, taking advantage of the discredit of the Spartans caused by the actions of Pausanias. Two years after the battle of Salamis, in the archonship of Timosthenes, Aristides made the first assessment of the tribute for each city and and took the oath of the Ionians, when they swore to share the same friends and the same enemies with the Athenians, and ratified the oath by casting the iron lumps into the sea.

After these events, as the city had grown confident and a considerable amount of money had been accumulated, Aristides took to advising the citizens to aim at the hegemony and to leave their farms and live in the city, where everybody would be able to make a living, some by serving in the army, some by serving in the garrisons or by taking care of the public affairs, and by these means they would become the leaders of the Greeks. Having acquired the leadership as advised by Aristides, the Athenians took to treating their allies despotically, all except the Chians, the Lesbians and the Samians, whom they held as guardians of the empire, and allowed to maintain their constitutions and to continue to rule the subjects which happened to be under their power. Aristides also advised them to create a generous food-supply for the populace, and so it occurred that more than twenty thousand men were living on the revenues and taxes paid by the allies: there were 6000 jurors, 1600 archers and 1200 cavalrymen, 500 councilmen, 500 guardians of the docks, and also 50 watchmen in the acropolis, and as many as 7000 officials at home and 700 abroad. And then, later on, when they went to war with the Spartans, 2500 hoplites, 20 guard-ships and other ships to collect the tribute, with crews amounting to 200 units; and also the prytaneum, orphans, and warders of prisoners, all these received public funds: all these were maintained on public funds.

[c] Thuc. 1.138.3: A portrait of Themistocles

Themistocles was a man who gave the strongest proofs of his natural qualities, and this makes him especially worthy of admiration. In fact, owing to a natural ability which was not the product of study or experience, he was able to formulate in the briefest time the best judgement on the events of the immediate present as well as those of the most distant future. Themistocles could expound the affairs which he had in hand, as well as express an absolutely competent judgement on those of which he had no experience. Also, he could discern in the clearest terms whether any action was turning for the better or the worse when its outcome was still uncertain. In sum, Themistoces, with the power of his natural qualities and the swiftness of his deliberation, surpassed all men in devising offhand what should be done.

[d] Fornara 55 = M&L 23 = SEG XXIV.444, XXVIII.400, XXIX.376, XXX.384, XXXI.332, XXXII.388, XXXIII.308: The decree of Themistocles

In the name of the gods.

Decree of the Boule and the People.

Motion proposed by Themistocles son of Neocles of the deme of Phrearrhioi.

The city shall be entrusted to Athena, the protectress of the Athenians, and all the other gods, for protection and defence against the Barbarian, on behalf of the country.

All the Athenians and the foreigners who live in Athens shall place their children and their women in Troezen under the protection of Theseus, the founder of the land. The elderly and the movable property shall be brought to Salamis for safety. The treasurers and the priestesses are to remain on the acropolis to guard the properties of the gods.

All the other Athenians and those aliens who have come of age shall embark on the two hundred ships which have been equipped, and shall resist the barbarian for the sake of their liberty and that of the other Greeks, jointly with the Spartans, Corinthians, Aeginetans and the others who are willing to have a share in the danger.

Beginning tomorrow, the generals shall appoint two hundred captains, one for each ship, from those who are owners of both land and homes in Athens and who have legitimate children. The captains shall not be older than fifty years and will be assigned by lot to a ship. The generals shall also enlist marines in the number ten for each ship, from men aged between twenty and thirty, and four archers. When they appoint the captains by lot, the generals shall also appoint by lot the special officers for each ship. A list shall also be drawn of the rowers, ship by ship, on notice boards: the Athenians shall be selected from the lexiarchic registers, and the aliens from the list of names registered with the polemarch. The generals shall write up their names, arrange them by divisions, up to a total of two hundred divisions, each consisting of up to one hundred rowers. The generals shall also attach to each division the name of the warship, captain and specialist officers, so that they may know on what warship each division shall embark.

Once the assignment of all the divisions has been completed, and they have been allotted to the warships, all the two hundred warships will be manned by order of the council and the generals, after they have performed the sacrifices to appease the almighty Zeus, Athena, Victory and Poseidon the Securer. Once the manning of the ships has been completed, one hundred will be dispatched to bring assistance to the Artemisium in Euboea, and the other hundred shall lie at anchor and guard the country around Salamis and the rest of Attica,

To ensure that all Athenians will ward off the barbarians in a spirit of concord, those who have received the ten-year ban shall leave for Salamis and remain there until the people come to a decision about them. Those who have been deprived of citizenship shall have their rights restored.

[e] Thuc. 1.89–96: The end of the Persian Wars and the birth of the Athenian empire

It is in the following manner that the Athenians reached the state of affairs in which they became powerful. After the Persians withdrew from Europe, having been defeated by land and sea by the Greeks, and those who had sought refuge to Micale on their ships were annihilated, Leontychidas, the King of Sparta, who was the commander of the Greek forces at Micale, resolved to return home with the allies from Peloponnese. But the Athenians and the allies from Ionia and the Hellespont, who had already revolted from the King, remained, and laid siege to Sestus, which was held by the Persians. The allies wintered there and when the Persians abandoned Sestus, they occupied it.

After these events, they sailed away from the Hellespont, each returning to their cities. As for the Athenians, as soon as the barbarians had withdrawn from their territory, they immediately began to carry over their children, their wives and all the property which had been left behind from the places where they had brought them for safety, and prepared to rebuild the city and the walls. For only small sections of the wall perimeter were still standing, and most of the houses were lying in ruins. Only a few had been spared, and these were the ones where the Persian notables had taken up their quarters.

The Spartans sensed what was going to happen, and so they dispatched an embassy to Athens, in part because they did not want to see Athens or any other city have a wall, but especially because they were urged to do so by their allies, who were worried by the size of the fleet recently acquired by the Athenians, and by the daring spirit they had displayed in the course of the Persian wars. Accordingly, the Spartans urged the Athenians not to rebuild their walls: rather, they should join them in demolishing the walls of the cities outside Peloponnese that were still standing. The ambassadors, however, made no mention of the real reason of their mission, or of the suspicions which had prompted it. Instead, they told them that, if the barbarians were to return again, they would not find any stronghold to use as their base, as they had lately done with Thebes. Also, they told them that Peloponnese was large enough for all, both as a place of safety and a base for operations.

After the Spartans said this, Themistocles advised the Athenians to dismiss them at once, on the understanding that they send an embassy to Sparta to discuss the matter. Furthermore, Themistocles told them that they should send him to Sparta immediately. As for the other ambassadors appointed as his colleagues, they should not send them to Sparta immediately, but wait until they had raised the wall to sufficient height for defensive purposes. All the population, even women and children, were to contribute to the building of the wall, without sparing any edifice public or private or public, which could be used to complete the work. All of them should be thrown down.

Having given these instructions, Themistocles said that he would personally take care of the matter in Sparta, and then departed. Once in Sparta, Themistocles did not go to meet the city's magistrates, but made excuses and tried to gain time. And whenever some of the authorities asked why he did not appear at the assembly, he said that he was waiting for his colleagues, who had been delayed by some undeferrable business. However, he said that he expected them to arrive soon, and in fact was surprised that they were not already there.

The Spartans trusted Themistocles because he was bound to them by friendship, but when other people arrived from Athens all clearly indicating that the rebuilding of the wall was underway and that it had already reached a certain height, they did not know how to disbelieve those reports. Once he realized what was going on, Themistocles bade them not to be misled by those rumours, but to send some reputable men to Athens to examine the situation there and give a trustful report on it. So the Spartans sent their observers, and Themistocles secretly sent a message to Athens concerning these men, giving orders to detain them as covertly as possible and not let them go until they had themselves had returned, for by that time he had been joined by his fellow-ambassadors: Abronichus, son of Lysicles, and Aristides, son of Lysimachus. These had come with the news that the construction of the walls was sufficiently advanced. In fact, Themistocles was afraid that the Spartans, if they heard what was going on, would not let them go. So the Athenians detained the Spartan envoys in accordance with his dispositions, while Themistocles had a meeting with the Spartans and at last openly told them that the rebuilding of the city's wall had reached a stage sufficient for the protection of its inhabitants. For the future, if the Spartans and their allies intended to send embassies to Athens, they should do so on the assumption that the Athenians could discern the common interest and their own. When the Athenians had resolved to leave their city and embark on their ships, they had taken that bold decision without consulting with them. On the other hand, whenever they had taken counsel with the Spartans, they had proved to be second to none in the exercise of discernment. The Athenians had thought it fit that the city had a wall in the better interest of their city and their allies. For, he said, it would not be possible to have equal weight in the common resolutions of the allies without having equal military power. Therefore, either all the members of the confederacy should be without walls, or the present resolution of the Athenians should be considered to be correct.

The Spartans, as they heard this, did not give any open sign of anger towards the Athenians, for in truth they had sent the embassy to Athens not to obstruct but to assist them in their decisions. Furthermore, at the time they were still well disposed towards the Athenians owing to the spirit with which they had fought against the Persians; still, they felt greatly frustrated at the failure of their purpose, even though they did not show it. By all means, the respective embassies returned home without making any formal remonstration.

In this way the Athenians walled their city in a short time; and even today it is clear that the work was completed in haste, for the foundations of the wall are laid of all possible kinds of stones, and in some places these have not even been wrought as to fit together, but just placed in the order in which the various workers brought them. A number of columns from tombs and engraved stones were also built into the wall. The perimeter of the city was extended in all directions and so in their haste they used whatever building materials they could find. Themistocles also persuaded them to complete the walls of the Piraeus, the building of which had begun in the year of his archonship, for Themistocles thought that its three natural harbours made it a particularly fine site, and that by becoming sailors the Athenians would have made a big step forwards to establish their power. In fact, it was Themistocles who first ventured to tell them to apply themselves to the sea, and so he immediately helped them to lay the foundations of their empire. Following his advice, the Athenians built the walls around the Piraeus of the thickness that can still be seen, for two wagons carrying stones could meet and pass each other. Between the walls there was no rubble or mortar, but large stones hewn square and fitted together, cramped to each other on the outside with iron clamps and lead. The walls were completed only to half of height which had been originally planned. For Themistocles wanted to ward off the assaults of the enemy by the thickness and height of the wall, his idea being that a small garrison of invalids was sufficient to defend it, leaving the others available for service in the fleet. Themistocles devoted his utmost attention to the navy, for in my opinion he saw that for the King's army it was easier to make approach by sea than by land. Also, he thought that the Piraeus was more strategic than the upper city, and often advised the Athenians, if one day they would be pressed by land, to come down to the Piraeus and resist all their enemies with their fleet.

Thus in this way the Athenians built their walls and all the other fortifications immediately in the aftermath of the Persian Wars.

In the meantime, while Sparta was still the supreme power in Greece, Pausanias son of Cleombrotus was dispatched from Sparta as commander of the Greeks with 20 ships from Peloponnese. Thirty ships of the Athenians, and a number of other allies were also sailing with him. They made an expedition against Cyprus and subdued most of the island. Then they sailed against Byzantium, which was held by the Persians, and forced it to surrender.

Pausanias however had already become violent and so he had become odious to the other Greeks, in particular the Ionians and those who had been recently liberated from the King. These took to call on the Athenians begging them as their kinsmen to assume the leadership and thus prevent Pausanias. The Athenians accepted their proposals, and were determined to put all their attention on the matter to make sure that they would not endure any other act of arrogance from Pausanias, and to settle everything else as it seemed best for their interests.

In the meantime, the Spartans recalled Pausanias wishing to interrogate him about the reports which they had heard. For the Greeks travelling to Sparta accused him of many wrong-doings, saying that he exercised his power more in the manner of a tyrant than a general. As it happened, Pausanias was recalled at the same time as the hatred mounting against him was driving all the allies over to the Athenians, with the exception of the Peloponnesian troops. Upon his return to Sparta, Pausanias was held to account for his personal wrong-doings. As for the most serious accusations, he was acquitted of any misconduct. One of the main charges against him was that of Medism, and this seems to have been well documented. At any rate, the Spartans sent him back as commander. Instead they dispatched Dorcis and some others at the head of a small force, but the allies did not intend to yield him the supreme command. Sensing this, they withdrew and the Spartans did not send out others to replace them. In fact, the Spartans were afraid that anyone whom they would send may be corrupted, as could be seen in Pausanias. The Spartans were also willing to disengage from the Persian wars. They thought that the Athenians were sufficiently competent to lead the operations and at that time were well disposed toward them.

Having obtained the leadership with the consent of the allies owing to their hatred for Pausanias, the Athenians made an assessment of the tribute both for the cities which were to provide the money for the war against the Persians and for those which were to supply ships. Their avowed goal was to retaliate for what they had suffered from the King by ravaging his territory. Then, for the first time, the Athenians established the office of Ellenotamoi, or 'Treasurers of the Greeks'. These were responsible for receiving the *phoros*, or 'tribute', as the collected money was called. The first tribute was assessed at four hundred and sixty talents; the treasury was at Delos, where the members of the league held their meetings.

7

Democracy Accomplished

20. *Pentekontaeitia*

The fifty years between the establishment of the League of Delos and the outbreak of the Peloponnesian War were the golden age of democratic Athens. This long period of imperial dominance, democratic development and cultural achievement usually goes by the name of *pentekontaeitia* ('fifty years' in Greek). The term is drawn from the final paragraph of the excursus on the imperial expansion of Athens contained in the first book of Thucydides' *Histories*.

Thuc. 1.118.2–3: From the Persian Wars to the conflict with Sparta, Athens' golden age

All these actions carried out by the Greeks against each other and against the barbarians took place in the fifty years between the retreat of Xerxes and the outbreak of the present conflict. In these years the Athenians made their empire more secure and raised their authority to a great height. The Spartans were aware of these developments. Occasionally they tried to oppose them, but for the most time they remained inactive. For they were traditionally slow to engage in wars, unless they were compelled by necessity, and at the present time they were constrained by internal conflicts. But when the rise of the Athenian empire could no longer be ignored, and had become a threat to their own confederacy, the Spartans then realized that they could not endure any longer, and so they resolved to do everything in their power to put down this hostile force by undertaking this war.

21. Democracy accomplished: The reforms of Ephialtes

The *Constitution of the Athenians* says that in the years after the Persian Wars the council of the Areopagus, the aristocratic conclave of the former archons, was in control of Athenian politics. The moral guidance of the Areopagus was important to rein in the bold enthusiasm engendered by democracy, the victory over the Persians and the growth of the *polis'* Aegean power.

This situation came to an end in 462, when the *ekklesia* approved Ephialtes' proposal to transfer the constitutional 'additional powers' of the Areopagus to the assembly and a newly formed body of *nomophylakes* ('custodians of the laws') [a, b]. These powers arguably concerned the procedure of *eisangelia*, a form of indictment for crimes against the state, and the so-called the examination of the conduct of magistrates at the end of their mandate. The Areopagus continued to operate exclusively as a tribunal for the trials of intentional homicide. Judging from the account of the *Constitution*, an epochal reform seems once again to have been inspired more by personal enmities than any far-reaching political vision. The curtailing of the powers of the Areopagus paved the way to a series of other reforms, which furthered the progress of democratization. This was somehow favoured by a certain lack of leadership within the faction of the notables following the ostracism of Cimon, who had been the leading figure of Athenian politics in the years of the ascendancy of the Areopagus. The atmosphere was tense in Athens in 461 Ephialtes was assassinated. Five years after his death, the citizens of the zeugitai class were admitted to the ballot for the office of archon.

Released from the moral and political guidance of the Areopagus, the Athenian populace inevitably grew more arrogant and less disciplined.

[a] [Arist.] *Ath. Const.* 25: Ascendancy and decline of the Areopagus

The constitution remained under the control of the Areopagus for about seventeen years after the Persian Wars, although its ascendancy gradually declined. For as the population increased, Ephialtes, son of Sophonides, a man reputed to be incorruptible and honest in political matters, having become the leader of the people, began to attack the council. Ephialtes first made away with many of its members by bringing charges against them regarding their administration; then, in the archonship of Conon, he stripped the Areopagus of all the additional powers which made it the guardian of the constitution. Some of these powers he transferred to the assembly and others to the law-courts. Ephialtes accomplished these things with the assistance of Themistocles, who was a member of the Areopagus, but was to be put on trial for conspiring with the Persians. Themistocles wanted the council to be put down, and so he told Ephialtes that the Areopagites were about to arrest him, and the Areopagites that he had information about a conspiracy to subvert the constitution. Also, he took some selected members of the council to the place where Ephialtes lived to show them the people who were gathering there, and talked with them intently. Ephialtes was dismayed at the sight of all this, so he rushed off wearing only a tunic, and sought sanctuary at the altar. Everybody was astonished by these events and afterwards, at a meeting of the Five Hundred, Ephialtes and Themistocles spoke against the Areopagus and then addressed the assembly in the same manner, until they deprived the council of its authority. After a short while however, Ephialtes was also made away with, when he was treacherously murdered by Aristodicus of Tanagra.

In this manner the Areopagus was deprived of its political responsibilities. Following these events, it so happened that the government of the city became more and more lenient owing to the zeal of the popular leaders. In those times the upper classes happened to be without leader, because the most prominent man among them, Cimon, son of Miltiades, was still very young and had only recently entered political activity. Add to all this the sufferings that the war had inflicted upon the populace: in those days expeditionary contingents were drawn from an enrolment register and put under the command of generals who had no military experience, but had been promoted only in reason of the reputation of their families. Therefore, any expedition would result in as many as two or three thousand casualties, and so both the upper classes and the commons got deprived of their most notable men.

In all respects the administration of the city was no longer conducted with the same attention to the laws as before. The method for the election of the nine archons was not modified, but five years after the death of Ephialtes they decided to include the zeugitai in the preliminary list for the election of the archons. The first of that class to hold the archonship was Mnesthides. All the archons had hitherto drawn from the knights and the pentacosiomedimni, whereas the zeugitai could only hold the ordinary magistracies, unless the dispositions of the laws were ignored. Four years later, in the archonship of Lysicrates, the thirty judges known as local justices were re-established.

[b] Philochorus FGH 328 F64b (= *LexRhetCant* p. 351, 10N nomophylakes)

The *nomophylakes*, or 'guardians of the laws' were seven in number, and were established, as reported by Philochorus, at the time when Ephialtes left the council of the Areopagus in charge only of the trials for intentional homicide.

22. The new democracy on stage: Aeschylus' *Suppliant Women* and *Eumenides*

Religion in ancient Athens was a public and political matter. Priesthoods were state magistracies, usually bestowed upon the members of the most prestigious families of the *polis*. Likewise, the annual festivals in honour of Athena and Dionysus were eminently political events, organized and financed by private individuals on behalf of the city community, to celebrate the *polis* and its identity.

Aeschylus is the earliest of the three tragediographers whose work has come down to us. His extant tragedies mostly date between 472 and 458, and feature many references to the development of democracy. Two tragedies, *Suppliant Women* and *Eumenides*, are particularly relevant in this regard.

The *Suppliant Women* was staged some time between 470 and 459. The suppliants in question are the daughters of Danaus, the mythical king of Egypt, who have reached their ancestral home of Argos to escape forced marriage with their cousins. The Egyptian women supplicate Pelasgus, the king of the city, to give them protection, but the king refuses to grant them sanctuary pending the sovereign verdict of the *demos*. The Argive people eventually decide to grant sanctuary to the suppliants. After the deliberation of the assembly, a messenger comes from Egypt to force the return of the suppliants, but Pelasgus replies that the women have been granted sanctuary by the vote of the Argive assembly, and invites them within the walls of his city. This tragedy is a celebration of the sovereignty of the assembly's decrees, of rule by public debate, and of the mighty power of persuasion. Upon hearing the supplications of the Egyptian women, the first concern of Pelasgus is that their unexpected arrival and request may bring disorder into the *polis* [a]. Then Pelasgus conducts Danaus to the Argive assembly to plead the case of his daughters, and he warns the suppliants that whether their father will succeed or not will depend on his ability to persuade the citizens of Argos with convincing arguments [b]. When Danaus returns on stage to announce the positive response of the assembly to his daughters, he praises the binding power of the assembly's decrees [c], and so does Pelasgus when the Egyptian messenger comes to abduct the suppliants: the assembly has decreed to grant them asylum, and nobody will ever take away from Argos without their consent [d].

In 458, Aeschylus won the first prize at the festival of the Dyonisia with a trilogy of tragedies on the story of Orestes, the son of Agamemnon who killed his mother Clytemnestra and her lover Aegystus to avenge the assassination of his father Agamemnon. *Eumenides*, the last play of the trilogy, is set in Athens, and shows Orestes lying at the feet of the statue of Athena as a suppliant. Orestes is chased by the Furies, the deities who punish matricide and patricide. As the Furies surround Orestes, Athena, the *dea ex machina*, descends onto the stage, accompanied by eleven Athenian citizens who will judge the case of Orestes. This is the first trial of history: Apollo speaks in Orestes' defence, and the Furies against him. At the end of the trial, the jurors and the goddess cast their votes in equal numbers for and against Orestes, and so the defendant is acquitted. The plot of *Eumenides* is clearly inspired by the reforms of Ephialtes and celebrates the new role of the Areopagus as a homicide tribunal. Before the jurors cast their vote, Athena delivers them (and to the Athenian audience) a warning: the new Areopagus may have lost its political prerogatives, but it is still there to serve as a guardian to the city, and to ensure that the citizens make good use of their new power and responsibilities [e].

[a] Aesch. *Supp.* 355–405: The sovereign people ruling the city

PELASGUS: I see an assembly of contending gods, under the shadow of fresh-plucked boughs. May this matter of claimants to the public friendship of our city bring no harm. May no strife fall upon the city from unforeseen and unexpected causes, for the city does not need such things.

CHORUS: Indeed! May Justice, the daughter of Zeus the Apportioner, guardian of the suppliants, look upon our flight. But you, who possess the wisdom of age, learn from a younger woman. If you are merciful to a suppliant ... from a holy man ...

P.: It is not my house at whose hearth you are sitting. If the city, the common home, is stained with pollution, let the people strive in common to find a cure. I will make no promise until I report these events to all the citizens.

C.: You are the city, you are the people, you are sovereign and subject to no judgment, you rule the altar, you accomplish everything by giving vote autonomously. Defend your sanctity!

P.: Pollution on my foes! I don't know how to bring aid to you without causing harm, but I cannot dishonour these supplications with a light heart. I don't know what to do, and fear has taken hold of my heart: to act or not to act, or take what fate brings?

C.: Look upon him, the man who looks down from above, the guardian of much-labouring mortals, who appeal to their neighbours, without obtaining the justice which they are entitled to obtain. The wrath of Zeus, the god of the suppliants, will remain, untouched by the wailing of a sufferer.

P.: If the sons of Aegyptus have power over you by the laws of your nation, as they claim to be your next of kin, who is going to oppose them? You should plead in your defence that, according to the laws of the country which you have fled, they have no authority over you.

C.: May I never fall subject to the will of these men. I am determined to escape the sorrowful union, and the stars will be my guide. Choose justice as your ally, and judge the cause honoured by the gods!

P.: This case is not easy to settle. Don't be the judge. I have already said that, even though I am the ruler, I cannot effect this without the consent of the people, lest later anybody might say, if the city is struck by evil: 'the foreigners you have honoured have brought destruction upon the city'.

C.: Zeus, related by blood to both sides, looks upon the two of them, inclining now to one and then to the other, and commeasuring the evil deeds of the unjust, and the good actions of the just. If you measure these in fairness, how can you feel remorse for acting unjustly?

[b] Aesch. *Supp.* 517–23: The democratic city and the importance of persuasion

KING: Your father will not leave you here alone for too long. Now I will summon the people of the country, and I will make the community benevolent to you. I will teach your father what is necessary to say. But now remain here and beg the gods of this land with prayers to give you what you desire, while I go to plead your cause. May persuasion and good fortune follow me!

[c] Aeschylus, *Supp.* 600–1: The power of the decrees of the assembly

DANAUS: Lift your spirits, my children: everything proceeds well on the part of the citizens. The people have passed all-powerful decrees.

[d] Aesch. *Supp.* 938–49: Pelasgus to the Egyptian messenger; the people are sovereign in Argos

PELASGUS: Why should I tell you my name? You will learn it in due time, you and your companions. As for these women, if you manage to persuade them with god-fearing words, and they consent to come with you by their own will and intention, you can take them. But a decree has already been passed on this matter by the unanimous vote of the people, that these should never be abducted by force from this city. The nail has been fixed tight and firm by their determination. These words have not been inscribed on tablets, nor have they been sealed in the pages of a book. But now get out of my sight immediately.

[e] Aesch. *Eum.* 681–710: The tribunal of the Areopagus

ATHENA: Hear my ordinance, people of Attica, as you are to pass your first verdict on a trial for bloodshed. This council of judges will serve the people of Agaeus, for the future and forever, on this Hill of Ares, the sitting-place camp of the Amazons, when, filled with resentment, they led their army against Theseus, and built this new high-towered citadel to rival his, and made sacrifices to Ares, who gave the name to this rock: Areopagus. Here, the reverence of the city, and fear, its cognate, will hinder them from committing injustice, by day and by night, provided that the citizens do not pollute the laws with malefic streams: if you stain clear water with filthy mud, you will never have anything to drink.

I ask the citizens to support and honour neither anarchy nor tyranny, and never to drive fear completely out of the city. For no mortal can be righteous when he fears nothing. As long as you stay in awe of this majesty, you will have protection for your land and a safety for the city such as no other man has, in Scythia or in the land of Pelops.

I hereby establish this venerable tribunal, untouched by greed, quick to wrath, vigilant for those who sleep, a guardian for the land.

This is my advice to my citizens for the future; but now you have to stand up and take a ballot to decide the case, in fulfilment of your oath.

My word has been spoken.

8

Building a Unique Community

23. Pericles' funeral speech: A citizen's manifesto

In the years of the *pentekontaeitia* Athens became the dominant power of the Greek Aegean. The city was a capital of culture and commerce, which attracted traders, intellectuals, scientists and artists from all over the Mediterranean. Athens of course was a democracy where power belonged to the people; yet, the city seemed to have lived its time of maximum splendour under the towering leadership of one individual, Pericles, son of Xanthippus, the political heir of Ephialtes, and the continuator of his democratizing policies.

Pericles held the *strategia* almost without solution of continuity between 443 and 429. In the winter of 430/429, a few months before succumbing to the epidemic which had broken out in the city, Pericles was called to deliver the traditional speech in honour of the Athenians who had died in battle in the course of the previous year. This speech was the central moment of the public funeral for the fallen soldiers which was held every year at the cemetery of the Ceramicus. This was one of the most important and solemn events in the city's calendar and had a central significance in shaping the identity of the Athenian citizens. Thucydides marks this by giving a brief account of how the ceremony unfolded.

According to French scholar Nicole Loraux, the funeral speech (*epitaphios logos*) was a unique rhetorical genre of the democratic *polis*, and was meant to express a dual political and cultural hegemony: on the one hand the supremacy of Athens over the rest of the Greek world, and on the other that of the demos over the whole of the Athenian citizen body. Pericles' funeral speech as reported by Thucydides is one of only six such texts extant. The content of these speeches reflects the solemnity of the occasion and generally focuses on the glorious past of the city and the noble deeds of the ancestors. Pericles, as he warns his audience, intends to follow a slightly different path by celebrating the sacrifice of the Athenian soldiers through a eulogy of the city's national character and the democratic constitution, which is the most original product of the Athenian genius, and a model for other Greek states to follow. Contrary to modern interpretations of democracy as a universal value, Pericles is adamant in linking the development of the Athenian democratic constitution with the specific character of the history and social and even ethnic identity of the city. Democratic Athens is great because it is different from all the other *poleis*. In this speech, Pericles famously says that the Athenian constitution is called *demokratía* because power is in the hands of the many, not the few. Even in the celebratory context of the funeral speech, therefore, the orator does not deny the fact that popular government implies the rule of one specific section of the population. The Athens described by Pericles is a well-balanced community of responsible citizens, who are willing to take part in the government of the polis and to defend it with the utmost bravery whenever needed. In Athens the laws apply equally to all, and citizens are rewarded on merit. Although the Athenians were proud of the purity of their lineage, they had turned their triumphant city into a cosmopolitan metropolis where one could experience the best that the world produced. Also, the democratic constitution allowed a good balance between the public duties of a citizen and the sphere of his private life: unlike the Spartans, the Athenians did not live under a constant state of military training, nor was service to the state the only horizon of their lives. This however did not make them less valiant soldiers, rather the opposite, for the military valour of the Athenian soldiers stems from their natural bravery, combined with their inventiveness and sense of freedom.

Thuc. 2.34–42.1: Athens, the school of Greece

In the same winter the Athenians, following the custom of their ancestors, celebrated at public expense the funeral ceremony of the first who had fallen in the course of this conflict, in the following manner. A tent is erected, and the bones of the fallen lie in state there for three days before the ceremony, and the people bring to their dead any offerings they wish. On the day of the funeral procession, coffins of cypress wood are carried on wagons, one for each tribe, and the bones of each soldier are placed in the coffin of his tribe. One empty bier decorated with crowns is also carried in the procession in remembrance of the missing whose bodies could not be recovered. Anybody who wishes to do so can join in the procession, citizens as well as foreigners, and the female relatives of the deceased soldiers are also present and mourn on the coffins. The bones are laid in the public mausoleum, which is located in the most beautiful suburb of the town. This is the place where the Athenians have always buried the men who fell in war, except those who died at Marathon, whom they buried in the site of the battle as a reward for their outstanding virtue. Once the corpses have been laid in the earth, a man selected by the citizens on account of his wisdom and reputation delivers a speech in honour of the fallen, as the occasion demands, and after the speech all depart.

This is how they celebrate the funeral: even in the course of this conflict, whenever the time came, they have kept to this custom. Pericles, son of Xanthippus, was selected to deliver the speech in honour of the first who had fallen in the course of this war. When the prescribed time came, he proceeded from the tomb and walked up to a high platform, built in such a manner that the voice of the speaker could be heard by as many of the crowd as possible. Then he spoke these words:

'Many of those who have spoken here in the past praised the man who made this speech part of our laws, for it is good to honour those who fell in war with a public eulogy. As for myself, I am of the opinion that, since these men have shown their bravery in deeds, it would be sufficient to honour it by deeds such as those you have witnessed honoured by the state, at this funeral and not to risk the bravery of many men on the words of one speaker who might make it more or less credible according to whether he speaks well or not so well. Indeed, it is difficult to speak with some sense of measure when it is so difficult to establish the truth of what one is saying. For the listener who knows the facts and was a friend of the deceased may think that the speech is inadequate in comparison with his desires and knowledge of the events. On the other hand, someone who is not so well informed, if he hears of actions that go beyond his natural abilities, may be influenced by envy to think that the speaker is exaggerating. Indeed, the eulogies of other men are tolerable only insofar as each of the listeners believes himself able to perform any of the exploits of which he is hearing, but whatever goes beyond that point excites envy and is deemed as unbelievable. However, since this practice has been set up and approved by our forefathers, it is my duty to comply with the law and do my best to satisfy the wishes and beliefs of each one of you.

I shall begin with our ancestors, for it is just and appropriate to honour their memory. They dwelt in this land in unbroken succession, generation after generation, and, by their virtue, they have given into our hands a free country. Indeed, they deserve to be praised, but even more so our fathers who, adding to what they had inherited, built the empire which we now possess, and spared no toil to bequeath it to us who are living today. As for ourselves, who are assembled here, mostly in the prime of our life, we have made this empire even stronger, and have supplied our city with all the necessary resources to support herself in peace as well as in war.

'The military exploits by which all our possessions were conquered, whether it was ourselves or our fathers who valiantly rebuffed our enemies, barbarian or Greek, I will not recount, for I have no desire to speak at great length of events which are known to you all. But first I want to talk about the sense of pursuit which has led us here, and the character of the constitution which has made us great, and the national customs from which it stemmed. Then I will proceed to the praise of these men: I think that such a speech would be worthy of this occasion and all this audience, citizens and foreigners alike, would benefit from listening to it.

'We follow a constitution which does not imitate the laws of our neighbours, but we are rather a model for others to follow. Its name is democracy because power lies in the hands of the many, not the few. Our laws afford equal justice to all in the settlement of their private disputes, but when it comes to reputation, we assign public offices on the basis of personal merit, and no citizen is preferred to another because he belongs to a higher social class, nor is lack of means a barrier from attaining renown and public honours for anyone who can be of service to the city.

'Not only do we enjoy freedom in the government of our city, we are also free from mutual suspicion in our daily activities; for we don't feel any resentment if our neighbour does as he pleases, nor do we give him that kind of sour look which might be harmless, but still is a cause of suffering. While we conduct our private life without causing offence to anybody, in public matters we abstain from wrong-doing chiefly through fear. And so we obey the magistrates and the laws, particularly those established to assist the oppressed, and the unwritten norms which, when contravened, give universal shame for the transgressor.

'Furthermore, we have devised many ways to give our minds repose from the toils of life: we celebrate games and sacrifices throughout the year, and the beauty of our private residence is a delight that drives out our daily worries. The greatness of our city conveys to our city every kind of produce from around the world, and it so happens that the enjoyment of exotic delicacies is as familiar to us as that of the fruits produced by our own country.

'We are also different from our enemies in our approach to military matters. We keep our city open to the world, and never expel foreigners to prevent them from learning or seeing anything which, when revealed, an enemy might find useful to know. For we place our trust less on deceit and machinations than the bravery of our men on the battlefield. If we turn to education, while our enemies since the earliest age have to undergo the most toilsome training in their pursuit of manly courage, we live a life free from constraints and yet are just as prepared to encounter the dangers of war. And here is the proof: when the Spartans invade our territory, they never come by themselves, but bring all their allies with them. On the other hand, we Athenians march into the territory of our neighbours on our own and with no difficulty prevail upon men who are fighting on their ground to defend their homes. In fact, none of our enemies has ever faced our combined forces yet, owing in part to our naval commitments, but also because on land we engage in a number of different operations. Yet, whenever they happen to engage with a division of our force and attain victory, they boast that they have defeated the whole of the Athenian army, and when they are defeated, they claim to have been defeated by us all. If we are still willing to encounter dangers with our easiness of temper more than toilsome exercise, and with a courage which stems not by the bond of laws but by natural bravery, we have the advantage of not being distressed for dangers which are not yet at hand, but when it comes to face them, we are as brave as those who are always weary with toil.

'So, our city deserves to be admired in these and other endeavours. For we love beauty without being extravagant, and culture without being weak. Wealth we use more as an opportunity for action than vaunting. And if we attach no dishonour to acknowledging poverty, we find it more shameful to do nothing to escape it. In the same man one might find an equal interest in public as well as private matters, and even those citizens who are mostly concerned with their private businesses, do not lack in knowledge of public affairs. For we are the only ones who consider the man who does not take part in public life not as someone who looks after his business, but as good for nothing. We are able to take political decisions by ourselves or submit them to thorough discussion, for we believe that debate is not an obstacle to action. Rather, we think that careful discussion is an essential preliminary to any wise action. Also, we differ from our enemies on this point: you can find men who are exceptionally ardent in their bravery and at the same time wise in deliberation, while with other people bravery brings about foolishness, and reflection hesitancy. But the men who can be easily considered the bravest are those who can best recognize the difference between pain and pleasure without turning away from danger. Again, we see virtue in a different way than most people, for we acquire our friends by doing good to them, not by receiving it. In fact, the giving man makes the stronger friend, because it is by continuing to show his goodwill that he keeps alive gratitude in him. On the contrary, a man who owes you something makes a duller friend, because he knows that whenever he repays your generosity, that will be the repayment of a debt, and not a spontaneous act of amity. For we alone render service to others in a spirit of full liberality, without thinking about what is in store for us.

'In a word, I say that our city is a school for Greece, and that, as it seems to me, each of us, with the greatest ease and versatility, could prove to be the perfect master of himself in the most various cases of life. And this is not just empty boasting for the present occasion. This is nothing but the truth, as the power of our city is there to demonstrate: a power that we have acquired in reason of these very virtues. For Athens alone, when its valour is put to the test, comes out to be superior to her own fame. Athens alone never gives cause of shame to her assailants, because they have been defeated by unworthy enemies, or to her subjects, because they are ruled by unworthy masters. We have left many monuments testifying the greatness of our empire; present and future generations will look in amazement at our achievements. We do not need a Homer to sing the praise of our city, or any other poets whose verses might delight us for the moment, but whose version of events is bound to be contradicted by reality. Our daring spirit has granted us access to every sea and every land, and we have set up everlasting memorials of the good we have done to our friends and of the pain caused to our enemies. It is a city of this kind that these men strove to defend, this is the kind of city for which they have valiantly fought and died. It is therefore befitting that all those who have been left behind should be prepared to endure pain on its behalf.

'For this reason I have talked for so long about our city: to make it clear that, in this war, we are not contending for the same prize as those who do not partake in these privileges as much as we do, and to give to my eulogy of these men the clarity which comes from incontrovertible evidence.'

24. Defining and protecting Athenian citizenship

In the course of his career Pericles promoted a number of measures to encourage popular participation in the government of the city. Most notably, he established a salary for a number of public duties, such as service in the jury-courts. The author of the *Constitution* is very critical of these developments, which are blamed on Pericles' need to find a countermeasure to the lavish personal expenditures with which his political rival Cimon tried to buy popular consensus. This, however, ultimately resulted in a deterioration of the quality of government [a].

One of the most notable effects of the international development of Athens was the steady growth of the foreign population residing in the city. This was to cause some serious problems, particularly as concerned citizenship entitlements: a more diverse city meant an increasing number of mixed marriages. Athenian citizenship was certainly a valuable asset and we might suppose that a number of people tried to obtain it even though they were not qualified. All this called for a more precise definition of Athenian citizenship, and in 451/450 a law was passed under Pericles' proposal establishing that citizenship was limited to those of legitimate Athenian birth on both father's and mother's side [b]. The destruction or alteration, either accidental or deliberate, of the citizens' registers was not an uncommon issue in ancient Athens, often resulting in court actions. More than one century after Pericles' citizenship law, in 346/345, a scrutiny for applicants to citizenship was formally instituted under the proposal of a Demophilus [c, d].

[a] [Arist.] *Ath. Const.* 27.4: Pericles makes the constitution more democratic

When Pericles became the leader of the people, having first distinguished himself when still a young man, he challenged the accounts of Cimon's generalship, it so happened that the constitution became even more democratic. For Pericles deprived the Areopagus of some of its powers and urged the city towards naval power. As a consequence of this, the populace became bolder, and brought all affairs of government into their own hands. Forty-eight years after the naval battle of Salamis, in the archonship of Pythodorus, the war against the Peloponnesians broke out. In the course of that conflict the people remained locked up in the city, and became accustomed to receiving their wages by serving in military campaigns, and so they came, at the same time by and against their will, to take charge of the government of the city. Pericles was also the first to establish a wage for service in the jury-courts. This he did in response to the populist lavishness of Cimon, for the latter owned an estate which was large enough for a tyrant, and could afford to discharge public services with great splendour. On top of that, Cimon maintained many of his fellow-demesmen, for any of the Laciadae who so wished was allowed to come to his house every day and get a moderate supply of what he needed. Also, his estates were left unfenced, so that anybody who liked could enjoy the fruits of the harvest. Now, since Pericles' fortune could not match such lavishness, he followed the advice of Damonides of Oea (who was believed to have inspired most of Pericles' measures, for which reason he was later ostracized): since his personal resources were inferior to Cimon's, Pericles should give the people what belonged to them, and so he instituted payment for service in the jury-courts, which according to some resulted in their decadence, because the common people were always more eager to cast their lot for this office than the men of reputation.

[b] [Arist.] *Ath. Const.* 26.3: Pericles' citizenship law of 451/450

In the archonship of Antidotus, due to the large number of citizens, the Athenians approved the proposal of Pericles, to the effect that only those of Athenian birth on both sides could partake of citizenship.

[c] Dion. *Isaeus* 16: The citizenship scrutiny, I

The Athenians passed a law that the scrutiny of the registered citizens was the responsibility of the demes, and anyone who had been rejected by the vote of his fellow-demesmen should not partake of the right of citizenship, but those who had been unjustly rejected could appeal against his fellow-demesmen, but if they were rejected again, they could be sold as slaves and their property confiscated.

Aes., *C. Tim.* 77–8: The citizenship scrutiny, II

Ballots have been taking place in the demes, and each of us had to vote on his person whether he was an Athenian citizen or not. Now, whenever I attend the law-courts, I notice that the same argument always carries the day with you: when the prosecutor says, 'gentlemen of the jury, the demesmen have under oath excluded this man. Nobody has brought a formal accusation or given testimony under him, but everybody knew that he is not a legitimate citizen'. At this point you all applaud, because the defendant has no claim to citizenship. For, I think, you assume that when someone knows something perfectly well on his own knowledge, he does not need corroborate his case with evidence or testimony.

25. Athenian democracy: An exclusive community, the ephebic oath

Pericles made Athens more democratic and cosmopolitan, but his citizenship law did not modify the exclusive nature of *polis* membership. Athens, like any other Greek city-state, was a close-knit community whose membership was primarily defined by birth and kinship [a].

The accession of young Athenians to the duties and entitlements of full citizenship was marked by a series of civic-religious ceremonies and rituals. At the end of his eight–tenth year of age, the young Athenian lad was officially registered as a citizen at his deme. The procedure was rather complex and involved a public scrutiny of the candidate's age and legitimacy. On successful completion of the scrutiny, the new citizen underwent a two-year period of military training, called *ephebia*. The coming of age was marked by a solemn ceremony at the temple of Aglaurus, located near the acropolis. Aglaurus was the patriotic daughter of the mythical king Cecrops, who, as Athens was embroiled in a long war, decided in compliance with an oracle to sacrifice her own life to bring peace to her city [b]. The Athenians honoured the memory of Aglaurus with the erection of a shrine, where the young Athenians solemnly swore to defend and aggrandize the city [c]. The text of the oath of the ephebi is known from a number of literary sources and an epigraphic monument datable to 334/333 or later. The oath puts across a very conservative image of a citizen's duties, still based on the ethics of hoplitism.

[a] [Arist.] *Ath. Const.* 42.1–2: Control and scrutiny of Athenian citizenship

Only those who are of citizen birth on both sides can partake of citizenship; at the age of eighteen they are registered in the roll of their deme. At the act of their registration, their fellow-demesmen take a vote on them under oath. Firstly they vote on whether they have reached the legal age, and if they have not, they return to the rank of boys. Secondly, whether they are freeborn of legitimate birth. Then, if the vote goes against the candidate, he can appeal to the jury-courts and the demesmen appoint five of them to plead against him, and if it appears that he has been rightfully denied the registration, the city sells him as a slave. If he wins, the demesmen are required to register him. After this, the council revises the lists of those who have been registered, and if anyone is found to be under eighteen years of age, they impose a fine on the demesmen who have registered him. Once the list of the ephebi have undergone this revision, their fathers hold meetings by tribes and elect three men over forty years of age from their tribe, whom they consider best suited to take care of the ephebi. From these, the assembly elect by show of hands one man for each tribe to serve as disciplinary supervisor, and appoint one citizen from all the other Athenians to serve as their director.

[b] Lyc. *Ag. Leoc.* 76: Perjury at the ephebic oath

There is an oath which all citizens are required to take when they are enrolled in the register of their deme as ephebi: not to bring shame to your sacred arms, not to desert your place in the line, but to defend your fatherland and to hand it over better than he found it. If Leocrates has sworn this oath, then he is clearly guilty of perjury, and not only has he injured you, but he has also committed sacrilege towards the gods. If he has not sworn it, then it is clear that he has intrigued to avoid his duty, and for this reason you would be right to punish him on behalf of yourselves and the gods. Clerk, please, read the oath:

'I shall never bring shame to the sacred arms, nor shall I desert the man beside me, wherever I stand in the deployment. I shall defend the rights of gods and men, and when I die, I shall not leave the fatherland smaller, but greater and better both to the best of my own abilities and with the help of all. I shall duly obey the magistrates in charge, and the laws currently in force and any law which may be established in future. If anyone intends to destroy the laws I shall oppose him to the best of my own abilities and with the help of all. I shall honour the ancestral cults. My witnesses shall be the gods Agraulus, Hestia, Enyo, Enyalius, Ares, Athena the Warrior, Zeus, Thallo, Auxo, Hegemone, Heracles, and the borders of my native land, wheat, barley, vines, olive-trees, fig-trees ...'.

Paus. 1.18.2: The sanctuary of Aglaurus

The shrine of Aglaurus is located below the sanctuary of the Dioscuri. They say that Athena gave Erichthonius, whom she kept hidden in a chest, to Aglaurus and her sisters, Herse and Pandrosus, telling them to abstain from prying into the content of the chest. Pandrosus, they say, obeyed, but the other two opened the chest and went mad when they saw Erichthonius, and threw themselves down from the steepest cliff of the acropolis. This was the place where the Persians climbed and killed the Athenians who thought that they had understood the oracle better than Themistocles and walled off the acropolis with a wooden fence.

26. The duties of a good citizen: Commitment and reward, the liturgy system

The democratic constitution of Athens gave all the citizens the opportunity to make their private affairs prosper. Also, democracy encouraged active participation in the government of the *polis* from all citizens, regardless of their social rank, and expected the wealthy to give their particular contribution to the life of the community. Healthy competition between those ambitious individuals who were willing to gain renown by looking after the common good was essential to the prosperity of the city. The Athenian system did not provide for any form of regular taxation on the income of citizens. Wealthy citizens contributed to the life of the community through the so-called liturgies. The liturgy was a form of civic duty whereby the richest citizens carried out services of public interest at their own expense. These services ranged from the organization of tragic performances and religious festivals to the fitting of warships. Naturally, the citizens who took charge of these onerous services expected something in return from the city. This is what made the orator Lycurgus say that the liturgies were public services carried out in the private interests of one's family [a]. A passage from Demosthenes' speech *Against Evergus and Mnesibulus* describes the procedure for the assignment of naval liturgies for the equipping of warships [b].

Demosthenes' speech *Against Leptines* is an interesting document for the study of the Athenian culture of euergetism. Sometime after 355, as Athens was lingering in near bankruptcy following the disastrous conflict against the allies of the second Athenian league (Social War, 357–355), Leptines had a law passed abolishing a series of privileges, such as exemptions from liturgy duties, which the city often granted to its benefactors and their descendants. The new norm, however, was challenged as unconstitutional (*graphe paranomon*) by the heirs of the great general Chabrias. The legal issues, however, play a very secondary role in the speech prepared by Demosthenes. According to the orator, the proposal of Leptines in fact would deprive the *demos* of one of the prerogatives of the demos, namely the authority to reward the benefactors of the city, either Athenian or foreigner, and, by doing so, stimulate competition for the gratitude of the *demos* [c, d].

Defendants appearing before the Athenian law courts often tried to obtain the sympathy of the jury by listing the liturgies and other public services which they had undertaken [e–g]. If wealthy citizens who took over liturgies enjoyed great popularity, those who did not were the object of great resentment, as hinted at in a passage of Xenophon's *Symposium* [h].

[a] Lyc. *Ag. Leoc.* 139–40: Lycurgus on liturgies

Having performed public services for the advancement of their own families, these people are now asking you for a public token of gratitude. The breeding of horses, a handsome payment for a chorus, and other expensive gestures do not entitle a man to any such recognition from you, since for these acts he alone is crowned, conferring no benefit on others. Instead, if he wants to obtain your gratitude, he should have distinguished himself as a trierarch, or built walls for the protection of his city, or used his money to contribute to the public safety. These are real services to the state, because they make a real difference to the welfare of the whole community and demonstrate the loyalty of the benefactors. While the others reveal nothing but the wealth of those who have spent the money.

[b] [Dem.] *Ag. Ev. Mnes.* 20–2: The naval liturgies

Charidemus proposed this decree in order that the equipment for the ships might be exacted and kept safe for the benefit of the city. Please read the decree:

When this decree had been passed, the magistrates appointed by lot those who owed the naval equipment to the city, and handed over their names, and the supervisors of the dockyards passed on their names to the trierachs who were then about to sail and to the overseers of the navy-boards.

The law of Periander prescribed and gave order to us to receive the list of those who owed naval equipment to the state. This is the law in accordance with which the navy-boards were established. Also, there is another decree of the assembly compelling them to assign to us the debtors so that we might recover from them his proportionate amount.

Now, I happened to be a trierach and overseer of the navy-board; Demochares of Paeania was also in the navy-board and he owed the state, in conjunction with this man Theophemus, the equipment of a ship, for he had served as a trierach with him. Accordingly, the names of both of them had been inscribed on the list of those indebted to the city for the naval equipment, and the magistrates, having received their names from those who had served in that office before them, handed them over to us in accordance with the law and the decrees.

[c] Dem. *Ag. Lep.*, 1–5: The importance of honouring benefactors, I

Gentlemen of the jury, I have agreed to plead the case of these men to the best of my possibilities chiefly because I believe that the city will benefit from the repeal of this law, and in part owing to my sympathy for the young son of Chabrias. There is no doubt, men of Athens, that Leptines and anyone else who may speak in defence of this law will have no just argument to support his case. Instead, he will point out the disrepute of some of those who have taken advantage of their exemptions to avoid public services, and this will be his main argument.

As for myself, I will not reply to that by saying that it is unfair to deprive everyone of this privilege because some have abused it, for this point has already been raised, and you certainly know how strong it is. However, I would like to ask Leptines why, if not some, but all those who have received this benefit were utterly unworthy of it, he considers you just as undeserving as them, for with the clause 'none shall be exempt' he has deprived of the privilege those who are currently enjoying it, but with the addendum 'nor shall be lawful hereafter to award it' he deprives you of the right to bestow this reward. In fact, he cannot certainly mean that, while he judges the recipients of this privilege unworthy of it, so he considers the people unworthy of the right to bestow it upon whomever they wish.

Perhaps, he might object that he framed the law in this way because the populace is easily manipulated. But then, by the same token, why should you not be dispossessed of all your rights, of the whole constitution in fact? You have often been deceived into voting decrees, sometimes you have been misled into choosing weak allies instead of strong. In general I think that the same thing will necessarily happen in many of your public affairs: should we therefore pass a law banning the council and the assembly from deliberating on any matter? I do not think so, because we must not be deprived of our rights, when we have been misled. Instead, we should learn how to avoid such mistakes, and we should pass a law not to deprive us of our own authority, but to punish those who mislead us.

But now you should leave all these things aside and consider the matter at stake, whether it is in your better interest that you should maintain the authority of granting this privilege, even though sometimes you are deceived into granting it to a crook, or that, by being dispossessed of this authority, you should not be able to grant rewards even to those who deserve them. Now, the former course, as you realize, is more profitable. Why? Because widespread rewards result in many being encouraged to do good to you, but if there are no rewards for anybody, the spirit of emulation is dead.

[d] Dem. *Ag. Lep.* 155: The importance of honouring benefactors, II

The law of Leptines, men of Athens, is unjust not only because it abolishes the rewards of benefactions, thus depriving us of the benefit of having ambitious men striving for honours, but also because it gives our city a shameful fame of illegality. For, as you are certainly aware, the law prescribes one specific penalty for each serious crime. In fact, the law explicitly says that 'at any trial there should not be more than one assessment of penalty, whatever decided by the court, either a personal punishment or a fine, but not both'. But this man has used a different kind of measure, and if anyone claims a return from you, 'he shall be disenfranchised, and his property made public'. So, there are two penalties here.

[e] Lys. *Corr.* 1–6: A man of many liturgies, I

Men of the jury, since you have received an exhaustive account of the accusations against me, I would like to give you some additional information so that you may understand what kind of person I am before you cast your verdict. I was certified of age in the archonship of Theopompus, and having been appointed to produce a tragic drama I spent 30 minae on it. Two months later I spent two thousand drachmae and won the first prize with a male chorus at the Thargelia. In the archonship of Glaucippus I spent eight hundred drachmae for a chorus of pyrrhic dancers for the Great Panathenaea. In the same year I also won the first prize with a male chorus at the Dionysia on which I spent five thousand drachmae, including the dedication of a tripod. In the archonship of Diocles, I spent three hundred drachmae on a cyclic chorus for the Little Panathenaea. In the meantime, I spent six talents on the equipment of triremes over a period of seven years. Although I have sustained all these expenses, and encountered dangers every day as I served abroad on your behalf, I have nevertheless contributed thirty minae and then four thousand drachmae for special levies. As soon as I returned here, in the archonship of Alexias, I spent twelve minae on producing games for the Promethea, and obtained a victory. Later on,

I was appointed to produce a chorus of boys and spent more than fifteen minae. In the archonship of Euclides I produced a comedy for Cephisodorus and won the first prize; I spent sixteen minae on it, including the dedication of the scene material. At the Little Panathenaea I spent seven minae on producing a chorus of beardless pyrrhic dancers. I have won a warship race at Cape Sunium, spending fifteen minae. Furthermore, I have been responsible for sacred embassies, ceremonial processions and other such duties, on which I have spent more than thirty minae. Of all the disbursements which I have enumerated, had I limited my public services to what was prescribed by the law, I would have spent less than a quarter.

[f] Lys. *Corr.* 13–14: A man of many liturgies, II

Gentlemen of the jury, consider the abysmal state of the city's finances, and how these have been depredated by their appointed guardians: you should therefore consider the fortunes of those who are willing to perform public services as the safest revenue for the city. So, if you are well advised, you should take the utmost care of our property as though it was your own, knowing that you will be able to benefit from all our resources, as you did in the past. Also, I believe that all of you will find in me a far superior controller of my own estate than those who control the treasury of the state on your behalf. On the other hand, if you make me poorer, you will make damage to yourselves, for others will divide up my estate among themselves as they have done with the rest.

[g] Lys[ias]. *Aristoph.* 60–2: A family of benefactors

Now, there have been aspects of my father's life which have not been beyond blame, but when it comes to money, nobody has ever dared to reproach him, not even his enemies. Therefore, it is not fair to give more consideration to the words of our accusers than the deeds of his life, or time, which you should consider the most reliable witness of truth. Had he not been the man that he was, he would not have left but a small portion of his large estate, and now, if you were deceived by these men and confiscated our property, you would not get as much as two talents. It would be therefore more profitable for you to acquit us, not only as reputation is concerned, but also money, for you will derive a higher advantage if we keep our estate.

Consider, as you consider the time that is past, all the money which appears to have been spent on behalf of the city. Right now I am equipping a warship from what remains of my wealth, my father was equipping one when he died, and I will try to do what I saw him doing, and raise, by degrees, some small amount to be spent on public services. My money therefore continues to be the property of the state, and while I will not think that I have been damaged for having been deprived of it, you will have in this way more benefits than you would obtain by confiscating it.

[h] Xen[ophon]. *Symp.* 4.45: The burden of public offices

'Oh Hera!' commented Callias, 'there are many reasons why I must congratulate you on your wealth, one is that the city does not give you orders, as though you were its slave, another is that the populace doesn't get angry at you when you don't make them a loan.'

9

Democracy and the Problem of Individual Leadership

27. Pericles the foremost citizen

When the Peloponnesian War broke out, in the Spring of 431, Pericles had been the dominant figure in Athenian politics for about three decades, during which he had served almost uninterruptedly in the board of *strategoi*. In the course of those long years the Athenians had strengthened their control of the Aegean Sea and the grip on their allies. Upon entering the conflict with Sparta, naval dominance and imperial revenues were the Athenians' main assets: Pericles envisaged the impending war as a struggle between two extremely different powers in terms of military capability, political organization and socio-economical conditions. Also, he realized the epochal importance of this conflict, and its extraordinary implications for the life of the cities of Greece. Upon entering the conflict, Pericles, the undisputed leader of Athens, was faced with the task of persuading his fellow-citizens of the deep-reaching consequences of naval imperialism, and of the need to rethink completely their understanding of war and conflict [a]. Relying on their unassailable naval superiority and on the financial revenues stemming from empire, the Athenians should drag the Spartans into a long, transmarine war, using their fleet to launch raids against the shore of Peloponnese to destabilize the social and political situation in the heartland of Sparta's power, and avoiding at any cost engaging the enemy land forces. To carry out this plan it was essential that the Athenians resisted the temptation of expanding their empire. Also and most crucially, Pericles advised the Athenians to abandon the rural districts of Attica, which were to become the targets of the raids of the enemy hoplites, and seek refuge within the walls of the city of Athens. Pericles' plan was as daring and innovative as it was inevitably controversial: as soon as the Athenians began to see the Peloponnesian troops lay waste to the land of Attica, Pericles became the object of harsh criticism, as the man responsible for what appeared as a suicidal strategy, and for his refusing, although he was one of the generals, to take the infantry onto the field and repel the enemy. In the second year of the conflict, the outbreak of the pestilence in the overcrowded city could not but deteriorate the situation [b].

The criticism to which Pericles was subject after the outbreak of the Peloponnesian War highlights one of the most important themes in the history of Athenian democracy, namely the difficult balance between the principle of popular sovereignty, demanding that any magistrate be subject to the supreme authority of the *ekklesia*, and the personal ascendancy of charismatic leaders. Owing to his extraordinary charisma and ability to understand and direct the feelings of the *demos*, Pericles was able to contain the inevitable excesses of popular rule and give a coherent direction to the affairs of Athens. Thucydides famously went so far as to say that under Pericles, viz. in the most flourishing years of the history of democratic Athens, the city was a democracy by name, but in fact was ruled by its foremost citizen. The death of Pericles would result in a steady decline of the city's political personnel [c].

[a] Thuc. 1.140–3: Athens and Sparta at the outbreak of the Peloponnesian War, two different kinds of power

'Athenian citizens, my opinion is the same as it always was: we must not give in to the Peloponnesians. I am aware that the spirit that inspires men as they are persuaded to undertake a war does not remain the same once they are engaged in it. For as the circumstances change so does our judgement. Now I see that I have to give you the same or almost the same advice that I have given you in the past, and I demand that those of you who will find my arguments persuasive support the resolutions that we take as a community even if we do not meet with success, or they should not to take credit for our wise deliberations if we meet with success. For sometimes the course of events follows a path as inscrutable as that of the human mind and this is why when things do not turn out as we expected we blame it on bad luck.

'Now, it was already clear before that the Spartans were contriving against us, and now it is as clear as ever. The treaty says that we should submit our mutual differences to an arbitration, and that in the meantime each party should keep what they have. Yet the Spartans have never made any such offer to us, nor would they accept an arbitration if we were to offer them one. Instead, they want to settle their remonstrations not by diplomacy, but war, and so here they are, dropping the tone of expostulation and adopting that of command. They order us to raise the siege of Potidaea, leave Aegina independent, and revoke the decree about Megara. Then they give us an ultimatum, ordering us to leave the Greeks independent. None of you should think that, if we refuse to revoke the Megara decree, we would be going to war for an insignificant matter, which is chief among their complaints, and say that there will be no war if we revoke it. Nor should you leave any sense of guilt longer in your hearts as if you were going to war for a minor issue. For this minor issue contains the warranty and trial of the resolution which you are going to take. If you acquiesce to them on this point, you will have to acquiesce on bigger issues, as though you had been frightened into submission. On the other hand, a firm refusal will make them understand in the clearest terms that they should rather treat you as equals. So make up your mind here and now whether you should submit to the Spartans before you get harmed, or, if we are to go to war, as I think we should, you should do so with the determination of never acquiescing on any matter big or small, without fearing that your possessions are in danger.

'As for the war and the resources of each side, listen to me carefully, and make up your minds that we are not at all in a position inferior to theirs. For the Peloponnesians till their own land and have no financial resources, either public or private. They have no experience of protracted or transmarine warfare, and owing to their poverty can only engage on minor conflicts against each other. Powers of this kind cannot afford to man ships or send out armies too frequently, for they cannot stay away from their homes and need to provide the funds for these campaigns themselves. Besides, they have been kept away from the sea.

'The costs of war are better supported through capital accumulated over time than taxes levied under the pressure of circumstances, and farmers as a class of men are usually more willing to risk their own bodies than their possessions; for while they are confident that they can survive the dangers of war, there is no guarantee that they will not exhaust their properties, particularly if the conflict lasts for longer than they expect, as seems the case with the present conflict.

'In a single pitched battle, the Peloponnesians and their allies can take on the whole of Greece, but they are unable to sustain a war against a foe different in character from what they are, for they do not have a common council to prompt steady and vigorous resolutions. Also, they have all equal rights of vote, but do not belong to the same race, and so they pursue each their own interests without ever accomplishing anything substantial. For, while some of them want to take revenge against a particular enemy, others are more interested in avoiding damage to their properties. They are always slow to assemble and when, after some long interval, they finally meet, they spend very little time addressing issues of common interest, and most of it to their particular concerns. None of them think that any harm may come from his personal neglect, as they assume that it is always somebody else's duty to take care of this or that for him. And since each of them is of this opinion, they don't realize that their commonwealth is in fact perishing.

'But the most important thing is that they will be hindered by their lack of money, for the slowness with which it will come to them will cause delay, but the opportunities of war never wait for long. And we should not be afraid lest the enemy may build a fort in our territory or use their fleet against us: in the first case, building a city large enough to rival another one is difficult even in time of peace, much more in a hostile country for which we have provided fortifications to guard it from the enemy, and in the course of a conflict. And even if they manage to build a fort in Attica, they may be able to cause some damage to our territory with their incursions, or to incite desertion, but this will not prevent us from sailing to their territory and building strongholds here, or retaliating with our fleet, because it is in the fleet that our strength lies. In fact, we can draw more advantage from our experience of naval warfare for our operations on land than them from their experience of land warfare for their naval operations. Nor could they easily acquire the art of seamanship. Consider this: you began to exercise it in the aftermath of the Persian Wars, and still have not yet brought it to perfection: how could a population of farmers and not sailors ever achieve anything of note if we'll prevent them from getting any practice by constantly keeping an eye on them with the deployment of a large fleet? Trusting that numbers can compensate for lack of expertise, they might risk an engagement if they are faced by a small fleet, but if they find themselves blocked by a large one, they will remain quiet, and this lack of practice will make them more maladroit and consequently more timid.

'Seamanship, like everything else, is an art that requires complete commitment, and cannot be taken up and practised occasionally as a pastime. Also, if they try to lay their hands upon the treasuries of Olympia and Delphi and try to turn our mercenary rowers away from us with the promise of higher pay, that would be a serious problem, but only if we were not as good rowers as they are and the metics were not also serving in our fleet. In fact this makes a match for them, and, most importantly our steersmen and sailors are citizens, and they make better crews than the rest of Greece could ever put together. As for our mercenaries, none of them would prefer to run the risk of being defeated and exiled from his fatherland, for the sake of a few days' extra pay.

'This is I think a fairly exhaustive account of the situation of the Peloponnesians. We Athenians are free from the faults which I have criticized in them, and have other advantages which our foes cannot match. And if they invade our territory with their army, we shall sail against theirs, and it will be clear that the destruction of the whole of Attica will not be the same as that of even a small portion of Peloponnese. For they will not be able to acquire other land if not by means of a pitched battle, while we have plenty of land both on the islands and on the mainland. The rule of the sea is a great thing indeed. Just consider this: would we be more secure from assaults if we were islanders? For the future, this is how we should consider ourselves at the best of our possibilities. Leaving behind our land and houses, let us guard the city and the sea. And even if we lose our land or our homes, we should not let our resentment against the Peloponnesians drive us to engage them in a pitched battle, because their land forces are far superior to ours. If we come out victorious we would still have to fight against them again in a position of inferiority, and if we are defeated we would lose our allies, on whom our strength lies. For they would not remain quiet a day if they see that we don't have enough troops to send against them. We should not mourn the loss of land or our houses, but that of our men. For land and houses do not provide us men, but it is men that provide us those things. In fact I would have told you to go and raze down your houses, had I known that I could persuade you to do so, and show the Peloponnesians that you will not submit to them for the sake of your material possessions.'

[b] Thuc. 2.59–60: Mounting criticism against Pericles' leadership

After the second invasion of the Peloponnesians, the Athenians changed their spirits, for their land had now been laid waste twice, and the combined evils of war and pestilence were pressing on them. They accused Pericles of having persuaded them to go to war and held him responsible for all their misfortunes. So they became eager to come to terms with the Spartans, and even sent ambassadors to them without however accomplishing anything. The Athenians were now completely despondent, and all their anger was turned against Pericles. When he saw that they were so exasperated by the situation and behaving exactly as he had foreseen, Pericles, who was still a general, summoned an assembly, with the purpose of pouring confidence into the Athenians and guiding them from this anger to a milder and calmer mood. So he came forward and spoke as follows:

'I was expecting this wave of indignation against me, for I know its causes. I have summoned this assembly expressly for this reason, to give you some reminders, and to complain that you are unreasonably angry towards me, or frightened by your sufferings. I am convinced that a flourishing state is more beneficial to private citizens than individual prosperity while the state is suffering. For even when a private citizen is doing well, if the city is ruined he will be ruined with it. On the other hand, a prosperous state always provides opportunities of salvation for struggling citizens. Since the state can assist the struggling citizens, but the citizens cannot assist the state, it is the duty of all of us to defend it, while now you are so afflicted by your domestic grievances that you have forgotten about the common safety, and blame me for having advised you to go to war, and yourselves for having approved my advice. If you are angry with me, you are angry with the man who, I think, knows better than anybody else what should be done in the interest of the city, and how to expound it, a man who loves his city and is incorruptible. Besides, a man who has this knowledge, but does not know how to explain it clearly, may as well not have any idea at all. If he has both the policies and the ability to explain them, but no love for his country, he could not give his advice with the same affection. And if he has love for the country, but this love is not incorruptible, then everything would be up for sale. Therefore if you thought that I was even blandly distinguished for these virtues when you followed my advice and went to war, you should not accuse me now of having harmed you.'

[c] Thuc. 2.65.1–10: Pericles' Athens, a democracy only by name?

Such were the arguments used by Pericles as he tried to release the Athenians from their anger and to divert their thoughts from their current sufferings. As a community, he succeeded in persuading them, and so they gave up the idea of sending to Sparta, and devoted themselves to the war with renewed energy. As individuals, however, they were still grieving over their misfortunes, for the populace had been deprived of the little that they had, while the richer citizens had lost their beautiful properties, residences and the magnificent buildings that they had in country. And worst of all, they had war instead of peace. The Athenians in fact did not desist from their anger against Pericles until he was given a fine. Soon afterwards, however, as is the way with the populace, they elected him general again and entrusted all their affairs to him. This they did because they were now less concerned about their domestic problems, and had realized that he was the best man for the needs of the state.

As long as Pericles was the leader of the city during the peace, he pursued moderate policies and kept Athens safe. Under his guidance the greatness of the city reached its height, and even when the war broke out, he seems to have made a right assessment of the city's power. Pericles lived for two years and six months after the outbreak of the conflict, and after his death his foresight in relation to the events of the war became even better known. For Pericles promised them that if they remained quiet, exposing the city to no hazards during the war, they would come out victorious. But the Athenians did the very contrary: driven by personal ambitions and private interests, they adopted policies damaging both to themselves and to their allies even in matters apparently unrelated to the conflict. And the success of these policies would have conferred honour and benefits only to some private citizens, but their failure would have meant certain disaster for the whole country in the course of the war. The reason for this was that Pericles, owing to his rank, ability, and undisputed integrity, exercised a form of individual control over the multitude, while formally respecting its liberty; to put it in one word, he led them instead of being led by them. For Pericles never sought power by dishonest means, or resorted to flattery, and enjoyed so high a reputation that he could freely contradict them and cause their anger. Whenever he saw them arrogant and confident in spite of the circumstances, with his words he would astound them to fear. On the other hand, if they were seized by panic, he was able to restore at once their confidence. In short, the government of Athens, a democracy by name, under Pericles' guidance became a rule of the foremost citizen. But the successors of Pericles were more on a level with each other and, each of them striving for supremacy, gave in to the populace and committed the government of the city to their whims.

This, as was to be expected in a great and imperial state, led to many blunders: one of these was the Sicilian expedition, which failed not so much through a wrong assessment of the power of those against whom it was sent, but because those who had approved the expedition failed afterwards to consider the requirements of the troops. Instead, they gave themselves to personal slanders about the leadership of the populace, which affected the conduct of the campaign, and for the first time brought about civil unrest at home. The Athenians lost most of their fleet and other forces in Sicily, and civic unrest had broken out at home: still, for ten years they stood their ground against the enemies against whom they had been fighting since the outbreak of the war and, in addition to them, the Sicilians, and most of their allies, who revolted in great numbers, and finally Cyrus, the son of the Great King, who gave money to the Peloponnesians to maintain the fleet, and they did not give in until they fell victim to their own internal quarrels. So abundant were the resources upon which Pericles based his forecast of an easy Athenian victory over the sole forces of the Peloponnesians.

28. Democracy, demagogues and adventurers: The cases of Cleon and Alcibiades

Pericles was an exceptionally charismatic leader who was able to control the passions of the Athenian masses and to address their decisions towards the common interests of the *polis*. After his death, however, politicians of a very different stamp came onto the scene: a new breed of mediocre aspiring leaders took to court the basest instincts of the masses to attain power and wealth, with little or no consideration for the common good. These were the so-called demagogues [a].

Cleon was arguably the first and foremost of these demagogues. A vocal opponent of Pericles and his policies, Cleon rose to prominence after his death by fiercely opposing any suggestion of appeasement with the Spartans. Although his family had noble roots, Cleon was the son of a tanner, who cleverly managed to turn the relative modesty of his upbringing to his political advantage. A clever public speaker, Cleon courted the support of the Athenian people by affecting a rough and unpolished demeanour and rhetorical style. Thucydides presents Cleon as the 'most violent' of the Athenians: in 427 this demagogue urged his fellow-citizens to put to death the whole of the male population of Mytilene, who had dared to revolt against Athens. Thucydides portrays him as he addresses the assembly. The speech which Cleon delivers is an eloquent manifesto of his radical, ruthless views on democracy and empire [b]. The policies of Cleon and the demagogues were a frequent target of satire in Aristophanes' early plays. In *Knights* (424) Cleon is directly portrayed as a greedy, heinous Paphlagonian slave at the service of Demos, an old Athenian man. Cleon is Demos' favourite slave and abuses this position to extort and retaliate the other members of the household, Nicias and Demosthenes [c, d].

The first phase of the war between Sparta and Athens dragged on for ten years. In 422, Cleon of Athens and Brasidas of Sparta, the main advocates of war in their cities, both found death in the course of the same engagement at Anphipolis. Some months later, in the spring of 421, the Peace of Nicias, so named after the main Athenian negotiator, was finally signed, but the two great cities were not to remain at peace for too long. In Athens, one of the most vocal opponents of the peace agreement with Sparta was the young and flamboyant Alcibiades, a scion of the noble house of the Alcmaeonids and former pupil of Socrates. Alcibiades was a man of extraordinary talents, fascination and ambition: this was an extremely dangerous mix, which contributed to polarizing public opinion in favour or against him. One of the most prominent and controversial figures in the years between the Peace of Nicias and the end of the war with Sparta, Alcibiades came to be seen as a man who believed himself to be greater than the *polis*, and used its institutions to serve his own interests and ego.

Having been excluded from the negotiating team that discussed the peace with the enemy, Alcibiades began to pave his way to prominence and power by following a different and autonomous foreign policy, and using his personal international connections to foster an alliance between Athens and Argos, Sparta's main rival in Peloponnese [e]. Some years later, in 415, as the city was still recovering from the first phase of the conflict, Alcibiades persuaded the Athenians to embark upon an over-ambitious campaign against the Sicilian town of Syracuse, which was an ally of Sparta. The plan was in blatant contradiction with the strategy laid out by Pericles at the outbreak of the war, and became the topic of heated debate in the city. What is certain, the plan greatly appealed to the adventurous spirit and fascination for the exotic of the younger Athenian generations. The debate on the campaign therefore sparked a sort of clash between generations, in which the experienced Nicias tried to urge the Athenians to follow the most cautious path and abstain from a potentially catastrophic enterprise, while Alcibiades appealed to the adventurous and bold spirit of the Athenians, a spirit which he claimed to embody to the utmost, as witnessed by his many sporting victories and the splendour of his public displays [f].

The build-up to the Sicilian campaign was marred by scandal and controversy. The night before the fleet was to set out, someone mutilated the phallic portraits of Hermae scattered around Athens for good luck. The episode was associated with the blasphemous parodies of the Eleusine Mysteries performed in the houses of the Athenian *jeunesse dorée*, which had been lately brought to light, and for Alcibiades' adversaries it was very easy to persuade public opinion that he was involved in those crimes, and that those actions were part of a conspiracy to overthrow democracy, of which Alcibiades was suspected of being the ringleader [g]. These suspicions followed Alcibiades as he set sail to Sicily with the biggest fleet ever prepared by the Athenians. So, to avoid the consequences of the hostility mounting against him, Alcibiades defected to Sparta, where he would gain a prominent role as a military advisor to the enemies of his fatherland. But that was not the end of his wanderings. Having fallen into disgrace with the Spartan king Agis, Alcibiades sought refuge in Persia at the court of the satrap Tissaphernes, then he re-joined the Athenian troops at Samos at the time of the coup of the Four Hundred. After a string of naval victories in the Aegean and a triumphant return to Athens, Alcibiades fell into disgrace again with his fellow-citizens following a maladroit engagement with the Spartans at Notium (407), and witnessed the disaster of the Athenian fleet at Aegospotami as an exile from his estates in the Thracian Chersonese.

[a] [Arist.] *Const. Ath.* 28.1–3: Popular leaders and demagogues

As long as Pericles was the leader of the people, the affairs of the city went better, but after his death they became much worse. For then, for the first time, the people chose a leader who was not esteemed by the upper classes, while in former times it was the respectable citizens who continued to have the leadership of the people: Solon was the first and original leader of the people; the second was Pisistratus, who was a man of nobility and repute. After the tyranny was overthrown, Cleisthenes, a scion of the house of the Alcmaeonids, became the leader of the people, having no adversaries, for the faction of Isagoras had been banished. After this Xanthippus was the champion of the people, and Miltiades of the upper orders, and after them Themistocles and Aristides. After them, Ephialtes was the leader of the people, and Cimon, son of Miltiades, of the notables. And then Pericles of the people and Thucydides, a relative of Cimon's, of the others. After the death of Pericles, Nicias, who died in Sicily, was the leader of the notables, and Cleon, son of Cleanaetus, held the leadership of the people. Cleon seems to have done the most to ruin the people by means of his angry outbursts, and was the first to have resorted to shouting and abuse on the speaker's podium, and to gird up his cloak before addressing the people, while others spoke in an orderly manner. After these, Theramenes son of Hagnon was the leader of the others and Cleophon the lyre-maker of the people: he was the first to introduce the two-obol allowance. He went on to distribute this for some time, until it was abolished by Callicrates of the deme of Paene. He was the first to promise to add another obol to the two-obol dole. Both Cleophon and Callicrates were later on sentenced to death, for even though the populace may be utterly deceived, later they get to hate those who have led them to act unjustly. From Cleon on, leaders of the people invariably became the men who were most willing to act audaciously and to court immediate popularity by pleasing the lower orders.

[b] Thuc. 3.36.6–37: Cleon, the most violent of the Athenians

A meeting of the assembly was summoned at once, several speakers giving their different opinions on the matter. One of these was Cleon son of Cleaenetus, who had carried the earlier motion to put the Mytilenaeans to death. Cleon was among other things the most violent of the citizens, and at that time was by far the most influential with the populace. Cleon came forward again and spoke as follows:

'On many other occasions in the past I have been convinced that a democracy is incapable of ruling over others, so much so today seeing your change of mind about the Mytilenaeans. Because your daily relations with each other are free from intrigue and fear, you have developed the same attitude towards your allies. And so you forget that whenever you are led into error by their words, or give in to pity, you are in fact putting yourselves in danger without obtaining the gratitude of your allies. What you are failing to realize is that the power you hold is in fact a tyranny, imposed upon recalcitrant subjects who are plotting against you. If they obey you, it is not because you go so far as to harm your own interest to please them, no: it is your superior strength, rather than their goodwill, that gives you power over them. But the most terrible thing is that your resolutions are never final; for you ignore the fact that a city with inferior but inviolable laws is stronger than one with beautifully concocted laws but without authority, and that ignorance combined with prudence is more useful than cleverness without discipline, and that the affairs of the community are often better entrusted in the hands of the simpler citizens than the very clever ones. For the latter always try to appear wiser than the laws, and to dominate the political debate, as though they cannot give proof of their wisdom in more important matters, by which conduct they generally drive their cities to ruin. On the other hand, those who have no trust in their own discernment, are content to be less intelligent than the laws, and less able than others to scrutinize the words of a clever speaker, and are fair judges rather than competitors, generally conduct affairs for the better. What we need is action, and not to be excited by combats of wits to take resolutions against your own judgement.'

[c] Ar. *Knights* 40–84: Paphlagon, deceiving slave of Demos

DEMOSTHENES: We have a boorish master; he is a very irascible man and
   an avid bean-eater. His name is Demos of the deme of Pnyx, a half-deaf,
   intractable old man. Last new moon he bought a slave, a tanner called
   Paphlagon, a truly wicked and slanderous fellow. This leather-Paphlagonian

knows the habits of his old master; he flatters, fawns and cringes to him
with little pieces of leather, saying things like: 'Oh Demos, try one single
case and have a bath. Eat, gulp down, and then have dessert: here are three
obols for you! Would you care for me to get your supper ready?' Then he
clinches the dish that some of us have prepared and graciously presents it
to the master. The other day I baked a Laconian barley-cake at Pylus, and
that wicked man comes around, seizes the cake I kneaded, and offers it
up to Demos as his own. He always drives us away, for none but himself
must attend to the master. When Demos is having dinner, he stands at his
side with a leathern thong in his hand, and scares away all the orators. He
is always singing oracles to him, so much so that the master gets all Sybil-
crazy. And when he sees the master drifting, he uses all his art to throw
lies and slanders at the household, and so we get flogged: Paphlagon on the
other hand runs around the slaves, begging, causing trouble, taking bribes,
and saying things like: 'See how I've got Hylas beaten? Do as I say, or you'll
die this very day! So we have to give, because if we don't, the old man will
beat us eight times as much. But now, my friends, let's see how we can put
an end to this and who is going to get us out of here.'

[d] Ar. *Knights* 864–70: Demagogues prosper when the city is in trouble

SAUSAGE-SELLER: (to Cleon) You are like those who fish for eels: in still waters
they catch nothing, but when they stir up the lime up and down, their
catching is good. Likewise, you prosper when the city is in troubled water.
But now tell me: you who sell so many skins, have you ever given Demos a
clout to patch his shoes? And you claim to be so fond of him!

[e] Thuc. 5.43–44.1: Introducing Alcibiades

As the differences between the Athenians and Spartans had reached this point,
the party at Athens of those who wanted to cancel the treaty immediately set
themselves in motion. One of them was Alcibiades, son of Clinias, a man still
young in age for any other Greek city, but who was already distinguished for the
glory of his ancestry. Alcibiades thought that an alliance with Argos would have
been more advantageous, although his wounded pride also led him to oppose
an agreement with the Spartans, for they had preferred to negotiate the treaty
through Nicias and Laches, overlooking Alcibiades in reason of his young age.
Also, they had not shown the respect due to the ancient links of hospitality
between his family and the Spartans, which his grandfather had renounced,

but he wanted to renew it by bringing assistance to their prisoners taken in the island. Considering himself disparaged in every way, Alcibiades first spoke against the treaty, saying that the Spartans could not be trusted, but had made a treaty only to get rid of the Argives and then move against the Athenians alone. Therefore, as soon as this disagreement emerged, he privately sent messages to the Argives, asking them to come to Athens as soon as possible with the Mantinaeans and the Elaeans, for the time was right and he would give them his fullest support.

Upon hearing this, and discovering that the Athenians were not hostile to an alliance with the Boeotians and had a serious disagreement with the Spartans, the Argives forgot about their own ambassadors whom they had sent to Sparta to negotiate a treaty, and began to incline more towards the Athenians, thinking that, if they were to go to war, they would have a city on their side which was an old friend of Argos as well as a sister democracy and a mighty power at sea. Accordingly, they immediately dispatched ambassadors to Athens to discuss a treaty, and these were accompanied by envoys from Mantinaea and Elaea.

[f] Thuc. 6.15.1–17.1: Alcibiades and the Sicilian expedition

These were the words of Nicias. Most of the Athenians who came forward and urged to make the expedition without repealing their vote, while some spoke in opposition to it. But the most enthusiastic advocate of the campaign was Alcibiades, son of Clinias. He was eager to stand up to Nicias, who was his political rival, in part because he had made some envious remarks about him, but most importantly because he coveted the command of the campaign and hoped to reduce Sicily and Carthage under his control and, in case of success, to foster his personal wealth and public esteem. For the reputation which Alcibiades enjoyed among the citizens led him to indulge in his appetites beyond his actual means, both in the breeding of horses and those other extravagances of his, which later on would play no insignificant part in the destruction of the city. Alarmed by the greatness of his licence and indulgence both in his private life and all the designs which he had undertaken, the masses became hostile to him as someone who aspired to tyranny. While in public his conduct of the war met with general approval, in private everybody was upset by his extravagant habits, and so they entrusted the affairs of the city to someone else.

Now however he came forward and gave the following advice to the citizens:

'Athenians, I have a better right than others to hold the command: I have to start from this point because Nicias has attacked me and because I consider myself worthy of it. The things for which I am criticized have brought fame to my ancestors and myself, as well as profit to the fatherland. The Greeks at first were hoping to see our city destroyed in the course of the war, but then, owing to the magnificent display which I have made at the Olympic games, they went under the impression that it was bigger than it actually is: for I sent seven chariots, a number never before sent by a single person, and I won the first prize, and was second and fourth, and arranged everything else in a manner worthy of my victory. Custom considers these displays honourable, and they cannot be performed without leaving behind an impression of power. And the splendour which I have displayed at home with the production of choruses and other public services, this has excited the envy of my fellow-citizens, but, again, what foreigners gather from these displays is an impression of strength. And it is not a useless folly at all when a private individual uses his wealth not only for his own benefit, but also for that of his city, nor is it unfair that a man proud of his achievements should refuse to be put on the same foot as the others. A man in misery cannot share his misfortunes with anyone, and in the same manner as nobody courts those who are badly off, a man should accept being looked down on by those who are more prosperous, or else, let him first mete out equal measure to all, and then demand to have it meted out to him.

'I am aware that men of this kind, and those who have achieved success in any field, can cause distress in the course of their lives, particularly to their peers, but they leave behind to future generations a desire of claiming connection with them, even when there is none, and are hailed by their fatherland not as strangers or scoundrels, but as fellow-countrymen and benefactors. This is what I want to attain; this is why I am abused in my private accomplishments. But what you should consider is whether anyone would be able to manage the public affairs better than me. I have brought together the most powerful states of Peloponnese without any serious danger or expense for you; I forced the Spartans to put everything at stake in one single battle at Mantinaea, and although they came out victorious, they have never since recovered all their confidence. And so my youth, combined with my supposed folly, found the right arguments to cope with the might of the Peloponnesians, winning their confidence with its ardour. Now, don't be afraid of it, but while I am still in the flower of my age, and Nicias has a reputation for good luck, make the most of the services of us both.'

[g] Thuc. 6.26.2–29: Alcibiades and the Hermae scandal

While the Athenians were engaged with the preparations for the campaign, it so happened that the statues of Hermes in the city of Athens, the typical square pillars which arc so common on the doorways of temples and private houses, in the course of the same night almost all of them had their faces mutilated. Nobody knew who had done it, but the state offered generous rewards to identify the culprits. Also, it was voted that anyone who was in possession of any information relating to acts of impiety having been perpetrated should come forward and disclose testimony in confidence, whether he was a citizen, a foreigner or a slave. The matter was taken very seriously because it seemed to be ominous for the expedition, and part of a conspiracy to bring about a revolution and overthrow the democratic constitution.

Accordingly, some metics and servants gave information not about the Hermae, but other previous mutilations of statues, perpetrated by some young men in a drunken rampage, and of mock celebrations of the Eleusinian Mysteries to be held in some private residences. Also, they said that Alcibiades was implicated in this affair. These accusations were taken up by the fiercest opponents of Alcibiades, who thought that he was the obstacle to them becoming the undisputed leaders of the people, and believed that, if he was removed, they would have the first place. Accordingly, they magnified the matter, shouting loud that the affair of the Mysteries and the mutilation of the Hermae were part of a scheme to overthrow the popular government, and that Alcibiades had been involved in all this, as demonstrated by the general, undemocratic indecency of his life and his conduct.

Alcibiades immediately defended himself from the accusations of the informers. The preparations for the campaign had been completed, and Alcibiades said he was ready before sailing to be tried if he had really been involved in any of these things. If found guilty he would pay a penalty, but if he was cleared, he should keep the command of the campaign. Alcibiades protested that they should not accept slanders against him in absence, and should rather put him to death, if he had done anything wrong. Also he asked whether if it was wiser not to send him at the head of such a large expedition, while such grave accusations were still pending upon him. His opponents however were afraid that, if he was tried immediately, Alcibiades would have the army on his side, and the populace would be softened in favour of the man owing to whom the Argives and some of the Mantinaeans had joined in the expedition. They did the utmost to have the trial postponed, bringing forward other orators who said that they should sail at once and not delay the departure of the expedition. As for Alcibiades, he should be tried upon his return at an established time. Their plan was to bring up a more serious charge, which they would more easily bring up in his absence. Accordingly, it was resolved that Alcibiades should sail.

10

Athens, the Democratic Empire

29. The nature and objectives of Athenian imperialism

In 478, the Spartans recalled the unpopular Pausanias home and the Athenians took over the command of the campaign against the Persians. Some time later, a new alliance was formed. This was a *symmachia* (*syn–*: 'together'; *mache*: 'fight'), i.e. a full defensive and offensive military alliance, established with the official purpose of carrying on the war against the Persians. The meetings of the allies were held at the sanctuary of Apollo in the island of Delos, which was also the seat of the league's treasury. As the leaders of the new organization, the Athenians decided which members were to contribute to the alliance by providing ships and which by paying an annual tribute in money. The magistrates responsible for the collection of the tribute were called *Hellenotamoi*, or 'treasures of the Greeks', and were of course from Athens.

According to Thucydides, the Athenians originally respected the autonomy of the allies, but soon began to abuse their leadership, especially when some allied states were unable to pay the tribute [a, b]. As we have seen in the previous section, the Athenians were quite aware that any power which exercises hegemony inevitably attracts the hostility of its subjects, and that hegemony cannot be exercised without a degree of coercion. In 429, in the wake of the second Peloponnesian invasion of Attica, Pericles addressed the Athenians and urged them not to close their eyes to the tyrannical nature of their rule over the allies: the Athenians ought to defend their city against their Peloponnesian enemy as well as against the hatred of their own allies [c].

Exercising a form of despotic rule over unwilling subjects, any hegemonic power was engaged in a continuing struggle to impose and demonstrate its military superiority. For any step back could be interpreted as a sign of weakness, and an encouragement for the allies to revolt. A significant episode took place in the summer of 416, when the Athenians landed on Melos, an island of the Aegean which had so far remained neutral. The mightiest naval power of Greece was challenging the independence of a very small *polis* of limited political and strategic relevance. The contrast inspired Thucidides to stage a dialogue between the Athenian commanders Cleomedes and Teisias and a group of Melian envoys. The latter ask the Athenians what advantage they hope to obtain from the submission of a small neutral city, which may decide to take sides with the Spartans as a result of this act of aggression. The Athenians reply that their only concern is the defence of their city and empire: justice cannot be a primary concern for any hegemonic power [d].

In the course of the fifth century, as the original military objectives of the alliance grew less urgent, it became increasingly clear that the Delian League was in fact an Athenian empire. In 454, the treasury of the alliance was transferred from Delos to Athens, and the allies were required to pay the tenth part of their tribute directly to the Athenians. Also, the allies had to refer to the Athenian tribunal for resolution of disputes, and this generated considerable income for the city [e]. Athenian influence on the internal affairs of the allied cities also increased. The so-called cleruchies became a symbol of Athenian imperialism: these were groups of Athenian settlers, usually drafted from the poorer sections of society, who received an allotment of land in the territory of some allied city. This procedure served the double purpose of maintaining a degree of social peace in Athens and preventing rebellions from the allies [f, g]. The Athenians also wanted to have a voice on the constitutional organization of the allied city. A decree of the *ekklesia* dated to the middle 460s or 453/2 required the citizens of Erythraea to bring gifts to Athens on the occasion of the Great Panathneanea and, most importantly, to set up a new 120-member assembly in imitation of the Athenian boule [h]. Some years later, in 440/439, the people of Samos were also forced to adopt an Athenian-style constitution [i]. Some time between 450 and 446 the assembly passed another decree requiring all the members of the League to adopt the currency, weights and measures in use in Athens [j]. Again, Athenian envoys were to visit the allied towns to make sure that the new norms were enforced, and all contraveners were to stand trial in Athens.

[a] Thuc. 1.97.1: Athenian hegemony between the Persian and Peloponnesian Wars

The Athenians at first were the leaders of autonomous allies, who all contributed to the deliberations of the common assembly. Then, in the interval between this war and the one against the Persians, they undertook the enterprises which I am about to relate, both in war and in the running of public affairs. These were directed against the barbarians as well as their own allies, when they tried to revolt, and against those Peloponnesian states against which from time to time they came into conflict in each of their attempts.

[b] Thuc. 1.99: Athenian despotism towards the allies

Now, there were various reasons which caused the allies to revolt, but the principal ones were failure to pay the tribute or to provide their quota of ships, and, in some cases, desertion. For the Athenians were extremely exacting in the collection of the tribute, and resorted to the utmost severity against those who were not accustomed or willing to endure the hardships of service. In other respects too the Athenians were no longer the popular rulers they originally were. For now they refused to serve on an equal footing with the other allies, and found it easy to subdue those who wanted to leave the confederacy. And the allies had nobody but themselves to blame for this, for most of them, willing as they were to avoid service, opted to pay their share of the tribute in money instead of sending ships. As a result of this, the Athenians could increase their fleet with the funds provided by the allies, and whenever the allies revolted, they would find themselves without the necessary preparation and experience to face a war.

[c] Thuc. 2.63.1–2: Athens as a tyrant?

Athenians, it is your duty to defend the honour which your city has gained through empire, for you all take pride in it, and you cannot refuse to sustain the burden of empire and still expect to have a share of its profits. You should bear in mind that this war is not merely about freedom or slavery, no: you are also fighting to defend your empire against the hatred incurred in the exercise of power. Some of you, in the fear of the moment, might think that withdrawing from empire would be just and prudent. But now it is too late for that. For the power you exercise, to speak frankly, is in fact a tyranny. It might have been wrong to acquire it first, but letting it go would be a risk.

[d] Thuc. 5.91–101: The dialogue of the Melians

ATHENIANS: The risk of losing our empire does not frighten us, if we are ever to lose it. For those who rule over others, like the Spartans do (even if the

Spartans were our real enemies), are less of a threat for a defeated power than its subjects, if these were to assault and overpower their rulers. But this is a risk which we are prepared to face. Now, what we want to do is to show you that we are here to defend the interests of our empire. What we are about to say is exclusively concerned with the safety of our city. For our desire is to rule over you without trouble, and see you safe in the interest of both of us.

MELIANS: And how could it be convenient for us to serve, while you rule?

A.: Because you would not suffer terrible pain before being subdued and it would be convenient for us not to annihilate you.

M.: So you will not let us remain neutral and quiet, friends rather than enemies, but allies of neither side?

A.: No. Because your hostility would not hurt us as much as your friendship would be a sign of our weakness, and your hostility one of our power.

M.: Is this your subjects' idea of justice? To consider those who do not belong to you exactly like those who have been subdued by you, most of whom were your own colonists, and others rebellious subjects?

A.: As far as justice is concerned, they think that one side has as much of it as the other. But then, ruling or being ruled, is not about justice, but power, and if we do not attack them, they think that it is because we are afraid of them. Therefore, if we subjugate you, on top of extending our empire, we will also gain in security. And since you are islanders and weaker than others, it is of the utmost importance that you should not baffle the rulers of sea.

M.: But can't you see the risks implied in all this? For if you prevent us from talking about justice and invite us to yield to your interests, we should also have the chance to explain what would be convenient for us and try to persuade you, if your interest and ours happen to coincide. How can you avoid making enemies of those who are neither your allies nor Sparta's, if, looking at what is happening to us, they conclude that one day you will attack them as well? Don't you think that what you are doing is nothing but giving strength to your current enemies and compelling others to become your enemies, people who would have never though of it?

A.: We do not think that the people of the mainland can cause any serious harm to us: the freedom which they enjoy will dissuade them from taking precautions against us. In fact, it is the islanders who are not under our rule, like you, and the more intractable among our allies that are most likely to make a thoughtless move and drive themselves and us into easily foreseeable danger.

M.: But if you are willing to risk so much to defend your empire, and your subjects to set themselves free from it, there would certainly be cowardice and baseness in us if, while we are still free, we do not everything to avoid being enslaved.

A.: No, if you consider the matter wisely. For the contest is not an even one, with honour for the winner and shame for the loser. Your very safety is at stake, and not succumbing to a far stronger power than you are.

[e] [Ps. Xen.] *Ath. Const.* 1.16–18: How the Athenians benefit from the empire

The people seem to be ill advised on this point: they compel the allies to sail to Athens for legal proceedings. Their answer is that the Athenian people benefit from this. Firstly, because throughout the year their deposits at law are used to pay for the service of the jurors. Secondly, because this system enables them to sit at home and govern the affairs of the allied cities without sailing off in the ships, and in the courts they protect the democrats and ruin and damage their opponents. If all the allies were to hold their trials at home, owing to their hatred of the Athenians, they would damage those who are on the friendliest terms with them. Furthermore, the Athenian people benefit for the following reasons from holding the trials involving the allies in Athens: first, the one per cent tax at the Piraeus brings in more money for the city; second, if anyone has a property to rent, he is better off, and so are those who have animals or slaves to hire. Also, the heralds of the assembly are better off when the allies are in town. If the allies were not compelled to sail away for their trials, they would show respect only for those Athenians who sail out from their city, such as generals, trierarchs, and ambassadors. Under the current system, the allies need to flatter the Athenian people, for they know that when you sail to Athens for a trial you are putting yourself in the hands of none other but the Athenian people: this is what the Athenian laws prescribe. And once in the courts they have to flatter whomever comes in, and grasp him by the hand. This is how the allies have become slaves to the Athenian people.

[f] Plut. *Per.* 11.5: Pericles' cleruchies

Pericles dispatched 1,000 settlers to the Chersonese, 500 to Naxos, and 250 to Andros, 1,000 to Thrace to settle with the Bisaltae, and others to Italy, when Sybaris was settled, which they named Thurii. He did this to relieve the city from the burden of a mob of lazy and idle busybodies. Also this policy allowed him to rectify the embarrassments of the poorer people, and gave the allies for neighbours an imposing garrison which should prevent rebellion.

[g] Thuc. 3.50: The submission of Mytilene

The other party whom Paches had dispatched as the initiators of the upheaval were put to death by the Athenians upon the motion of Cleon. The number of these men was well above a thousand. The Athenians also demolished the walls of Mitylene, and took possession of the city's fleet. Afterwards tribute was not imposed upon the Lesbians; but all their land, except that of the Methymnians, was divided into three thousand allotments, three hundred of which were consecrated to the gods, and the rest assigned by lot to Athenian shareholders, who were sent out to the island. With these the Lesbians agreed to pay a rent of two minae a year for each allotment, and cultivated the land themselves. The Athenians also took possession of the towns on the mainland which belonged to the Mitylenians These cities therefore became for the future subject to Athens.

These were the events that took place at Lesbos.

[h] IG I³ 14 = Fornara 71 = M&L 40 = SEG XXVI.3, XXXI.5, XXIX.820, XXX.1866, XXXI.811, XXXII.867, XXXIII.731: Measures concerning Eretryae

It was decided by the council and the people, in the pritany of [*missing words*] presided, in the archonship of Lysicrates. The Erythraeans shall bring wheat for the Great Panathenaia worth not less than three minae. The Hieropoioi will distribute the wheat to the Erythraeans who are present, half a chous each. If they bring less than three minae, the Hieropoioi shall buy wealth, in accordance with this decree, and the Erythraeans will owe them ten minae. It shall be lawful for any Erythraean who so wishes to furnish the wheat. One hundred and twenty men will be appointed to the council by lot; the men who are allotted for office will undergo examination in the council, and it shall be unlawful for any foreigner to be a member of the council or for anyone under thirty years of age, and those found guilty will be prosecuted, and no one shall be a member of the council twice within four years. The Athenian envoys and the commander of the garrison will carry out the lot and the establishment of the present council, in the future the council and the commander of the garrison, no less than thirty days before the term of office of the council expires. The councilmen shall take the oath by Zeus, Apollo and Demeter, invoking destruction upon themselves and destruction upon their sons if they swear falsely. The oath will be ratified by the burning of sacrifices. The council shall make the sacrifice by burning at least a cow as victim, otherwise it shall pay a fine of 1,000 drachmas, and when the people swear, it will burn nothing less.

This shall be the oath of the council:

'I shall deliberate as best and as justly as I can for the Erythraean people and the Athenian people and the allies and I shall not revolt from the Athenian people and from the allies of the Athenians, nor shall I be persuaded by someone else, nor shall I desert or be persuaded to do so by someone else, nor shall I welcome the exiles nor shall I be persuaded to do so by someone else, namely those who went over to the Persians without the permission of the council and the people of the Athenians. Nor shall I expel any Erythraean citizen without the consent of the council and the people of the Athenians. If any Erythraean citizen assassinates another Erythraean, he shall be put to death, if judged guilty. If he is sentenced to exile, he shall be banned from all the allies of Athens and his property shall become the public property of the Erythraeans. If someone betrays the city to the tyrants, he shall be put to death with impunity and his children. If it is clear that his children are friends of the people of the Erythraeans and to the people of the Athenians, they will be spared and his entire property shall be declared by the children and they shall take half of it and half will be confiscated. The commander of the garrison will establish the necessary garrison anywhere in Erythrae […].'

[i] Thuc. 1.115.3: The submission of Samos

The Athenians sailed to Samos with forty ships and established a democracy, took as hostages fifty boys and as many men, put them down in Lemnos. Hence they left a garrison in the island and returned home.

[g] IG I³ 1453 = ATL II D14 = Fornara 97 = M&L 45 = SEG XXVI.6, XXVIII.2, XXIX.7, XXXI.7: Athenian decree enforcing the use of Athenian coins (c. 450–449)

The governors in the cities […] the treasurers of the Greeks […] to inscribe […] of any of the cities […]

Who wishes shall immediately bring before the law-courts of the lawgivers those who have acted against the law. The lawgivers shall institute procedures for the denouncers of each malefactor within five days. If someone, either citizen or foreigner, other than the governors in the cities, does not act in compliance with the decrees, he shall be declared dishonoured, his possessions shall be confiscated and made public and the tenth part will be dedicated to the goddess. If there are no Athenian governors, the magistrates of each city will do what is prescribed in the decree. If they do not act in compliance with the decree, they shall be directed to Athens to face a procedure of dishonouring.

In the mint, after receiving the money, they shall mint no less than half and [...] the cities. The fee taken by the superintendents will always be three drachmas for each mina. They shall convert the money [...] or be liable [...] Whatever will remain of the money shall be minted and handed over either to the generals or to the [...] When it is handed over [...] and to Hephaestus [...] If anyone proposes or puts to a vote a proposal regarding these things that it be legal to borrow or lend foreign currencies, an accusation shall be immediately lodged before the Eleven, and the Eleven shall sentence him to death. If he appeals against the charge, they shall bring him to the law court. The people shall elect the heralds, one to the Islands, one to the Hellespont, one to the Thraceward region. They shall dispatch [...] They shall pay a fine of ten thousand drachmas. This decree shall be inscribed on a marble stele and set up by the governors in the cities, in the agora of each city and by the superintendents in front of the mint. All this will be enforced by the Athenians if the peoples of the cities are not willing. The herald making the travel to the cities shall require of the peoples that they shall comply to what the Athenians prescribe. The following addition shall be made to the oath of the council by the secretary of the council for the future: if someone in the cities coins money and does not use the Athenian currency or weights or measures, I shall punish and fine him in compliance with the decree of Clearchus. Anyone shall be allowed to hand in the foreign currency which he possesses and convert it in the same manner as he wishes. The city will give in place of it our own currency. Each citizen will bring his money to Athens and deposit it at the mint. The superintendents shall make a record of everything yielded up by each citizen and set up a stele in front of the mint to be read by anyone who wishes. They shall make a record of all the foreign currency, keeping the gold separate from the coins, and the total of our money [...].

30. Athens' imperial democracy and the other Greek powers

The great war between Athens and Sparta of 431–404 is one of the most traumatic and defining events in the history of classical antiquity. Our knowledge and understanding of that epochal event largely depends on the work of one historian, Thucydides of Athens. The events of his life brought him to gain a very direct insight of the event of the conflict and its actors [**a**]. In 424–423, he was serving as *strategos* in the Thracian region, where his family held some mining estates, when the important town of Amphipolis fell to the Spartans. Although Thucydides claimed no responsibility for the debacle, he was banished from Athens for twenty years, during which time he had opportunity to visit the various cities involved in the conflict, including the allies of Sparta.

In the famous *proemium* of his work, Thucydides claims to have begun to write the history of the war as soon as it broke out, as a series of military and geo-political considerations induced him to think that Greece was about to witness the greatest upheaval of its history: the two main contestants had reached the peak of their military preparedness and international influence; the growing rivalry between Athens and Sparta had polarized the whole of Greece, and its effects were felt outside Greece as well [**b**]. In the first section of the first book, the historian gives an account of the grounds of complaint between Sparta and Athens which brought about the termination of the peace treaty signed in 460. Thucydides however thinks that the imperial rise of Athens since the end of the Persian Wars, and the Spartans' growing concern for it, had made war inevitable [**c**]. The Spartans were understandably concerned lest the spectacular growth of Athens could destabilize their traditional hegemony within Peloponnese. Furthermore, democratic Athens was an innovative and dynamic kind of power, which was calling into question the traditional values embodied by the Spartans. The development of a large naval empire was a completely new experience in the history of Greece, which the Spartans seemed to be struggling to decipher. The wake-up call for the Spartans came from their allies Corinth, who, like the Athenians, were an important naval power. In the summer of 432, after the Athenians laid siege to Potidaea, an ally of Corinth, an assembly of the Peloponnesian League was held in Sparta to address their remonstrances against the Athenians. Thucydides reports the speeches delivered on this occasion by the Corinthian and Athenian representatives, by the Spartan king Archidamus, and Sthenelaidas, one of the ephors in charge. More than addressing the actual grounds of complaint of the Peloponnesians, these speeches serve the purpose of introducing the readers to the different national characteristics of the main powers of Greece.

The meeting had been called by the Corinthians, whose representatives accuse the Spartans of having contributed to the growth of Athens by failing to take resolute action against them. What is worse, the Spartans have failed to understand that the Athenians are no ordinary foe: they are swift, innovative, dynamic and adventurous. The challenge they pose to the Spartans is military, political and cultural: will the Spartans be able to move out of their Peloponnesian comfort-zone and face this new kind of enemy [d]?

Two Athenian envoys happened to be in Sparta at the time of this meeting, and made a request to the Spartans to address the assembly and reply to the accusations of their allies, lest their anger might drive them to take hasty resolutions and step into a potentially destructive war. The speech of the Athenian envoys addresses two topics: the circumstances that led Athens to become the dominant naval power of the Aegean, and therefore a challenge to Spartan hegemony, and what they have been compelled to do to maintain their leadership. The ambassadors remember the Athenians' vital contribution to the defeat of the Persians, both at Marathon, and at the naval battle at Salamis [e]. In the latter battle in particular, the Athenians gave proof of their courage, patriotism and loyalty to the Greek cause [f]. After the battle of Micale, they took over the command of the war by common consent of the allies when the Spartans decided to return to Peloponnese and withdraw from the conflict. At this point, the envoys say that their rise to hegemony was less the result of a precise design than the product of a concatenation of circumstances, in which the Athenians found themselves under the compulsion of two mighty forces: fear, at the time of the struggle against the Persians, and honour, when the allies urged them to take over the leadership of the Greek coalition. Thereupon, once the Athenians had taken over the burden and responsibility of hegemony, their actions were to be determined by another: self-interest. For every power exercising hegemony over others has to defend itself from the envy and resentment that its position of supremacy engenders in those who are subject to it. The exercise of hegemonic authority therefore requires a degree of coercion: this is an all-important rule of relations between different powers, which applies to Athens' dominance of the Aegean Sea as well as to Spartan hegemony over Peloponnese [g]. The speech of the Athenian envoys is a masterpiece of elaborate rhetorical art and political cynicism. Nothing could be more remote from the Laconic frankness of the Spartans. The Spartan king Archidamus is left astonished by the Athenians' words, and wonders why they did not even try to deny the accusations brought against their city. Far from indulging in the Machiavellian disquisitions of the two Athenians, his understanding of international relations revolves around two basic categories: what is good and what is bad [h].

[a] Thuc. 5.26.5: Thucydides and the events of the Peloponnesian War

I lived through the whole of the war, and was of an age to understand events. So I gave my attention to them, to know the exact truth about this conflict. Also, it befell me to be banished from my fatherland for twenty years following my strategy at Amphipolis, and so, being acquainted with both sides, and in particular with the Peloponnesians owing to my exile, I had the leisure to acquire a deeper understanding of these events.

[b] Thuc. 1.1.1–2: The incipit of Thucydides' *Histories*

The Athenian Thucydides wrote an account of the war fought by the Peloponnesians and the Athenians against each other. He began his task as soon as the war broke out, for he believed that it would be a great conflict, and more worthy of narration than the previous ones. The proof of this was that both powers were in every respect at the peak of their preparedness and he could see that the other Greek nations were taking sides in the dispute, some immediately, others intending to do so. In fact, this war was the greatest upheaval ever experienced by the Greek world as well for some of the barbarians, that is to say for most of mankind.

[c] Thuc. 1.23.6: The real cause of the Peloponnesian War

The truest cause of the conflict, and the least spoken of, I believe to have been the growth to power of the Athenians, which brought fear to the Spartans and made war inevitable.

[d] Thuc. 1.68.3–69.4: The opposing characters of Spartans and Athenians

'Spartans: the confidence you have reposed in your constitution and commonwealth makes you more suspicious towards us if we make any comments on other powers. Hence comes your moderation, but also your ignorance of foreign affairs. For although we have often warned you of the damage which the Athenians were going to inflict on us, you have never taken steps to ascertain the veracity of our warnings. Instead, you have raided suspicions on those who were warning you, as though they had been moved to talk by their private interests. And so you have summoned the present meeting of allies not before the blow was struck, but only when we are already in the midst of a crisis. Of your allies, we are certainly not the least entitled to speak, for we have been the most vocal in protesting about the arrogance of the Athenians, and your own neglect.

'Now, if the Athenians had been perpetrating their abuses in secret, and you were unaware of what was happening, you would have needed someone to give you a clear exposition of the facts. But now there is no need for long speeches, for you see with your own eyes that they have enslaved some of us and are plotting against others, particularly our allies, and have been long making preparations for war. Otherwise they would not have seized Corcyra, which they still hold against our will, and would not be besieging Potidaea, the latter being conveniently located for launching attacks against Thrace, while the former would have contributed a very large fleet to the Peloponnesians.

'You, and not others, are responsible for this: for you permitted them, in the first instance, to fortify their city after the Persian Wars, and then to build the Long Walls, while up to this moment you have always deprived of their freedom not only those who had been enslaved by them, but now even your allies. For who are the truer subjugators? Those who have enslaved a city, or those who failed to do what was in their power to prevent it, and still claim the honour of having been the liberators of Greece? Now at last we have assembled, albeit not without difficulty, and without a clear purpose. Now we should no longer discuss whether we have been injured, but look at how we should defend ourselves. For men of action make their plans and put them into practice with no hesitations, while their opponents are pondering their options. We are well aware of how the Athenians advance against their neighbours: a little here and a little there. As long as they think that they can carry out their plans unnoticed owing to your lack of attention, their actions are less bold, but once you make them understand that you know what they are doing, but don't care to interfere, they will press on more aggressively. Spartans: of all the Greeks, you alone remain inactive and defend yourselves not by using your power but by showing the intention to use it; you alone intend to dissolve the power of your enemies not as its outset, but when it is doubling itself. People used to say that you were a reliable nation, but now your reputation goes beyond the truth. The Persians, as we know, managed to reach Peloponnese from the ends of earth without you sending out any force worthy of this name to meet them. But now you disregard the Athenians, who are not a distant enemy, as the Persians were, but your neighbours. You prefer to act on the defensive against them, and not on the offensive, and leave this matter to chance by engaging in a struggle with an enemy which is twice as powerful as it originally was. And yet you are aware that the barbarian failed mostly by his own fault, and in our engagements with the Athenians we owed our successes more to their mistakes than the aid we may have received from you. Many a state has been ruined by the expectations that they placed on you, for, trusting on your help, they neglected military training. And let none of you think that these words are spoken out of hostility, and not as a remonstrance. For one remonstrates with a friend who is in error, while accusations are made against enemies by whom we have been injured.

'We believe that we are as entitled as anybody else to highlight the faults of our neighbours, particularly if we consider the great contrast between your national character and theirs. A contrast which you do not seem to perceive, for you have not considered what kind of men the Athenians are, whom you are going to fight, and how utterly different from you.

'The Athenians are men devoted to innovation: they are quick to put their plans into execution, while you tend to defend what you have, while you never devise anything new, and when action is required, you never go as far as is needed. Furthermore, they are daring beyond their strength, and adventurous beyond their judgment, and high-spirited in front of perilous situations, while you always do something less than would be in your power. You put no trust even in what your judgement considers safe, and believe that there is no release from danger.

'Also, they are resolute in action, while you are procrastinators; they are not afraid of venturing abroad, while you are tied to your homes, because they hope to gain something from their absence, while you are afraid that you may put at risk what you have by going abroad. When they overcome their enemies, they strive to pursue their advantage as far as possible; when they are defeated, they fall back as little as possible.

'In the service of their city, they use their bodies as though they were the bodies of other men, and their minds as though they were wholly their own. When they conceive a plan but fail to accomplish it, they think to have been deprived of some of their possessions, but when they go after something and attain it, they consider it very little compared to what the future has in store for them. When they fail in some undertaking, they set their minds on a new goal, and so they make up for the loss. Only the Athenians are so swift in putting their plans into practice that they can consider what they hope for as already obtained. And so they spend every day of their lives amid dangers and toils. They have less opportunity to enjoy what they have, because they are always engaged in the pursuit of something else. Doing their duty is their holiday, and unproductive idleness they regard as more calamitous than toilsome activity.

'In sum, if someone said that the Athenians were born never to have rest, nor to let others have it, he would say nothing but the truth'.

[e] Thuc. 1.73.4–74.2: Athenian heroism at Marathon and Salamis

We affirm we have single-handedly braved the barbarians at Marathon, and when they later returned, since we could not defend ourselves on land, we resolved to embark *en masse* and confront them in the sea-fight at Salamis. This prevented them from sailing against you, city by city, and ravaging Peloponnese, for you would not have been able to succour one another against such a large fleet. The best proof of this was provided by the enemy: for, having been defeated, they immediately withdrew with most of the army, as though their fleet was no longer the power that it used to be.

This is was the outcome of the battle; this clearly proved that the fate of the Greeks depended on their fleet. To that effort we contributed three very important elements: the largest number of ships, a most intelligent admiral and our untiring dedication. For almost two-thirds of the whole four hundred ships came from Athens; Themistocles was the commander and the man chiefly responsible for the decision of fighting the battle in the straits, a decision which ultimately saved Greece. For this reason you welcomed him with more honour than any other foreigner who ever visited your city. At Salamis we gave proof of our zeal and unremitting bravery, for when no one could come to our aid by land, since all the states up to our borders had already been enslaved, we resolved to leave our city and surrender our households. Even in those extreme circumstances, we did not desert our surviving allies nor did we make ourselves useless to them by dispersing our forces. Instead, we embarked on our galleys and braved the enemy, and we were not angry at you because you had not come to our rescue. Therefore, we claim to have given you more than we have happened to receive.

[f] Thuc. 1.75: How the Athenians obtained their empire

'Spartans: considering the dedication and vision which we displayed in those circumstances, do you really think that we deserve to be regarded with such extreme jealousy by the other Geeks on account of the empire which we possess? For we did not obtain it by means of coercion, but it so happened that you were no longer willing to carry on the struggle against what remained of the barbarian army, and so the allies came to us of their own accord, and begged us to take over the leadership. Hence circumstances have brought us to advance our empire to its present state being driven first by fear, then by sense of honour and finally by interest. But once we became the object of hatred for many of our allies, and some of them had revolted and then been subdued, and you were no longer as friendly as you used to be, but had become suspicious and turned against us, it no longer seemed safe to us to risk loosening our grip, for all the rebel allies would have turned over to you. And no one should be blamed for looking after his own interest when facing the most serious dangers.'

[g] Thuc. 1.76.1–77.6: How an imperial power has to defend itself

'Spartans, you rule over the cities of Peloponnese by settling their affairs according to your advantage. And if in the days of the war against the Persians you had persevered to the end, and grown unpopular owing to the exercise of leadership, we know for sure that you would have been no less obnoxious to the allies, and would have been forced to choose between iron-fisted government and danger to yourselves. Therefore, our conduct was not extraordinary or alien to human nature: we were offered an empire, and accepted it, and then, driven by the three strongest forces, honour, fear and self-interest, we refused to give it up. And we are not the first to have followed this course, for it has always been a law that the weaker must succumb to the more powerful. Also, we consider ourselves worthy of our standing, and so you used to consider us, until you began to calculate what was your interest and to use the argument of justice, which so far nobody has ever put before force when the opportunity arose to gain anything by force. Praise is certainly due to those who follow human nature and rule over others, and at the same time respect justice more than their strength would compel them to do. Therefore, we believe that if others were to take over our empire, the way in which they would exercise power would be the clearest proof of our moderation, but strangely enough in our case our moderation has won us more contempt than admiration.

For although we are at a disadvantage with our allies in lawsuits arising from commercial agreements, and we are subject to the same laws as them in the tribunals which we have established, still we are considered to be fond of litigation. As for our allies, they fail to consider that those who hold the leadership elsewhere and are less moderate towards their subjects are not reproached on this account, because those who have strength on their side don't need to appeal to right. Yet our allies have grown so accustomed to being treated as our equals that whenever they suffer even the most insignificant loss in what they consider right, be it in a trial or in reason of the power we exercise upon them, they forget to be grateful for not having been deprived of most of the advantages which our empire brings them, and feel more bitterly about that small mark of inferiority than if we had from the start deliberately put aside any legal principle and unashamedly enriched ourselves to their detriment, in which case they would not say that the inferior should not yield to the superior. Men, as it seems, are more angered by legal wrongs than physical oppression, for the former gives the impression of an act of arrogance from a peer, while the latter is a form of constraint exercised by someone superior. At any rate, our allies had to endure much harder sufferings when they were under the Persians, but now our rule seems to be much harder to bear. This however is not surprising, because the present always weighs heavy on the subjects.'

[h] Thuc. 1.86.1: Archidamus on the Athenians

'I cannot understand the long speeches of the Athenians, for although they have spoken at great length in praise of themselves, nowhere have they tried to deny that they are injuring our allies and Peloponnese. If they acted valiantly against the Persians in the past, but are wronging us now, they deserve a double punishment, because they used to be good and now have become bad.'

11

Democracy and the Effects of the Peloponnesian War: Crisis and Reconstruction

31. Popular criticism of democracy: The Sicilian debate

The Athenian expedition to Sicily of 415–413 was the greatest single military operation ever carried out by a Greek city (see Thuc. 7.87). Two years after landing in Sicily in the highest hopes, the Athenians were routed by the combined forces of the Syracusean and their Spartan allies. In spite of the total destruction of their once mighty fleet, the Athenians resolved to carry on the fight against the Spartans and their allies. The disaster however had important consequences on the morale of the Athenians and their trust in the democratic constitution. A council of ten *probouloi* ('revisors of the laws') was appointed to draft constitutional reforms.

Thuc. 8.1: The Athenians' reactions to the Sicilian disaster

When the news of the disaster came to Athens, the citizens remained for a long while in a state of disbelief. For, although the soldiers who had escaped from the action were giving reliable accounts of the events, such an utter destruction was simply deemed impossible. But when at last they realized what had happened, first they grew angry with those politicians who had joined zealously in promoting the expedition, as though they had not voted for it themselves; then they were angry with the oracle-mongers, the soothsayers and all the others who, through the practice of divination, had made them hope that they could really conquer Sicily. Everything around them was pain, and, after what happened, they were overwhelmed by a sense of fear and enormous consternation. The Athenians, both as a city and as a community, were seized by grief: so many hoplites had been lost, and cavalrymen and troops in the prime of their age that nobody could replace. Also, they were seeing that there were no sufficient ships in the docks, or money in the common treasury, or crews for the fleet, and so they began to despair for salvation. In fact, they were convinced that their enemies in Sicily, now that they had won such a resonant victory, would soon be sailing against the Piraeus, while their enemies at home would be doubling their preparations to attack them by land and sea simultaneously, and that their allies would revolt and join them. In spite of all this, the Athenians came to the conclusion that they should not surrender. They were determined to equip a new fleet with such means as they had, procuring timber and money from anywhere they could, and to secure the loyalty of their allies, particularly those of Euboaea. Also, they resolved to reform the city's constitution so as to make it more efficient and to appoint a board of elders who would advise upon the affairs of the city as a convenient opportunity should arise. And so, as is customary with democracies, in the panic of the moment they committed themselves to observe discipline in all their affairs.

32. Conservative criticism of Athenian democracy: The 'Old Oligarch'

The anonymous treaty on the *Constitution of the Athenians* traditionally attributed to an 'Old Oligarch' or 'Pseudo-Xenophon' is a trenchant analysis of the Athenian constitution written in the later decades of the fifth century, probably around the outbreak of the Peloponnesian War. Democracy is described as a wicked yet diabolically efficient system, deliberately devised to give the highest degree of power and licence to the worst citizens, whose service in the fleet had been instrumental to the imperial rise of Athens, while the political and financial burden of the administration of the city is left on the shoulders of the wealthy and respectable. The weakness of the Athenian infantry reflects this [a–c]. The development of democracy caused a proliferation of offices and magistracies which are the main source of revenue for many citizens. As a consequence of this, the political calendar of the city is incredibly packed, to the detriment of the quality of the government's daily operation [d].

Democracy also spoiled the athletic competitions and religious festivals of the city, which have become occasions for feasting at the expense of the good citizens [e, f].

[a] [Ps. Xen.] *Ath. Const.* 1.1–9: Democracy favours the worst citizens

As for the fact that the Athenians have opted for the kind of constitution that they have, I do not commend their choice, because, by adopting democracy, they have deliberately chosen to make the worst citizens better off than the best. This is why I do not praise what they have done. But since this is what they have resolved, I will show how well they defend their constitution and accomplish all the other things for which the other Greeks criticize them.

First let me say that it is right that in Athens the populace and the poor have more than the noble and the wealthy, because it is the people who man the ships and make the city strong. The steersmen, the boatswains, the sub-boatswains, the look-out officers: all these contribute to the strength of the city much more than the hoplites, the noble and the respectable men. For this reason, it is right that everyone has a share in the magistracies, both those allotted and those elective, and that anybody who wants to do so is entitled to speak his mind.

The populace however claim no share in those magistracies which bring safety to the whole city when they are well managed, or danger when they are not (for instance, they do not think that they should have an allotted share in the board of generals or the command of the cavalry). For the populace is aware that they have more to gain from not holding those offices and leaving them to the most powerful men. But those magistracies which are salaried and lucrative, the people want to hold them.

Now, some might find it extraordinary that the Athenians always assign more to the scoundrels, the poor and the demagogues than the better citizens: this clearly goes in the direction of preserving democracy, because if the poor, the extremists and all the men of the baser sort are well off and numerous, they will increase democracy. But if the wealthy and notable men are doing well, the popular leaders will create a strong opposition against themselves.

Everywhere in the world the most honourable citizens are against democracy. For in the best citizens there is a minimum of wantonness and injustice, and the greatest attention for what is good. On the other hand, among the populace there is a maximum of ignorance, disorder and wickedness. For poverty drives them to commit disgraceful acts. Also, poverty causes some to be uncultured and ignorant.

Some might say that they should not let everyone speak at the assembly on equal terms, or serve in the council, but only the best and most righteous men. But even in their letting the worst men address the assembly they are in fact acting very sensibly: for if the best men were to address the assembly and offer their advice, this would be good for the likes of them, but not so good for the men of the people. But now any scoundrel who wants to do so can stand up and obtain what is good for him and the people like him.

Some might also say: 'what good advice could such a man give for himself and for the people?' But they know that the ignorance, the wickedness and benevolence of this kind of men are more profitable than the virtue, wisdom and reproaches of the good men. Now, a city will never be the best on the basis of these principles, but this is how democracy can be best preserved. For the people do not want to be slaves in a well-governed city, but to be free and to rule. They are not interested if the city is badly governed: in fact, what you consider bad government is the source of the strength and the liberty of the people. If good government is good government, you should look for a city where the best men establish laws in their own interest. Then you will see the best men punish the worst, and legislate in the interests of the city. They will not let the worst men speak in public and take part in the assembly. But all these good measures will swiftly make the people fall into slavery.

[b] [Ps. Xen.] *Ath. Const.* 2.1: Weakness of the Athenian infantry

The Athenian infantry is rightly considered to be very weak, and has been deliberately left weak. For the Athenians consider themselves weaker and fewer in numbers than their enemies, but they are in fact stronger, even on land, than their allies who pay the tribute, and they consider it sufficient to have a stronger infantry than their allies.

[c] [Ps. Xen.] *Ath. Const.* 2.19–20: Good and bad citizens in democratic Athens

Now, I want to say that the people of Athens know who are the good citizens and who are the bad, still they show their support to those who are friendly and useful to themselves, even if they are bad, and as a norm they tend to hate the good people. For they think that the respectable people are naturally virtuous not for their benefit, but for their hurt. On the other hand, there are men who genuinely care for the people, even though they are not democrats by nature.

But I pardon the people for their democracy, as one should always pardon someone for looking after his interests. Having said that, whoever does not belong to the people and still chooses to live under a democracy rather than an oligarchy, well, this person is preparing himself to do wrong and has realized that a scoundrel is more likely to escape notice in a democracy than in an oligarchy.

[d] [Ps. Xen.] *Ath. Const.* 3.1: The busy political calendar of democratic Athens

As for the Athenian constitution, I do not praise its form, but since the Athenians have decided to have a democracy, I must say that they have defended it well by behaving in the manner which I have described. And I see that the Athenians are criticized because sometimes it is impossible for a man holding an office for one year to be heard by the council or the assembly. This happens in Athens because, owing to the amount of business on the agenda, they are not able to deal with all the officers before sending them away. In fact, how could they do that? For they have to celebrate more festivals than any other Greek city, and when these are being celebrated, it is even less possible for them to deal with the city's business. Then they have to preside over public and private trials, and the public examinations of the magistrates, to a degree beyond that of any other city; then the council has to deliberate on a number of matters concerning war, finances, legislation, and other issues concerning the city as the circumstances demand, and then the many matters concerning the allies, the collection of the tribute, the maintenance of the dockyards and the temples. It therefore comes as no surprise that, owing to the quantity of business, they are unable to deal with all the magistrates before sending them away.

[e] [Ps. Xen.] *Ath. Const.* 1.13: The people of Athens have spoiled the sport and musical competitions

The people have ruined every athletic and musical endeavour, because they judged them inappropriate (in fact, because they knew that they could not do them). When it comes to organizing dramatic choruses and athletic contests, and fitting out triremes, the people know that it is the wealthy who lead the choruses, while the people are led, and it is the rich who preside over the athletic contests and command the trireme, while the people are presided over and commanded. At any rate, the people think they deserve money for their singing, running, dancing, and sailing in the ships, so that they may become wealthy and the wealthy poorer.

And even in the courts they care less about justice than their own interests.

[f] [Ps. Xen.] *Ath. Const.* 2.9-10: The people of Athens have spoiled the religious rites of the city

The people know that each of the poor cannot afford to offer sacrifices and feasts, to set up shrines and to dwell in a beautiful and great city. Still they have found out how to get sacrifices, shrines, banquets and temples. They sacrifice at public expense many victims, but it is the people who enjoy the revels, and to whom the sacrificed victims are allotted.

There are wealthy citizens who own private gymnasia, baths and dressing-rooms, but the people have built for their own use many wrestling-quarters, dressing-rooms and public baths, and the lower orders have more enjoyment of these things than the few and the well-to-do.

33. The Four Hundred, the oligarchic experiment and the myth of the *patrios politeia*

The political crisis engendered by the Sicilian disaster culminated with the oligarchic coup of the spring–summer of 411. The oligarchic movement set off among the crews of the Athenian fleet at Samos, mainly through the machinations of Alcibiades. His promise to the crews was to persuade the Great King to lend support to the Athenians, but this could happen only if they would adopt an oligarchic constitution. In Athens, the constitutional change was supported by the members of the elite clubs known as *etairiai*. In the spring of 411, the assembly approved the decree of Pythodorus, providing for the appointment of a college of twenty *syngrapheis*, including the ten *probouloi* appointed after the Sicilian disaster, to prepare a draft of the new constitution. This was meant to be inspired by the so-called 'constitution of the fathers' (*patrios politeia*), the moderate regime in place at the time of Solon. The *boule* was to be replaced by a council of four hundred members, political rights were to be limited to the five thousand wealthiest citizens, i.e. those able to provide themselves with arms. Pay for any magistracy was abolished [a].

The oligarchic coup is the main theme of Book VIII (unfinished) of Thucydides' *Histories*, where great attention is paid to the interaction between the oligarchic conspirators and the crews at Samos [b, c], and their reaction to the coup. The crews, mostly (but not completely) composed of Athenian citizens, came to serve as a sort of *ekklesia* in exile. An assembly was held and the generals suspected of oligarchic sympaties were duly deposed. Other officials were appointed in their place [**e–f**]. Athens was a split city: the oligarchs in Athens, and the democratic government proclaimed by the crews at Samos. The events of Samos undermined the stability of the regime at home. Following an unsuccessful naval clash against the Spartans and the loss of Euboea, a meeting of the *ekklesia* declared the Four Hundred deposed. All the powers were to be handed over to the Five Hundred, who had not yet been nominated. A college of *nomothetai* ('legislators') was appointed to carry out a revision of the legislative body of the city.

The Five Hundred governed for a brief period between the deposition of the Four Hundred and the full restoration of democracy. Very little is known about this regime, but both Thucydides and the Aristotelian *Constitution* praise it for its moderation [**g, h**].

[a] [Arist.] *Ath. Const.* 29–30: Political developments after the Sicilian disaster; the decree of Pythodorus

As long as the vicissitudes of the war continued to be in balance, the Athenians maintained their democracy. But following the disaster in Sicily, the Spartan side became much stronger owing to their alliance with the king, and so the Athenians were compelled to abolish the democratic constitution, and established in its stead the regime of the Four Hundred. Melobius delivered the speech in support of this resolution prior to the vote; the motion had been drafted by Pythodorus, of the deme of Anaphlystus. And the people gave their approval to it in the belief that, if they changed the constitution to an oligarchy, the king would support them more in the war. This was the content of the motion of Pythodorus:

'The assembly shall appoint twenty citizens over forty years of age in addition to the ten preliminary advisors already in charge. These shall swear under solemn oath to draft whatever proposals they consider best for the city, and to prepare motions for the safety of the city. Any other citizen who intended to do so will be entitled to make proposals, so that the people might choose the best from them all.' Cleitophon proposed an amendment to the motion of Pythodorus: that the appointed advisors should also investigate the laws set by Cleisthenes when he established the democracy in order that having these before their eyes they might take the best decisions having also these laws in mind, on the assumption that the constitution of Cleisthenes was not altogether democratic, but more similar to that of Solon.

Once the advisors were appointed, their first proposal was that it should be compulsory for the prytanes to put to the vote any motion that was presented in the interest of public safety. Then they repealed the procedure of indictment for illegal proposal, and all the impeachments and public prosecutions, so that any Athenian who wished might offer his advice on the current circumstances. Also, they established that if anybody would try to punish them, or fine or bring to court for so doing, he would be liable to information and immediate arrest before the generals, and these should hand him to the eleven to be put to death.

After this, they arranged the constitution in the following manner.

The city's revenues were not to be spent for any other purpose except the war. All the magistrates were not to receive any pay until the end of the war with the exception of the serving prytanes and nine archons. These should receive three obols a day each. All the other public offices were to be put in the hands of the citizens most capable of serving the city in person or with their property for the duration of the war. The number of these should be not less than five thousand. These would have power to sign treaties with whomever they wished. And they should appoint a board of ten men over forty years of age from each tribe, who should draw the list of the Five Thousand after taking oath over unblemished victims.

These were the measures drafted by the appointed committee. Once they had been ratified, the Five Thousand elected one hundred of their members to draw up the constitution, and this is what they delivered:

'The council shall consist of men over 30 years of age and will hold office for one year, serving without pay. The following offices shall be appointed from the council: the generals, the nine archons, the amphictyonic registrar, the taxiarchs, the hipparchs, the phylarch, the garrison commanders, the ten Treasurers of Athena and the other gods, the Treasurers of the Greeks, the twenty Treasurers of the other non-sacred moneys, the ten officers of the sacrifices and the ten superintendents of the mysteries. The council shall appoint these offices from a larger preliminary list of candidates chosen from its current members. All the other offices were to be assigned by lot and not from the council. The Treasures of the Greeks who manage the funds shall not sit with the council. Four councils of men of the approved age shall be established for the future. And a section of these shall be appointed by lot to take office immediately, and the others shall serve in turn, in an order decided by lot.

The hundred commissioners shall divide themselves and all the others into four parts as equal as possible, and cast lots among them, and those selected by the lot will serve in the council for one year. The members of the council shall pass resolutions as seemed best to them to secure a safe custody of the funds and their expenditure for the necessary purposes, and on all the other matters to the best of their ability. And if they desire to consider other matters in added numbers, each member of the council shall have the authority to summon as a co-opted councilman another man of the same age as himself, whomever he may wish.

The council shall meet once every five days, unless further meetings are required. The council shall cast the lot to appoint the nine archons. The five tellers shall be appointed by lot from the councilmen, and one of these shall be selected by lot every day to serve as president. And the appointed five tellers shall cast lots among those who desired to confer with the council, first for religious matters, then for heralds, third for embassies, fourth about other any other business. But whenever they have to discuss matters relating to the war, the tellers shall introduce the generals without casting lots. Any councilman who fails to arrive at the council-house at the prescribed time shall receive a fine of one drachma for each day, unless he is away on leave of absence from the council.'

[b] Thuc. 8.47–8: Alcibiades and the Four Hundred

This is the advice that Alcibiades gave to Tissaphernes and the king at the time when he was their guest, in part because he thought that this was the best course to follow, but also because he was preparing his way to return home. For he knew that, if he did not spoil it, he could one day have the opportunity to persuade his fellow-citizens to recall him, and he thought that the best way to persuade them was by letting them see that he enjoyed the friendship of Tissaphernes. And this is exactly what happened. When the Athenian troops at Samos sensed that Alcibiades had great influence with the satrap, mainly by their own initiative, but also because Alcibiades was sending words to the most influential people among them to tell the best men of the army that if there was an oligarchy instead of that wicked democracy which had exiled him, he would be happy to return home and to make Tissaphernes a friend of the Athenians, most of the leaders of the navy and the Athenian trierarchs at Samos set in motion to overthrow the democracy.

The plot set out in the camp, and from there it reached the city. Some men crossed from Samos to confer with Alcibiades, and since he told them that he could make first Tissaphernes and then the king their friends, if only they were ready to give up democracy, for in this way the king would have more trust in them, the most prominent citizens, who had been severely affected by the war, began to entertain great hopes that they would gain control of the situation and prevail over their opponents. When the envoys returned to Samos, they organized their supporters into a club, and so they took to tell the crews that, if Alcibiades returned and democracy were abolished, the king would become their friend, and give them money. At first the mass of crewmen were annoyed by all this plotting and scheming, but then the lucrative prospective of getting their pay from the king served to keep them quiet. As for the oligarchic conspirators, after they exposed their designs to the people, they once again considered the plan proposed by Alcibiades among themselves and with many of their acolytes, and while most of them found it ingenious and reliable, Phrynicus, who was still general, did not approve it at all. Alcibiades, as he rightly thought, had no real preference for oligarchy over democracy. His only objective was to be recalled home by his friends, in one way or another, by changing the present constitution, while their only concern should be to avoid civic strife. Also, an alliance with the Athenians would not be in the interest of the king, for the Spartans had now become a naval power to match the Athenians, and had added some important cities to their empire: why would the king take sides with the Athenians, whom he did not trust, when he could be friends with the Spartans, who had never injured them?

As for the allied cities which were to be offered oligarchy, because Athens itself would not be a democracy any longer, Alcibiades, he said, knew well that those who had seceded from the league would not come back any sooner, nor would those who have remained loyal become steadier in their allegiance. For they would never prefer living in servitude under an oligarchy or a democracy over enjoying freedom under their own constitution, whichever that happened to be. Also, the allies thought that the rule of the so-called good and proper citizens would be no less oppressive than the rule of the populace, for they had been the originators, proposers and main beneficiaries of those actions of the commons which had damaged the confederates. In fact, if it depended on these men, the allies would be put to violent death without trial, while the commons would be their protectors and the chastisers of these men. All this the allies had learned by experience, and he knew for certain that this was their opinion. This is why he could never approve of Alcibiades' plans of and all the current intrigues.

[c] Thuc. 8.54: Popular reactions to Pisander's proposal

The people were at first outraged when they heard oligarchy being mentioned, but when Pisander explained to them in the clearest terms that there was no other way of safety, they got scared and finally gave in, hoping that one day they could change the constitution again. So the assembly resolved that Pisander should sail with ten other men and make the agreements which they considered the most convenient with Tissaphernes and Alcibiades. At the same time, when Pisander brought false accusations against Phrynicus, the people dismissed him and his colleague Scironides from their command, and sent Diomedon and Leon to replace them as commanders of the fleet. Pisander said that Phrynicus had betrayed Iasus and Amorges, because he thought that he was not well disposed towards the plans of Alcibiades. Pisander also went around the clubs operating in the city to seek their support in the lawsuits and the elections, urging them to make a common front and unite their efforts to dismantle the democracy. Having made all the preparations required by the circumstances, so as to avoid any delay, he set off with the other ten colleagues on his travel to Tissaphernes.

[d] Thuc. 8.67–8: The assembly of Colonus

At this juncture Pisander and his colleagues arrived in Athens, and immediately set out to finish what remained to be done. Firstly they summoned the assembly and proposed electing a board of ten men with full powers to draft a new constitution. After completion of their work, the ten men should on a stipulated day appear before the assembly to lay out their thoughts as to how the city would be best governed. When the day came, they convened the assembly at Colonus, a shrine of Poseidon, located about ten stadia outside the city. Then the ten commissioners brought forward nothing else but this single proposal: that any Athenian was entitled to advance whatever proposal he wished without fear of punishment, and harsh penalties were imposed upon any who would indict the proposer for illegality or damage him in any other manner. Then it was clearly said that all the magistracies and paid services existing under the current system were no longer in place, but five men were to be appointed as presidents, and these were to elect one hundred men, and each of the one hundred three each, and this body of four hundred would enter the council with full powers and govern the city as they deemed best, and they were to convene the Five Thousand whenever they pleased.

Pisander was both the proposer of this motion and the man who, to all appearance, gave the most enthusiastic contribution to the dismantling of democracy.

But the man who orchestrated the whole operation and paved the way to the disaster, and devoted himself to this plan for the longest time, was Antiphon, a man second to none for virtue in the Athens of his time. Antiphon had a remarkable skill for devising schemes and knew how to recommend them, but was always reluctant to come forward at the assembly or any other public meeting, for the populace looked at him with suspicion, owing to his reputation for cleverness. Yet, when asked for advice, he was the single most talented man when it came to lending advice to any man embroiled in a dispute at the law-courts or the assembly. Later on, following the restoration of democracy, when the Four Hundred, having been overthrown, were being severely dealt with by the people, Antiphon, who was under charge of having taken part in this coup, gave the best plea in his defence ever delivered by anybody up to this time.

Phryniscus also went beyond everybody in his enthusiasm for the oligarchy. For he was afraid of Alcibiades and knew that he was informed of his intrigues with Astyochus at Samos. Indeed, Phrynicus thought that, once oligarchy was established, Alcibiades would never be recalled by the new regime. And so, once the plot was set in motion, and dangers were to be faced, he proved to be one of the most dependable men.

Theramenes, son of Hagnon, a man of considerable intellectual and rhetorical ability, was also one of the foremost conspirators in the destruction of democracy. In fact, it was no surprise than an enterprise led by so many sagacious men, in spite of its magnitude, went forward. For it was a difficult task indeed to deprive the Athenian people of its freedom, and almost a hundred years had passed since the deposition of the tyrants, during which period the Athenians had never been ruled by anyone, and for more than half of it had accustomed themselves to rule their own subjects.

[e] Thuc. 8.73: Democratic reaction at Samos, I

At Samos the vicissitudes of the oligarchic regime took a completely different turn. The following events took place at the same time as the four hundred were carrying out their plot in Athens.

Those of the Samians who had earlier risen against the upper class, and were the democratic faction, had changed sides again, and having been persuaded by the words of Pisander, when he visited Samos, and of those of the Athenians present in the island who were involved in the plot, bound themselves by oaths to the three hundred and were preparing to attack the rest of their fellow-citizens, whom they now called 'the democrats'. Meanwhile, they put to death an Athenian citizen, name of Hyperbolus, a depraved man who had been ostracized, not because they were afraid of his power or influence, but because he was a scoundrel and a shame for their city. This they did with the support of Charminus, one of the generals, and by some Athenians who were with them, to whom they had sworn friendship. With these men they had already perpetrated other such acts and were now eager to overthrow the popular government. When these men got news of what was about to happen, they informed Leon and Diomedon, two of the generals, who were ill-disposed to the oligarchy owing to the credit which they enjoyed among the commons, and also Thrasybulus and Thrasyllus, a trierarch and a hoplite, and some other individuals who had always been among the most outspoken enemies of the conspirators. They implored them not to look on and see them ruined, and Samos, the only remainder of their empire, alienated to the Athenians. Having heard this, they approached each one of the Athenian soldiers and urged them to resist, particularly the crews of the Paralus, who were all Athenians and freedmen and had from time immemorial been hostile to oligarchy, even when such a thing did not exist. Leon and Diomedon left some ships behind in their defence. Then, when the three hundred attacked the populace, they all came to the rescue, particularly those of the Paralus, and the Samian people came out victorious. Some of the three hundred were put to death, three of the ringleaders were banished, while the rest were granted an amnesty, and lived together under a democracy for the time to come.

[f] Thuc. 8.75.2–3: Democratic reaction at Samos, II

After this Thrasybulus, son of Lycus, and Thrasyllus, who were the chief leaders of the upheaval, and had been very public in their support of a change of government of Samos to a democracy, made all the soldiers, and particularly those of the oligarchic faction, take the most solemn of oaths to accept a democratic government, to live in harmony, to carry on zealously the war against the Peloponnesians and to be hostile to the Four Hundred and not to communicate with them. The same oath was also taken by the Samians of full age and the soldiers who were associated with the Samians in their affairs and in their common dangers, for they thought that there was no other way of safety for themselves or for them, and if the Four Hundred or the enemy at Miletus were to prevail, they would be ruined.

[g] Thuc. 8.97: The deposition of the Four Hundred and the regime of the Five Thousand

When they heard the news, the Athenians manned 20 ships and called immediately a first assembly, which was summoned at the Pnyx where they used to meet before the coup. The people deposed the Four Hundred and voted to hand over the government to the Five Thousand, that is all who could supply themselves with a full armour. They also decreed that no one should receive pay for serving in any office, or if he did he should be held accursed. Many other assemblies were held afterwards, in which supervisors of the laws were appointed and all other measures pertaining to the constitution were taken. It was in this phase that the Athenians appear to have enjoyed the best government that they ever had, at least in my time. For it consisted in a wise mixture of democracy and oligarchy, which for the first time enabled the Athenians to raise their heads after their many sorrows. They also voted for the recall of Alcibiades and the other exiles, and sent to him and to the camp at Samos, and urged them to apply themselves to the war.

[h] [Arist.] *Ath. Const.* 33.2: The well-governed Athens of the Five Thousand

In this critical phase, Athens seems to have been well governed, although the war was still raging, and political rights were limited to those able to bear arms.

34. The Arginusae scandal and the excesses of democracy

In the spring of 406, the Spartans blockaded Conon, the commander-in-chief of the Athenian fleet, in the port of Mytilene. Once the news reached Athens, the assembly voted exceptional emergency measures to prepare a rescue mission: new ships were built, and the gold objects offered to the Goddess were melted to issue new coins and finance the operation; slaves were enrolled as rowers, even the citizens of hoplite rank were exceptionally enrolled for service in the fleet. Extraordinary powers were granted to the eight available generals to prepare and conduct the campaign.

The new fleet engaged in battle with the Spartan admiral Callicratidas at the Arginusae, a group of three small islands between Lesbos and the shores of Asia Minor. The Athenians came out victorious and Conon was liberated. After the battle however a violent storm broke out and the Athenian officials failed to recover the bodies of the dead and shipwrecked. This was cause of great outrage in Athens: the generals in charge of operations were deposed and the six who returned to Athens had to stand trial before the assembly and were sentenced to death. The trial of the Arginusae generals is one of the most controversial episodes in the history of the Athenian democracy. Xenophon insinuates that the trial was triggered by the machinations of Theramenes, one of the leading politicians of the time, who sensed the opportunity to get rid of his political enemies. Ancient sources and modern scholars alike agree that the execution of the generals was a tragic mistake that deprived the *polis* of its most experienced officials and ultimately caused Athens' defeat in the war against Sparta. To the critics of democracy, the Arginusae trial was exemplary of the violent and volatile temper of the Athenian *demos*.

Xen. *Hell.* 1.7.1–35: The trial of the Arginusae generals

Those at home deposed the above-mentioned generals, except Conon, and appointed as his colleagues two men, Adeimantus and Philocles. Two of the generals who had taken part in the naval battle, Protomachus and Aristogenes, did not return to Athens. But when the other six returned, Pericles, Diomedon, Lysias, Aristocrates, Thrasyllus and Erasinides, Archedemus, who was then the leader of the popular faction in Athens and was in charge of the two-obol fund, brought an accusation against Erasinides and asked for a fine to be imposed on him, claiming that he had taken money from the Hellespont which belonged to the people. Furthermore, he accused him of misconduct during his term as general. The court eventually decided that Erasinides should be arrested. After this, the generals made a statement in front of the *boule* concerning the battle and the violent storm, and Timocrates put forward a motion that the others should also be arrested and turned over to the assembly to stand trial, and so the *boule* had them arrested. Then a meeting of the assembly was held, at which Thermanenes and others spoke against the generals, saying that they ought to give an explanation as to why they did not rescue the shipwrecked. As a proof that none but the generals were responsible for what happened, Theramenes showed a letter sent to the *boule* and the *ekklesia*, in which they put all the blame on the storm. After this, the generals briefly spoke each in their defence, for they had not been granted a hearing as prescribed by the law, and gave a full account of their actions, claiming that after the battle they had set off to sail against the enemy, and that they had assigned the duty of recovering the shipwrecked to some of the triearchs, who were experienced and had already been generals in the past: people like Theramenes and Thrasybulus. These men, and no one else, were to blame for the failed recovery, for this duty had been assigned to them. The generals said that they would not put the blame on those who had falsely accused them: it was the violence of the storm that had prevented the recovery. Also, they presented as witnesses the pilots and many others of those who were sailing with them. The people were persuaded by these arguments, and many of the citizens rose and offered to give bail for them. The assembly, however, decided to defer the matter to another meeting, for it was already late in the day and they could not distinguish the hands in the vote. Also it was resolved that the *boule* should draft and bring in a proposal concerning the mode of trial for the men under arrest. Then the Athenians celebrated the Apaturia, where the fathers and kinsmen of the deceased sailors could meet together. Accordingly, Theramenes and his supporters organized a large group of men, clad in mourning veils, their hair skin-shaven. These were to attend a meeting of the assembly, claiming to be relatives of those who had perished in the battle. They also bribed Callixeinus to accuse the generals before the council. Henceforth they convened the assembly, and Callixeinus presented the proposal drafted by the council: 'It has been resolved: since the Athenians have heard at the previous assembly both the accusers who had brought charge against the generals and the generals themselves speaking in their own defence, they shall now all cast their vote by tribes. Two urns shall be set at the voting-place of each tribe, and in each tribe a herald will announce that whoever considers the generals guilty for not recovering the men who had triumphed in the naval battle shall cast his vote in the first urn, and whoever considers them innocent, in the second. And if they are found guilty, they shall be punished with death and handed over to the eleven, and their property be confiscated and the tenth part shall be given to the goddess. At this point a man came before the assembly: he claimed that he had been saved by a floating metal-tub, and those who were dying asked him, if he found safety, to tell the people that the generals did not recover the men who had fought so valiantly in defence of the fatherland. Euryptolemus, son of Peisianax, and some others called for an indictment against Callixeinus, alleging that he had made an unconstitutional proposal. Some of the assemblymen commended this action, but most of them cried out that it was terrible if the people were prevented from doing whatever they wished. At this point, Lyciscus proposed that these men should be judged by the same vote as the generals, unless they withdrew their summons. The mob then broke out again, and so they were forced to withdraw the summons. Now, since some of the prytanes refused to put the question to the vote because it was against the law, Callixeinus rose again to the podium and urged the same charges against them, and the mob cried out again that the prytanes who had refused to put the question to the vote should be brought to court. At this point the prytanes, shaken with fear, agreed to put the question to the vote, all of them except Socrates, son of Sophroniscus. He said that he would never perpetrate any act contrary to the laws. After this, Euryptolemus rose to the platform and gave the following speech in defence of the generals:

'Athenians, I have come here to accuse Pericles, although he is my kinsman, and Diomedon, an intimate of mine, but also to advise what policies I consider best for the city as a whole. I accuse them because they persuaded their colleagues to change their purpose when they wanted to send a letter to the council and the assembly, in which they stated that the duty of recovering the shipwrecked had been assigned to Theramenes and Thrasybulus, with forty-seven triremes, but they failed to rescue them. Now, should the generals share the blame with Theramenes and Thrasybulus, who in fact are the only culprits? And should they pay for the humanity which they showed then, and put their lives at risk, through the intrigues of these men and some others? Certainly not, if you follow my advice and act in accordance with the human and divine law. For if you follow my advice, you will best learn the truth, so you will not repent your decision later, when you'll find out that you have committed the gravest sins towards the gods and yourselves. If you follow my advice you will not be deceived by me or anyone else, but, having learnt who are the real culprits, you will punish them with whatever penalty you wish, either all of them together, or each one individually, and firstly you'll grant them one day, if not more, to speak in their own defence, and then you'll put your trust in yourselves more than anybody else.

'Athenians, you are all aware that the decree of Cannonus is excessively severe: it provides that if anyone does wrong to the Athenian people, he shall plead his case in chains before the assembly, and if he is found guilty, he shall be put to death by being thrown into the pit, his property be confiscated and the tenth part of it given to the goddess. Now, I urge you to try the generals under this decree, and, by Zeus, you should try my kinsman Pericles first, if it so pleases you, for it would be shameful of me to be more concerned about him than the whole city. And if you don't want to follow this course, try them under the following law, which applies to temple-robbers and traitors: "If anyone betrays the state or steals the sacred property, he shall be tried before a tribunal and if found guilty, he shall not be buried in Attica and his property will become public."

'Let these men be tried, Athenians, under whichever law you choose, each of them separately. The day be divided into three parts, one for you to hold assembly and vote whether they are guilty or not; another for the prosecutors to present their case and the third for the defendants to plead their case. Athenians, if this course is followed, the guilty will incur the harshest punishment, and the innocent will be released by you, and will not unjustly be put to death. You will grant them a fair trial, standing true to the laws, religion and your oaths, and you will not be fighting alongside the Spartans, by putting to death without a trial and in violation of the laws the very men who captured seventy of their ships and defeated them in the naval battle. So, why are you acting so hastily? What are you afraid of? Are you afraid of losing the right to put to death or release anyone you wish if you try these men in accordance to the law, by following the procedure which Callixeinus convinced the council to bring in to the assembly, that is by a single vote? But perhaps you might be putting to death someone who is not guilty, and you will repent later. Remember how painfully unavailing repentance is, particularly when mistakes result in the death of a man. In the past you gave Aristarchus, the very man who destroyed democracy and then betrayed Oenoe to the Thebans, your enemies, a whole day to defend himself as he wished, and all the other rights prescribed by the law, and certainly it would be a terrible thing if you were to deny the same rights to the generals who did everything in accordance with your opinion and defeated the enemy. No, men of Athens, don't follow this course. Defend your laws, the laws that have made you above everything else, and do not try to do anything outside their jurisdiction.

'But let us now return to the actual circumstances under which the generals supposedly committed their mistakes. When they sailed to the shore after winning the battle, Diomedon ordered that they should all put out to sea in line and recover the wreckage and the shipwrecked seamen, while Erasinides urged that they should all sail as speedily as possible against the enemy at Mytilene. Thrasyllus however said that they could do both these things by leaving some ships there and sailing against the enemy with the rest. If they approved of this plan, he said that each of the eight generals should leave three of his ships behind, and in addition to these the ten ships of the taxiarchs, the ten of the Samians and the three of the nauarchs. The total number of these ships was forty-seven, four for each of the twelve which had been lost. Among the officers who were left behind were Thrasybulus and Theramenes: these were the same men who accused the generals in the course of the previous assembly. The generals sailed against the enemies with the remaining ships. Now, is there anything that they did not perform in a satisfactory and adequate manner? It is therefore fair that those who were assigned to sail against the enemy should give account for their lack of success, while those who were assigned to the recovery of the shipwrecked should be tried for failing to recover them, if they did not comply with the orders of the generals.

'This is what I have to say in defence of both parties: the storm prevented them from doing anything of what the generals prescribed them to do. And those who were fortunate enough to find safety are here as your witnesses. Among them there is one of our generals, who found safety upon a disabled ship, and they now are urging you to judge him by the same vote, even though at the time he had to recover himself, by which you judge those who did not perform the tasks, which had been assigned to them by order of the generals. Citizens of Athens, in the day of victory and good fortune you should not behave like men who are beaten and unfortunate. Nor should you give the impression of acting unfairly, by giving a verdict of treachery instead of helplessness, for the storm prevented them from complying with the assigned task. It would be much more just for you to honour these men with garlands, than yield to wicked men and punish them with death.'

Thus spoke Euryptolemus. Then he presented a motion that the men should be tried under the decree of Cannonus, each one separately, while the proposal of the council was to try them all by a single vote. The Athenians then cast their vote between these two motions, and they first decided in favour of the one proposed by Euryptolemus. At this point however Menceles interposed an objection under oath and a second vote was taken, and this time they approved the motion of the council. After this they condemned the eight generals who had taken part in the battle, and the six who were in Athens were put to death. After a short time, the Athenians repented, and decreed that all the men who had deceived the people should furnish bondsmen until they were put to trial, and Callixeinus should be one of them. Complaints were also lodged against four men who were put into confinement by their bondsmen. Then the city entered a phase of factional strife, during which Cleophon was put to death, and these men escaped before they were put to trial. Later on Callixeinus returned, when the faction of the Piraeus had already returned to the city, but he was hated by everybody, and died of starvation.

35. The moral crisis of the Athenian democracy: Aristophanes' *Frogs*

In 405, as the Peloponnesian War was drawing to a close and the defeat of Athens looked more and more inevitable, Aristophanes won the first prize at the comedy competition at the Great Dionysia with his comedy *Frogs*.

The recent deaths of Euripides and Sophocles provide the background of the comedy. Grieved by the decline of Athenian tragedy, the god Dionysus decided to travel to the Underworld to bring back Euripides to Athens, but the poet is engaged in an argument with Aeschylus to decide who should be awarded the seat of the 'best poet'. Dionysus is called to judge the contest, and decides to award the palm to the poet who would give the best piece of advice to the people of Athens, and Aeschylus comes out victorious. Before leaving for Athens, Aeschylus decides to give the throne of best poet to Sophocles, not Euripides.

The decline of Athenian theatre that followed the almost contemporary death of Sophocles and Euripides is a reflection of the wider military, political and moral crisis of the city. The enfeebled voice of the Athenian stage is no longer able to provide moral guidance to the city. Athens seems to have lost direction.

Upon entering the stage, the chorus of the frogs of the Acheron delivers a heartfelt invective against the traitors of the city, the men who have ruined democracy and brought back *stasis* by using public offices for their private interests [a]. The piece of advice that wins Aeschines the contest with Euripides is very simple: to save Athens, the citizens should stop following the bad people and start trusting the good ones, and refrain from the excesses of imperialism [b].

[a] Ar. *Frogs* 354–71: An invective against the enemies of Athens

CHORUS: Let him be mute and stand apart from our choruses who is ignorant
of this language and of impure mind, or has never seen the sacred rites of
the noble Muses and never danced in them, or has never been initiated
to the Bacchic mysteries of Cratinus the beef-eater, or rejoices in coarse
language when it is not time to do so, or whoever does not dissolve odious
strife, and is not well-disposed towards the citizens, but, thirsty with greed,
stirs and fans civic disorder, or who takes bribes while they should guide
the city through the storm, or betrays the garrisons or the galleys, or trade
contraband goods from Aegina, as Thorcyon did, the heinous tax-collector,

who sent leather pads, sails and pitch to Epidauros; or persuades people to send money to the ships of our enemies, or pollutes the shrine of Hecate by singing circular choruses, or any orator who nibbles the wages of the poets for having been lampooned in the ancestral festivals of Dionysus. To all these people, I give the same advice again and again: stand aside from our mystical choruses. As for you, rouse the song and start the dances of this night-festival of ours.

[b] Ar. *Frogs*, 1457–90: How Athens can be saved

AESCHINES: How could anyone save a city like this, that doesn't like the goatskin blanket or the cloak?

DIONYSUS: Find out something, by Zeus, if you want to come up again.

A.: I will talk when I get there; I don't want to say anything right now.

D.: Don't say that, but try to bring up some pieces of good advice from here.

A.: When they think that the land of the enemy is their own, and our land the enemy's, their ships are a revenue, and the revenue is a loss.

D.: Well said. Problem is, the judges will swallow it themselves.

PLUTO: It's time you made your decision.

D.: This will be my decision for them: I will choose whomever my soul wants.

E.: Now, don't forget the gods by whom you swore to bring me home, and choose your friends.

D.: It was my tongue that swore; my choice is Aeschines.

E.: What, you most disgraceful of men?

D.: Me? I have decided that Aeschines is the winner. What's wrong with that?

E.: You have perpetrated the most shameful of deeds and still dare to look at me in the face?

D.: Why shameful, if the audience is pleased with it?

E.: You, abominable man, are you neglecting me now that I'm dead?

D.: Who knows if living is not dying? Breathing is dining and sleep is a rug?

P.: Go inside, then, Dionysus.

D.: For why?

P. So I can give a little entertainment to both of you before you sail off.

D.: Well said. I am not grieved by that.

CHORUS: Blessed is the man of perfect intelligence, who can learn in many ways. This man is known for his wisdom, and will return home again for the good of the citizens, of his relatives and his friends because of his wisdom.

12

Democracy Abolished and Restored

36. The Thirty and the amnesty

In the summer of 405 the Spartan admiral Lysander defeated the Athenians at Aegospotami, in the waters of the Hellespont. After the battle, Lysander proceeded to seize the important Athenian strongholds of Byzantium and Calcedon, and then set sail towards Attica, while the kings Agis and Pausanias were preparing to besiege Athens by land. The Peloponnesian War was over and democratic Athens had been defeated. When the messenger-ship Paralus landed at the Piraeus bringing news of the disaster of Aegospotami, the grieving Athenians realized that the days of empire were over, and that they were soon to suffer the same harsh treatment that they had inflicted to many of their enemies and subjects [a].

Besieged by land and sea, the Athenians were starved into signing a humiliating peace treaty, providing for the demolition of the Long Walls and the fortifications of the Piraeus, and the decimation of the fleet. Athens was forced to join the Peloponnesian league [b].

With Lysander in town, democracy was formally abolished. The Athenian assembly appointed a new commission of 30 men loyal to Sparta, whose formal mandate was to draw up a new constitution based on the ancestral laws. Political rights were limited to the 3,000 wealthiest citizens, and the powers of the popular tribunal were transferred to a committee of 300 members. The Thirty however never prepared any constitutional draft, nor did they pass power to the new assembly of the Three Thousand. Instead, they ruled the city as tyrant. Firstly they arrested those who were known as scoundrels and enemies of the aristocracy, then began to target the properties of rich metics. One of these was the father of the great orator Lysias. The men suspected of hostility towards the tyrants were arrested and murdered. After a few months, the junta, marred by internal divisions, decided to tighten its grip on the city: all those who did not belong to the body of the three thousand were banned from the *asty* [c, d]. The city of Thebes became the centre of the Athenian resistance. In the winter of 404/403, troops under the command of Trasybulus moved south and occupied Munichia, a mound near the Piraeus, where they successfully engaged in battle with the men of the Thirty. At this point, the Spartans also moved into Attica, but they did not provided the decisive help that the Thirty were hoping for. Rather, King Pausanias mediated a truce between the two parties: the old democratic constitution was to be restored and Athens would remain an ally of Sparta. The men of the two factions committed themselves to live in peace with each other, while Eleusis, the old stronghold of the tyrants, would be granted a semi-independent status, for those who were not willing to join their fellow-citizens in the restored democracy. A general amnesty was passed for the crimes perpetrated under the junta, except for those of the tyrants themselves and their closer associates.

The restoration of democracy after the overthrow of the Thirty is a milestone in the history of ancient Athens. The text of the oath sworn by the two factions is reported in a speech by Andocides [e]. The Aristotelian *Constitution* has an accurate account of the terms under which democracy was restored [f]. As the author highlights, the process was carried out commendably smoothly, and without violence.

[a] Xen. *Hell.* 2.2.3: The news of Aegospotami reaches Athens

The night that the ship Paralus arrived at Athens bringing news of the disaster, a cry of grief ran from the Piraeus through the Long Walls and into the city, one man passing the news to another. Nobody slept that night, for they were all mourning not only the loss of men, but also their own fate, thinking that they would have to endure the same treatment that they had inflicted upon the Melians, colonists of the Spartans, after taking them by siege, and then the Histiaeans, and the Scionaeans and the Toronaeans and the Aeginetans and many other Greeks.

[b] Xen. *Hell.* 2.20.2–3: The humiliating peace with Sparta

The Spartans said that they would not enslave a city which had done great service to Greece in the time of the greatest danger. So they offered to make peace on the following conditions. The Athenians should demolish the Long Walls and the walls of Piraeus, surrender all their ships except twelve, allow their exiles to return. Also, they should have the same friends and enemies as the Spartans, and follow them by land and by sea wherever they should lead the way.

So Theramenes and his fellow-ambassadors reported this to Athens. And as they were entering a city, a great crowd gathered around them, fearful that they had achieved nothing. For it was no longer possible to delay, owing to the number who were dying of the famine. On the next days the ambassadors reported to the assembly the terms on which the Spartans intended to make peace. Theramenes spoke on behalf of the ambassadors and urged that it was necessary to yield to the Spartans and demolish the walls. Although some spoke against him, a far greater number approved of his resolution, and so it was voted to accept the peace. After this, Lysander sailed into Piraeus, the exiles returned, and the Peloponnesians began to tear down the walls with great enthusiasm to the music of flute-girls, thinking that that day was the beginning of freedom for Greece.

[c] Xen. *Hell.* 2.3.1–3: The Thirty take power

In the following year, when it was celebrated an Olympiad, and Crocinas of Thessaly was victorious in the stadium, Endius was ephor at Sparta and Pythodorus archon at Athens. However, since Pythodorus was chosen during the time of the oligarchy, the Athenians do not use his name to mark the year, but call it instead the 'year of anarchy', or 'the year without archon'. And this oligarchy came into being in the way hereafter described.

This is how the oligarchy was installed: it was voted by the people to choose thirty men to prepare a new constitution based on the ancestral law and to conduct the government under this constitution. The following men were chosen: Polychares, Critias, Melobius, Hippolochus, Eucleides, Hieron, Mnesilochus, Chremon, Theramenes, Aresias, Diocles, Phaedrias, Chaereleos, Anaetius, Peison, Sophocles, Eratosthenes, Charicles, Onomacles, Theognis, Aeschines, Theogenes, Cleomedes, Erasistratus, Pheidon, Dracontides, Eumathes, Aristoteles, Hippomachus, Mnesitheides. After this, Lysander sailed off to Samos, while Agis withdrew the land force from Decelea and dismissed the several contingents to their cities.

[d] Xen. *Hell.* 2.3.11–12: Excesses of the Thirty

At Athens the Thirty had been appointed as soon as the Long Walls and the walls round Piraeus were demolished. Although, however, they had been chosen for the purpose of writing a constitution for the government of the city, they continually delayed the writing and publication of it. Instead, they appointed a council and other magistrates as they deemed fit. Then, as a first measure, they began to arrest and bring to trial for their lives those men who by common knowledge had made a living in the time of the democracy by acting as informers and had been hostile to the aristocrats. And the council was glad to vote these people guilty, and the rest of the citizens, or at least those who knew that they were not like them, were not displeased at all.

[e] And. *Myst.* 90: The amnesty oath

'... and I will bear no grievance against any of the citizens, except only the Thirty, the Ten, and the Eleven: and even among them against none who shall agree to give account of his office.'

[f] [Arist.] *Ath. Const.* 39.1–2: Reconciliation and amnesty after the fall of the Thirty

The reconciliation took place in the archonship of Euclides, under the following agreement:

'The Athenians who have remained in the city but are willing to emigrate, can move to Eleusis remaining in possession of their rights. They will be sovereign, and independent, and will enjoy the profits of their revenues. The temple will be shared by both parties and will be administered by the Cheruches and Eumolpides in accordance with the ancestral laws. But those at Eleusis are not permitted to move to the city, nor those in the city to Eleusis, except for both of them on occasion of the Mysteries. Those in Eleusis are required to contribute to the military expenses like the other Athenians. Those who leave the city and take a home in Eleusis will be assisted to convince the owner. If they cannot find an agreement, each party shall choose three assessors and accept whatever price they quote. And of the people of Eleusis those whom the settlers want to dwell with them will be allowed to do so. The registration of those who want to emigrate and reside in the countryside shall take place within ten days from the swearing of the oath, and they shall move to Eleusis within twenty days. The same procedure shall apply to those who are abroad, from the date of their return. It will not be permitted to any of those who take residence in Eleusis to hold any of the offices in the city until he registers to live in the city.

The trials for homicide will take place in accordance with the ancestral laws, if a man has killed or wounded another one with his own hands. There will be an amnesty for all the crimes of the past, applying to everyone except the Thirty, the Ten, the Eleven and the magistrates at the Piraeus, if they do not render account. And the magistrates at the Piraeus shall render account before the courts at the Piraeus, and those in the city before a court of citizens who can provide an account of their property. Those who do not render account on these terms shall migrate. Each party shall repay separately the loans contracted for the war.'

The reconciliation took place on the above terms. Those who had fought with the Thirty were alarmed, and many considered emigrating, but did not register until the very last days, as everybody always does. And so Archinus, seeing how many they were and wishing to keep them in Athens, cancelled the days that remained for the registration, so that they would be compelled to remain against their will, until they regained courage. This seems to have been an act of good government from Archinus, and so was what he did later, when he indicted as illegal the decree of Thrasybulus granting a share in the citizenship to all those who had returned together from exile at the Piraeus, some of whom were clearly slaves. His third statesmanlike act was that when a certain individual began to bear grudges against those who had returned, he brought him before the council and persuaded the councilmen to put him to death without trial, telling them that the time had come for them to show if they wanted to save the democratic constitution and keep the oaths. For if they let him go, they would encourage the others to do the same, but if they got rid of this man they would make him an example to all. And this is what really happened, for since the moment that man was put to death, nobody has ever broken the amnesty, but they appear to have come to terms with their past misfortunes in the most honourable manner, as good citizens should do, both as concerned their private and public affairs. In fact, the Athenians not only obliterated all the disputes concerning the events of the past, but also gave public restitution to the Spartans of the funds which the Thirty had taken for the war, even though the treaty provided for the parties in the city and at the Piraeus to give back the funds separately. For the Athenians thought that this should be the the first step towards civic harmony, whereas in the other cities the leaders of the people do not contribute out of their own property, and also redistribute the land. Furthermore, in the archonship of Xenaenetus, they made a reconciliation with those who settled at Eleusis, two years after they migrated.

37. Plato, the death of Socrates and the debate on democracy

The aftermath of the fall of the Thirty was a time of lively debate on the principles and forms of Athenian democracy. In his first public address following the overthrow of the junta, Thrasybulus reassured the Athenians that they would return to live under the old laws [a]. A decree was also proposed to grant full citizenship rights (*isoteleia*) to the foreigners who had fought against the Thirty. The assembly however did not approve it. Pericles' law on citizenship was duly restored [b].

The restoration of democracy was achieved without bloodshed, but this does not mean that it was immune from witch-hunting, the most famous victim of it being Socrates, who was made pay for his proximity to some of the leaders of the oligarchic coups of 411 and 404, such as Critias and Theramenes. In 399, the philosopher Socrates was brought to trial and judged guilty of corrupting the youth and blasphemy. The death of Socrates was an important turning point in the life of the young Plato, who decided to put aside his ambitions of a political career to devote himself to philosophy and thus contribute to the moral regeneration of the *polis* [c].

[a] Xen. *Hell.* 2.4.40–2: Thrasybulus and the restoration of democracy, the men of the city and the men of the Piraeus

'Citizens, this is my advice for you: know yourselves. And you would best learn to know yourselves if you were to consider why you are so arrogant as to claim that you should rule over us. Because you are more just than us? But the people, although they are poorer than you, have never done any wrong to you for the sake of money. While you, although wealthier than any of them, have done many shameful things for the sake of gain. And since you have no special claim to justice, consider whether you are entitled to pride yourselves on your courage. And what better test of your courage could there be than the way we fought against each other? Or maybe you think you are more intelligent, you who had a wealth of weapons, walls and money, not to mention the Peloponnesians as allies, and yet have been defeated by men who had none of those things? Or maybe it is your friendship with the Spartans that you are so proud about? What? They handed you to the outraged people as someone would put a collar around the neck of a biting dog, and hand him to the keepers. Yes, they have turned their backs to you and gone away. But, gentlemen, it is not for me to ask you to violate any of your solemn oaths. Rather I beg you to show this other virtue in addition to all the other virtues that you have: show the world that you can be faithful to your oaths, and flawless in your conduct.'

When he had said these things and more to the same effect, and had told them that there was no need for them to be worried, but that they had only to live under the laws that had previously been in force, he dismissed the assembly.

[b] FGH 4.358 F11 (= Athen. *Deip.* 13.577b): The law of Aristophon

Aristophon the orator, in the archonship of Euclides, passed a law that everyone who was not born from an Athenian mother was illegitimate.

[c] Plato *Lett. VII* 324b–326b: The young Plato and the crisis of the Athenian constitution

When I was young I went through the same experiences as many others. My intention was to enter into the public life of the city as soon as I could become my own master. But then it so happened that the following changes had befallen the state. The existing government, vilified as it was by many, underwent a revolution, and fifty-one men were at the head of this revolution: eleven of them were in the city, and ten in the Piraeus. These two groups were in control of the market-square and all the matters relating to the city. Then there was a group of thirty, who had full powers over all. Some of these men happened to be familiar and known to me, and they did invite me to take a share in their project. The feelings which I then experienced were not at all surprising, if one considers my young age: I was convinced that those men would govern the city by leading it out of an unjust life into a just one, and so I devoted my mind to them with enthusiasm, I was eager to see what they could do. But then I saw these men in a short lapse of time make the old regime appear as a golden age, above all the way in which they treated my friend Socrates, an old man, whom I would certainly not hesitate to call the most just of the men then living, when they sent him along with others to fetch a man by force to put him to death, so that he would have a share of their actions whether he wished or no. But Socrates refused to obey; he risked incurring the heaviest punishments rather than being an accomplice of their crimes. I could no more endure to be a witness of all these grave actions, and others not inferior, so withdrew myself from all the evil actions which were going on. After a short while, however, the junta of the Thirty and the whole government then in place fell altogether. At this juncture I felt once again a desire to take part in the common and political affairs, though more hesitantly. Many other unbearable events were taking place in those troubled times, and it is not surprising that, in the midst of these disorders, some individuals were taking revenge upon their foes with excessive severity, even though those who were then returning from exile gave proof of considerable equity. But then something quite unfortunate happened: some of those in power brought my friend Socrates before a court on a most ignominious charge, which Socrates least of all deserved. For they brought him to trial on the charge of impiety, and others voted him guilty and sentenced him to death: the same man who, when they themselves were in the unfortunate situation of being exiles, had refused to take part in the unholy arrest of one of their exiled friends. And when I considered all these events and who were the men in charge of the affairs of the city, and their laws and customs: the more I considered them and the older I grew in age, the more difficult it appeared to me to administer the affairs of the city. For it was impossible to take any action without friends and companions worthy of one's trust, and these were not were not easy to find ready at hand, because our city was no longer governed according to the principles and customs of the fathers, and it was impossible to acquire new friends with some ease. The written laws and the ancestral customs were being corrupted with incredible rapidity. So, while at first I was full of desire to engage in political activity, when I considered all these things, and the way in which the affairs of the cities were being swept about in all directions, I finally became dizzy, and although I did not stop considering how the city's constitution and the general state of affairs could be improved, I resolved to postpone action till the right opportunity should arise. Finally, it became clear to me, with regard to all existing cities, that they were all badly governed. For their laws had reached a state of almost incurable illness without some extraordinary reform, and good luck to support it. And so in my praise of true philosophy I was compelled to say that it is what makes men discern justice both in public and private affairs.

38. Socrates' trial and the power of rhetoric

The *Apology of Socrates* is one of the earliest, if not the earliest, work written by Plato. The text is a version of the speech which Socrates gave in his own defence on the charges of corrupting the youth and blasphemy. In the opening lines Socrates says that he recognize himself in the Socrates sketched out in the speech of his accusers, and tells the jury that he has no intention of persuading them by means of clever speaking, of which he is incapable: he wants them to be persuaded by the truth of facts [a]. Socrates presents himself as the most law-abiding of citizens, who was not afraid of defying public opinion, as he did at the time of the Arginusae scandal, when he stood against the decision of trying all the generals together, or at the time of the Thirty Tyrants [b].

Socrates was often (and wrongly) associated with the activity of the so-called sophists, the 'teachers of wisdom', usually foreigners who taught young and wealthy Athenians how to succeed in the assemblies and law courts by means of rhetorical persuasion. The deceiving power of rhetoric and the fallacies of a political system based on public debate is one of the main themes of Plato's early works, like the dialogue *Gorgias*. Discussing the true nature of rhetoric with the namesake of this dialogue, the famous sophist Gorgias of Leontini, Socrates argues that the goal of rhetoric is not to improve the citizens and set them on the path to virtue and truth, but simply to court their favour, with little regard for the truth, or the common good of the *polis* community [c].

[a] Pl. *Ap.* 17a–b: Socrates and the power of rhetoric

Athenians: I don't know whether you have been persuaded by my accusers. As for me, they spoke so cleverly that I have almost forgotten who I am. And yet there is hardly a word of truth in what they said. Of all their lies, one I found particularly shocking: when they said that you should beware of being deceived by me, because I am a clever speaker. This, I think, was the most shameful part of their conduct because I will soon show them guilty of falsehood by the evidence of fact, when I show myself to be not in the least a clever speaker, unless indeed they call a clever speaker him who speaks the truth; for if this is what they mean, I would agree that I am an orator, not after their fashion. Now, as I say, they have said little or nothing true; but you shall hear from me nothing but the truth.

[b] Pl. *Ap.* 32b–33c: Socrates' defence

Athenians: I have never held any public office, except for serving in the council for one term. And it so happened that my tribe, the Antiochis, was holding the prytany when you decreed to try not individually, but all in the same trial, the ten generals who had not recovered the shipwrecked after the battle: this was an illegal procedure, as you all acknowledged afterwards. On that occasion I was the only one of the prytanes who refused to do anything against the laws. The city was against me, the orators were ready to impeach and arrest me and you were shouting your support for them: but I thought that I must run all risks with law and justice on my side, rather than being on your side, fearing imprisonment or death, when you were wishing for unjust things. At that time democracy was still standing, but once the oligarchy was established, the Thirty sent for me and four others to come to the rotunda, and ordered us to bring Leon the Salaminian from Salamis to be put to death. They gave such instructions to other people as well, wishing to associate as many people as they could in their misdeeds. And on that occasion I demonstrated once again with my actions, and not in words only, that I don't care about dying, if this is not too vulgar an expression, but not doing anything unjust or unholy: that is what I really care about. That government, in spite of all its power, did not scare me into doing anything unjust, but when we got out of the rotunda, the other four sailed off to Salamis and arrested Leon, while I went home, and perhaps I should have been sentenced to death for it, if the government had not been overthrown shortly afterwards. You have many witnesses of these events.

Now, do you think that I could have lived so many years if I had been active in politics and behaved as an honest man is supposed to behave, by giving my aid to just causes, and considering this of the highest importance? Certainly not, Athenians, nor could have any other man. Yet, you will find that throughout my life I have always behaved as I am doing now, both in public and in private, and have never yielded to anyone unjustly, whether it was any other person or any of those who are said by my accusers to be my pupils, but I have never been anyone's teacher: if anyone, young or old, desires to hear me talking while I pursue my interests, I have nothing to object. I do not converse with people only when I get a fee, or do not when I don't, but I talk with the rich and poor indifferently, and whoever wishes may answer and hear what I have to say. And whether any of these discussions turns out to be useful or not, I should not be held justly responsible, for I have never promised anything or given orders to any of my listeners. And if anybody says they have learnt or heard anything from me in private conversations, of which everybody else was in the dark, he is certainly lying.

[c] Pl. *Gor.* 502d–504a: Socrates, Gorgias and the power of rhetoric

SOCRATES: Very well. But now, what can we make of the kind of rhetoric addressed to the Athenian people, or to the other assemblies of free men in the other cities? What can we make of them? Do you think that the orators are always speaking with a view to what is best, and, having this in mind, to make the citizens as good as possible through their speeches, or are they set to court the favour of the people, just like poets do? And do they treat these assemblies like children, by simply trying to please them, neglecting the common good for their personal interest, and not consider whether the citizens will be better or worse in consequence of their speeches?

CALLICLES: The question you ask is not an easy one. For some of the orators speak with the interest of the citizens in mind, while others are just as you say.

S.: That is enough for me. For if oratory is a twofold business, on one part, I assume, you will have flattery and clap-trap of the basest sort, and on the other there will be the noble endeavour to make the citizens' souls as good as possible, and a constant effort to say what is best, be it pleasant or fastidious to the audience. But this is a kind of oratory which you have yet to see, or if you have in mind any such orator, you should tell me his name at once!

C.: No, by Zeus, I cannot tell you of anyone among the orators of today.

S.: So what? Can you mention any of the orators of the past to whom the Athenians should be grateful for having begun to improve them with his speeches, from the worse state in which he originally found them? Personally, I don't know who such a man might be.

C.: What? Haven't you heard of Themistocles, how good he was, and Cimon and Miltiades and the great Pericles, who has recently passed away, and whom you heard yourself?

S.: Certainly, Callicles, but only if true virtue was what you are talking about now: the satisfaction of one man's desires and of those of other men. But if that is not so, and the truth is, as we had to recognize in the following discussion, that only those desires that improve men through their fulfilment should be satisfied, while those which make them worse should not, and that this is a kind of art, then for one I cannot tell you of any man of such qualities having lived among them.

C.: Well, if you search well, you will find one.

S.: Then we should ponder the matter with some calm, and see whether any such orator has ever existed. So please tell me: the good man, the man who speaks aiming at what is best, will not speak at random, but with a definite goal in mind? Well, this orator is like all the other craftsmen, who, having a specific object in mind, chose the things necessary for that work not randomly, but with the purpose of giving a certain appearance to whatever they are working on. Look for instance at the painters, the builders, the shipwrights, or any of the other craftsmen, you name it, and see how each of them arranges everything in reason of a given order, and compels all its parts to fit together, until he has combined the whole into a well-ordered and well-arranged object. And those who deal with the human body, like trainers and doctors, they too bring a coherent order into the body. Isn't that so?

13

Athenian Democracy in the Fourth Century

39. The path to a second Athenian league

Sparta held the hegemony of the Aegean for ten years. The ephemeral experience of Spartan naval imperialism came to an end in 394, when the Persian fleet, under the orders of the Athenian admiral Conon, defeated the Spartans in a naval battle fought off Cnidus. This battle ignited, to use the words of Diodorus Siculus (14.84.3), an 'eagerness for change' amongst the subjects of Sparta, to whom Conon and Pharnabazus promised independence and freedom. Conon was the man of the hour. After his victory, the general triumphantly returned to Athens. The general employed his men to complete the rebuilding of the so-called Long Walls, the fortification which linked the asty to the Pyraeus. The walls were a famous symbol of the city's naval dominance, which the Spartans had forced the Athenians to demolish as part of the peace terms imposed at the end of the Peloponnesian War [a, b].

The principles of liberty (*eleutheria*) and autonomy (*authonomia*) were to redefine the relationship between the *poleis*, and between the Greek world and Persia. In 386, the representatives of the major Greek powers gathered at Sardis to sign a peace treaty dictated by the Great King. Persia claimed possession of all the Greek cities of Asia and of the islands, while all the others were to remain autonomous: the time of the large symmachiai, like Sparta's Peloponnesian League and the Delian League, was now over [c]. The years after the signing of the Peace saw a recrudescence of Sparta's aggressive imperialism, culminating in the occupation of the Cadmaea, the acropolis of Thebes. Conversely, many cities began to attach themselves to Athens. The allies formed a new league (*synedrion*) of free and independent *poleis*, inspired by the principles of the peace of 386 [d]. In the late winter of 377, these principles were formally ratified by the Athenian *ekklesia* [e]. The decree of Aristoteles marked a notable departure of the new coalition from the excesses of fifth-century imperialism, which however occasionally resurfaced [f].

[a] Diod. 14.84.3–4: Athenian resurgence after Cnidus

After the naval battle Pharnabazus and Conon put out to sea with all their ships against the allies of the Spartans, and first they drove the people of Cos to secede, then those of Nisyros and Teos. And then the Chians expelled their garrison and joined the cities with Conon, and smilarly the Mitylenaeans and Ephesians and Erythraeans also changed sides. A kind of eagerness for change fell upon all of the cities, and some of them expelled their Spartan garrisons and maintained their freedom, while others attached themselves to Conon. As for the Lacedaemonians, from this moment they lost the hegemony of the sea. Conon, having decided to sail with his entire fleet to Attica, put out to sea, and after winning to his cause against the Cyclades, he sailed against the island of Cythera.

[b] Xen. *Hell.* 4.8.9: Pharnabazus, Conon and the revival of Athenian imperialism

Conon said that if he would let him keep the fleet, he would maintain it with the contributions from the islands and in the meantime he would sail down to his fatherland and aid the Athenians in the rebuilding of the Long Walls and the wall around the Piraeus. Conon said that nothing would be more grievous for the Spartans than this. 'So', he said, 'at the same time you will do a favour to the Athenians and take vengeance upon the Spartans, by making all their efforts to attain what they most desired useless.' Having heard this, Pharnabazus eagerly dispatched him to Athens and gave him additional funds to rebuild the walls.

[c] Xen. *Hell.* 5.1.30–1: The King's Peace

When Tiribazus invited to be present those who wished to hear the peace treaty, which the King had sent down, they all immediately presented themselves. Once they had gathered together, Tissaphernes showed them the King's seal and then read the text, which ran as follows:

'King Artaxerxes thinks it just that the cities in Asia should belong to him, as well as Clazomenae and Cyprus among the islands, and that the other Greek cities, small and great, should be left independent, except Lemnos, Imbros and Scyros, which should belong to the Athenians as of old. Whichever of the two parties does not accept the peace, I will wage war upon them, together with those who desire to do this, by land and sea, with ships and money.'

[d] Diod. 15.28.2–5: The second Athenian league

The Athenians sent their most respectable citizens as ambassadors to the cities which obeyed the Spartans, and urged them to adhere to the cause of common liberty. For the Spartans, relying on the size of their military force, were ruling their subjects contemptuously and oppressively. For this reason, many of those subject to their power were turning to the Athenians. The citizens of Chios and Byzantium were the first to answer the plea to secede, and were followed by the Rhodians, the Mytileneans and some other islanders. As this movement gathered pace throughout Greece, many cities sided with the Athenians. The people, buoyed up by the good-will of the cities, established a council of all the allies, and appointed representatives for each city. It was agreed by common decision that the council should hold its meetings in Athens, but all the cities, big or small, should be equal and sovereign and each have one vote, accepting the Athenians as their leaders. The Spartans, seeing that it was impossible to control the cities' movement to secede, nevertheless eagerly strove to reconcile their alienated subjects by means of embassies, friendly speeches, as well as promises of benefits. At the same time, they devoted all their thoughts to the preparations for war, foreseeing that the Boeotian War would be long and troublesome for them, since the Athenians and the other Greeks who took part in the council were allied with the Thebans.

[e] IG II³ 43 = Tod II 123: The decree of Aristoteles

In the archonship of Nausinicus.

Secretary: Callibius sono of Cephisophon of the deme of Paeania.
    In the seventh prytany of the tribe Ippotontis.
    The boule and the assembly decreed.
    Carinus of Atmos was president.
    Aristoteles proposed: to the Good Fortune of the Athenians and of the allies of the Athenians; in order that the Spartans may leave the Greeks in peaceful enjoyment of liberty and autonomy and in secure possession of [the whole of their territory], and so that [the joint peace sworn to by the Greeks] and the King according to the agreements may be valid and [last forever].
    The people have decreed: If any Greek or barbarian, either living on the mainland or an island, and is not subject to the King, so wishes, he is permitted to be a free and autonomous ally of the Athenians and of their allies, keeping to whatever constitution he wishes, neither admitting a [garris]on nor resident

official nor paying tribute, on the same terms as the Chians, the Thebans, and the rest of the allies. To those who have made an alliance with the Athenians and their allies, the people will surrender all landed property privately or publicly owned by Athenians in the t[erritory of those join]ing the alliance, and the people is to give them a guarantee [of this. If there] exist at Athens stelai unfavourable to any of the cities allied with the Athenians, the council of the year shall have the authority to destroy them. From the archonship of Nausinikos it is forbidden, either privately or publicly, for any Athenian to acquire in the territories of the allies either a house or land, either by purchase, mortgage or in any other way. If anyone buys, obtains possession of or mortgages property in any way whatsoever, it is permitted for any of the allies who wishes, to give information to the allies' representatives. The representatives are to sell the property, giving one half of the proceeds to the informant, while the other half is to belong to the joint funds of the allies. If anyone wages war either by land or sea, against those who have joined the alliance, the Athenians and their allies are to help them both by land and by sea with all possible strength. If anyone, either a magistrate or a private individual, proposes or puts to the vote any measure contrary to this decree so as to necessitate the repeal of any of the provisions stated in the decree, the people will punish him with the loss of citizen rights and the confiscation of his property, and the tenth part will be given to the Goddess, and he is to be put on trial before the Athenians and their allies on the charge of aiming to destroy the alliance; his punishment shall be death or exile from the territories of Athens and the allies. If he is condemned to death, he shall not be buried in Attica or in the territory of the allies. The Secretary of the Council is to record this decree on stone and set it up beside the statue of Zeus Eleutherios. Money towards the cost of inscribing the stele, sixty drachmae, is to be given from the Ten Talents fund by the Treasurers of the Goddess. On this stele are to be recorded the names of the cities at present allied and of any other city which may join the alliance. This is to be the inscription. But the people are to choose three envoys to go at once to Thebes to persuade the Thebans of whatever beneficial measures they can. The following were chosen: Aristoteles of the deme Marathon, Pyrrhander of the deme Anaphlystos, Thrasybulus of the deme Collytus. The following cities were allies of Athens: Chios, Tenedos, Thebes, Mytilene, Chalcis, Methymna, Eretria, Rhodes, Poiessa, Arethusa, Byzantium, Carystus, Perinthus, Icus, Peparethus, Pal..., Skiathos, Maroneia, Dion, Paros, Athenae, Diades.

[f] IG II³ 111 = Tod II 142: Athens punishes the rebels of Iulis

Since the citizens of Iulis brought back to their fatherland by the Athenians have reported that the city of Iulis owes the Athenians three talents in silver according to the decree of the Athenian people proposed by Messenus, it has been decreed that the citizens of Iulis shall return this sum to the Athenians in the month of Scirophorion in the archonship of Caricleides.

In accordance with the treaties, all the public and private trials for sums superior to one hundred drachmas shall be carried out in Athens.

40. After the empire I: Imagining Athens as a capital of trades and peace

The Peloponnesian War put two different models of *polis* one against the other. In the post-bellum period, the ephemeral experience of Spartan naval imperialism and the renewed Aegean activism of Athens were followed by the emergence of new powers, like Thebes, and new patterns of social and political organization, which developed in the peripheries of the Greek world, from the federal state of Thessaly to the kingdom of Macedonia.

The experience of the second Athenian league came to an end in 355, when a group of rebellious members, supported by Mausolus, satrap of Caria, defeated the Athenian fleet off Embata. Athens came out of the 'Social War' impoverished and humiliated in its international ambition; the failure of empire inevitably called into question the validity of the traditional democratic government. What new role for the *polis* now? In a treaty called *Poroi* ('*Means*'), Xenophon proposes to make the necessary investments to transform Athens into a vibrant cultural and economic hub, by taking advantage of the underused mines of Laurium and of the strategic location of the Piraeus. Isocrates' speech *On the Peace* has a more political take on the crisis of Athens: the fall of the second Athenian league was the natural effect of the degeneration of the system based on radical democracy and aggressive foreign policies. In this fictitious speech to the *pnyx*, the orator criticizes the current state of Athenian democracy, where the most highly regarded orators are those who deliver the most calamitous advice, by calling for new wars and raising false hopes of Aegean domination. The Athenians may make the best orators in Greece, but they are unable to uphold clear and consistent policies. Isocrates then urges his fellow-citizens to listen to the grievances of their allies, and become the standard bearers of peace.

[a] Isoc. *Pac.* 3–9: War and peace in fourth-century Athens

I notice that you do not apply the same attention to all the speakers, but while you follow some with interest, others you cannot suffer to hear their voices. This behaviour of yours is not surprising. For in previous times you became accustomed to sending away all other orators, except those who advocate your desires. And someone might justly censure you, because you are well aware that many great houses have been ruined by flatterers, and while in your private affairs you hate those who practise this art, in the management of public business you are not so badly disposed towards them. On the contrary, while you denounce those who welcome and take pleasure in the company of these men, you appear to trust them more than your other fellow-citizens.

Indeed, it is you who made the orators take care of and study not what will be profitable to the city, but how to please you with their speeches, and most of them are now resorting to this kind of oratory, since it was clear to all that you are more delighted with those who call you to war than those who advise for peace, because the former create the expectation of regaining our possessions in the cities and of recovering the power which we happened to possess in the past, while the latter do not hold out such hopes, but say that we should stay in peace and not set our hearts upon great conquests contrary to justice, but be content with our present possessions, which is the most difficult thing to achieve for most men. We are so dependent on our hopes and so insatiably greedy in pursuing what we consider our advantage that not even those who possess the greatest fortunes are willing to stick to what they have, but are always running the risk of losing what they have for their desire of getting more. It is therefore appropriate that in the current circumstances we are afraid lest we might be trapped in this madness. For some of us seem to be excessively eager for war, as though they had heard not by improvised counsellors but by the gods themselves that we will succeed in all our enterprises and will easily overcome our enemies.

But wise people should not take advice when dealing with matters about which they are competent, for that would be superfluous, but act like men who know what to do, whereas in dealing with matters upon which they do need to take advice, they should not suppose that they have a perfect understanding of what the outcome will be, but to be minded towards these circumstances, like men who exercise their best judgement, but are not sure what the future may hold. But you are not doing either, and are in the most turbulent state of mind. For you have assembled as though you had to select the best course from those proposed by the orators, yet you are not willing to listen to anyone except those who are haranguing you for your pleasure, as though you had a clear idea of what ought to be done.

[b] Isoc. *Pac.* 49–56: The idiosyncrasies of democratic government

If one was to observe that the domestic policy of Athens were well managed, he might be confident as to our other affairs, but should not we be especially aggrieved about this very thing? For we claim to be autochthonous and that our city was founded before all the others, but although we should be an example of good and orderly government to everyone, we run our city in a worse and more disorderly manner than those who are just founding theirs. We magnify and take pride in the fact that we were born superior to the others, yet we share this noble birth with anyone who desires it more easily than the Triballians or the Leucanians share their low birth. We pass an enormous quantity of laws, but we care so little about them – for if you hear about one case you will judge of the others as well – that although we have established the death penalty for anyone who is judged guilty of bribery, we elect men who are most blatantly guilty of this crime, such as our generals, and we appoint to the most important offices the man who has managed to destroy the greatest number of citizens. We are no less concerned about our constitution than the safety of the whole city, and are aware that our democracy flourishes and endures in peace and security, while it has been overthrown twice in time of war, yet we do not like those who desire peace, as though they supported oligarchy, and consider those who advocate war benevolent, as though they cared for democracy. We are the best masters of public speaking and politics, but we are so inconsiderate that we do not hold the same opinion on the same matter in the same day. Rather, what we criticize before entering the assembly we vote for once we have gathered, and shortly afterwards, on departing for the assembly, we disapprove of the measures which have been voted for there. We pretend to be the wisest of the Greeks, but we resort to the sort of advisers whom anybody would despise, and we give these same men, whom nobody would put in charge of any of their private affairs, sovereign powers upon all public matters.

But the most miserable thing of all is that we consider those whom we should all regard as the most depraved of the citizens as the most faithful guardians of our constitution, and we consider the metics to be such as their chosen patrons, but do not expect that we shall be judged by the character of our leaders. We are so different from our ancestors because they appointed the same men to be leaders of the city and generals, thinking that the man able to give the best advice from the platform could also take the best decisions when he was alone. We do the very opposite: for the men we use as advisors in the most important matters we do not consider worthy of being appointed as generals, as though we did not trust their intelligence, while those whose advice nobody would seek for his private affairs or those of the state, we dispatch them to the field with plenipotentiary authority, as though they will be wiser there and will take counsel about the business of the Greeks more easily than on the matters put under discussion here. I say these things not in relation to all, but only to those who are liable to the charges which I have made. However, what remains of this day will not be enough, if I were to try to examine all the mistakes, which have been made in the running of our affairs.

41. After the empire II: Revamping the international role of Athens

Isocrates' *On the Peace* is a call for moderate policies, against the excesses of empire-fuelled radical democracy. In the moment of deepest scepticism over the workablility of traditional democracy, the young orator Demosthenes urged the Athenians to take back their role of defenders of democracy, and answer to the call of a group of exiled democrats from Rhodes, who had taken part in the Social War, but had been now driven out of their town by the satrap of Caria. Any war against any democratic city is also a war against Athens.

Dem. *Rhod.* 17–18

You should also observe, Athenians, that you have waged many wars against both democracies and oligarchies, as you know well. But perhaps none of you considers what were the causes of war with either. So, what are these causes? With democracies, either private complaints, when these could not be settled by the city, or an issue concerning portions of land or boundaries, or an eager rivalry or a struggle for ascendancy; but with oligarchies, none of these things: you fight for your constitution and liberty. I should therefore not hesitate to say that I think it a more advantageous situation if all the Greeks were your enemies under democratic governments than your friends, but ruled by oligarchies. For I think that it would not be difficult for you to make peace with free men whenever you wished, but I do not think that friendly relations with oligarchies could ever be stable, since the few can never be well disposed to the many, nor those who want to rule to those who have chosen to live in equality.

42. The conflict against Philip: *Polis* v. tyranny

Demosthenes was one of the leading Athenian politicians at the time of the wars against Philip of Macedon, and had a key role in the pan-Hellenic coalition that would be defeated by the Macedonians at Cheronaea. The celebration of the superior civic spirit and patriotism of the democratic citizens is one of the most recurrent themes of his political oratory. Philip was a military maverick, who thought fast and acted fast. Still, he was not a genuine leader, heading an army of responsible citizens. He was like a master leading a posse of slaves [a]. Democracy had to be Athens' main asset in the war against Macedon; if the Athenians were biting the dust, that was because they were failing to act as a healthy democratic community. As Pericles says in the funeral speech, the system based on public debate allowed the Athenians to take informed decisions quickly and efficiently, but that was no longer the case [b]; the orator accuses his fellow-citizens of having turned the democratic decision-making process into a parody of itself.

[a] Dem. *Phil. III* 72: **The city against a tyrant**

Since this war is against an individual and not against the might of an organized city, this delay is not unprofitable, nor were the embassies sent around the Peloponnese last year and those denunciations, when I and your good friend here, Polyeuctus, and Hesegippus and the other ambassadors went from city to city and managed to keep him in check, so that he never invaded Ambracia nor even set off against the Peloponnese.

[b] Dem. *Answer Phil.* 17: **Philip misses no opportunity**

You wonder why Philip was more successful than us in the past war? I will be frank with you: because he always serves in first person, sharing the toils and dangers of the campaign, never misses an opportunity, never wastes any season of the year, while we – if I have to tell the truth – sit here, wasting time, we cast our votes and go to the agora to learn what is news. And what could be more astonishing news than a Macedonian insulting the Athenians and sending to them such a letter as the one you have just heard read a moment ago?

43. Protecting democracy after Chaeronea

One thousand Athenian soldiers fell at Chaeronea and twice as many were made prisoners. One of them was the orator Demades, who, according to Diodorus, witnessed a curious act of hubris from Philip, when the King, raising the glass to his victory with his inner circle, scoffed at the Athenians' obsession for democratic politics by singing the opening words of an imaginary decree of the *ekklesia*: 'Demosthenes, the son of Demosthene proposed...' (Diod., 16.87; Plut., *Dem.* 20.3). After the battle, the Athenians took every measure to defend the city from the inevitable attack from the Macedonians and to protect its democratic constitution from any attempt at setting up a tyrannical regime in support of Athens' enemies, as in the aftermath of the Aegospotami [a, b].

[a] Lyc. *Ag. Leoc.* 36–7: Emergency measures after Chaeronea

So much for the challenge and the crime. I think you have clearly understood what can be taken for granted. But now I want to remind you of the circum-stances and the situation of grave emergency which the city was facing when Leocrates betrayed it. Please, clerk, take the decree of Hyperides and read it [Decree].

You hear the decree, gentlemen. It provided for the council of the Five Hundred to go down to the Piraeus in arms and deliberate with regards to the defence of the harbour and be prepared to do whatever they considered expedient for the people. And yet, if the men who had been exempted from military service so that they could deliberate upon the state of the city were serving in the role of soldiers, do not you think that the alarms by which the city happened to be held down were indeed serious?

[b] SEG 12.87 (law against tyranny, 337/336)[1]

In the archonship of Phrynichos.
  In the ninth prytany of Leontis,
  Chairestratus, son of Ameinias, of Acharnai, was secretary;
  Menestratus of Aixone, of the *proedroi*, put the question to vote;
  Eucrates, son of Aristodimos, of Piraeus, proposed;
  For the Good Fortune of the Athenian people. Be it resolved by the Nomothetai: If anyone rise up against the people to establish tyranny or join in establishing the tyranny or overthrow the Athenian people or the democracy

in Athens, whoever kills him who does any of these things shall be blameless. It shall not be allowed to anyone of the Councilors of the Council from the Areopagus – if the people or the democracy in Athens has been overthrown – to go to the assembly or sit in the Council or deliberate about anything. If the people or the democracy in Athens have been overthrown and anyone of the Councillors of the Areopagus goes up into the Areopagus or sits in the Council or deliberates about anything, both he and his descendants shall be deprived of civil rights and his substance shall be confiscated and a tenth given to the Goddess. The secretary of the Council shall inscribe this law on two stelai of stone and set one of them by the entrance into the Areopagus, that entrance, namely, near where one goes into the Bouleuterion, and the other in the assembly. For the inscribing of the stelai the treasurer of the Demos shall give 20 drachmai from the state funds for the inscription of decrees.

44. Athenian independence and Alexander the Great

One of the most interesting aspects of the Athenian history after Chaeronea is the remarkable stability not just of the democratic constitution of the city, but also of the democratic culture of the citizens. It is significant that the proposal of granting citizenship to the metics and slaves who were willing to defend Athens in case of a Macedonian attack was turned down as contrary to the principles of the *politeia*.

Philip of Macedon was assassinated in 336. The following year, his son Alexander was proclaimed king. A conference of the Greek cities was then held at the Isthmus of Corinth in preparation of a new pan-Hellenic campaign against Persia. On that occasion, a new common peace was signed, whereby Alexander committed itself to respecting the independece and autonomy of the cities. In 331, while Alexander was in Asia, the king of Sparta Agis promoted a pan-Hellenic upheaval against the Macedonians. In the oration *On the Treaty with Alexander*, the anonymous orator replies to another politician who had spoken before him against joining the Spartans and the other Greeks in respect of the agreements of the Isthmus. For this proud democrat, Alexander, like any other tyrant, was a natural enemy of Athenian democracy [a].

In 336, Ctesiphon proposed to honour Demosthenes with a golden crown in recognition of his work for the city. In 330 Aeschines brought Ctesiphon to trial for a number of procedural irregularities in relation to the award of the crown. Demosthenes himself took over the defence of Ctesiphon, but his oration is first and foremost a passionate defence of his political activity and his struggle to protect the independence of Athens [**b**].

[a] [Dem.] *Answer Alex.* 8–12: Debate on the treaty with Alexander

The first article of the treaty provides that the Greeks shall be free and independent. For this reason, is it not absurd that, while the clause about freedom and autonomy stands first, one who has enslaved people is not thought to have acted contrary to the agreement? Athenians, if we are to abide by our oaths and the agreement and to behave justly, as the orators are urging you to do, as I said, it is our duty to take the arms and fight against the transgressors with those who are willing to join us. Or do you think that immanent circumstances sometimes are so powerful that expediency is pursued with no regard to justice: now, if justice, contingencies and expediency gather at the same place, will you really wait for another opportunity to claim your liberty and that of all Greeks?

I come to another principle established by the agreement. The text says: 'If any of the parties shall overthrow the constitutions established in the various states at the time of the swearing of the oaths of the peace, they shall be held as enemies by all the parties who have sworn the peace.' But note, Athenians, that the Achaeans in the Peloponnese had a democratic constitution, and the Macedonian has overthrown the democracy of Pellene by expelling the majority of the citizens, and has given their substances to their slaves and established Chaeron, the wrestler, as their tyrant. But we ourselves have sworn the peace treaty, which orders treating as enemies those who commit such acts. Therefore, we have to obey these dispositions and treat them as enemies, or will anyone be beastly enough to say no, someone in the paybook of the Macedonians, grown rich at your expense? Be assured that they are aware of these facts, but they have reached such heights of impudence, having the tyrant's troops for their bodyguards, that they compel you to observe the oaths which have already been violated, as though he had absolute power overupon the crime of perjury as well, and compel you to abrogate your own laws, by releasing men who had been declared guilty by your courts, and forcing you to sanction a quantity of other illegalities.

[b] Demosthenes, *On the Crown* 61–5: The struggle against Philip

Among the Greeks, not some but all of them invariably, it happened that a crop of traitors and bribe-takers, odious to gods and men alike, had sprung up, more numerous than they have ever existed within human memory. Philip took these men as his accomplices and assistants. The Greeks were already at loggerheads and quarrelsome with one another, and he made the situation worse by cajoling some men, bribing others and corrupting some others in every possible way. Philip divided the Greeks into many factions, although they all had one common interest: to prevent him from becoming so powerful. Now, since all the Greeks were in such a dire situation, and ignored this growing and ever-gathering evil, you, men of Athens, should ask yourselves what policy or course of action was fit for the city to choose, and to hold me responsible for this, for I had taken over the responsibility for the constitution. Do you think, Aeschines, that the city should have let her pride and dignity fall, ranking itself with the Thessalians and Dolopians, and help Philip to establish his ascendancy over Greece, to obliterate the fine and just accomplishments of our ancestors? Or if Athens should not have done this – which would have been really atrocious – should she have looked on, while all that she saw would happen, if no one prevented it – all that she realized, it seems, at a distance – was actually taking place? But now, I would like to ask to the harshest critics of my actions which party he would have liked the city to join: the party of the accomplices in the miseries which has fallen upon the Greeks, let us call it the party of the Thessalians and their supporters, or the party of those who looked on these events, in the hope of gaining some advantage for themselves, in which we should place the Arcadians and Messenians and Argives? But in the end we have fared better than most of these, let us say all of them. For had Philip withdrawn immediately after his victory, and remained in peace, giving no trouble whatsoever to any of his allies or the other Greeks, then there would have been some ground for anger and accusations against those who had opposed his machinations. But seeing that he has deprived all of them of their dignity, ascendancy, and liberty, and so much so of their constitutions, wherever he could, can it be denied that the policy, which you adopted under my guidance, was the most glorious policy possible?

45. The decline of democratic politics and the last democratic hero

Fourth-century Athens could not count on the financial revenues of empire, and the control of the city's finances became a pressing issue in its agenda. The city's treasury was replaced by a number of funds, called *merismoi* ('partitions'), allocated to different budgets; in 378/377 the richest citizens who paid the *eisphora*, a sort of income tax used to finance military operations, were organized into groups called *symmories*. A new elective body of magistrates was created to manage the *theorikon* fund. This turn had notable effects on the face of Athenian politics: gone were the days of the great leaders such as Pericles who brought together in themselves the roles of the orator and of the *strategos*. The new situation called for a higher degree of specialization. In the aftermath of the Social War, a time of great financial difficulty for Athens, the *theorikon* commissioners acquired great political relevance. Eubulus was the champion of this new breed of finance specialists, who opposed interventionist policies and focused their activity on restoring prosperity at home. Although Eubulus and others were successful in putting the Athens' treasury back in shape, Demosthenes was very critical of such policies, which he considered unworthy of the *polis'* past and international role as leader of the Greek democracies [a].

Athens briefly recovered its leading role among the *poleis* of Greece in the months following the death of Alexander, when the general Leosthenes led the insurgency against the Macedonian lieutenant Antipater. Leosthenes was killed while besieging the town of Lamia. The funerary oration in his honour was delivered by Iperides, one of the leading orators of the time. Leosthenes is celebrated as the worthy heir of Miltiades and Themistocles, and a symbol of the autochthnous virtues of Athens [b–d].

[a] Dem. *Org.* 30–1: The new democracy of fourth-century Athens

Today, men of Athens, while our city likes to provide roads, fountains, whitewash and balderdash out of the public treasury, and I do not blame those who proposed these measures, not at all, but you, if you think that this is all that is required of you. Some of the private individuals who are in control of any of the public funds have erected private residences, which are not just better than those of the majority of citizens, but even more stately than our public buildings, others have purchased and farmed estates bigger than they ever hoped for before. The cause of all this is that back then the people were master and sovereign of everything, and the others were happy to accept honours, offices and rewards as dispensed by them. Now, on the contrary, those men are in charge of all the goods, while the people are relegated to the role of lackeys and aiders, and you are happy to accept whatever they give you.

[b] Hyp. *Ep.* 2–3: Leosthenes' heroes

Time itself will be witness to the words which are about to be spoken upon this grave, in honour of Leosthenes the general and the others who fell with him in the war, for they behaved as brave men … For time has never seen better men than these who are now dead or more magnificent actions. Indeed, what I am most afraid today is that my words may appear unfit to describe their deeds. This thought, however, gives me confidence: that you, who are listening, will add to what I say, for my words will not fall upon a random audience, but those who were the very witnesses of the actions of these men. It is indeed appropriate to praise this city of ours for having chosen a course of action on a par with its past achievements, if not more venerable and splendid, and the fallen for their bravery in battle, and for not dishonouring their forefathers. Leosthenes the general is twice worthy of praise: for he served as a guide to the city in its choices, and besides the commander of the citizens on the battlefield.

[c] Hyperides, *Fun. Speech* 6–7: Brave Athenian soldiers

As I said, I will not endeavour to describe the common achievements of the city; my speech will deal with Leosthenes and the others. Where shall I start my story from? Which exploit shall I remember first? Shall I pass through their ancestry? That would be guileless, I suppose. If one is celebrating men of a different stamp, such those who have gathered together from different places in one city where they now live, each bringing his own lineage into the common stock, then one should trace back their ancestry man by man. But for one who is speaking of the Athenians, a people born of their own land, with a lineage of unsurpassable nobility, celebrating the lineage of each man would be, I think, redundant.

[d] Hyperides, *Fun. Speech* 35–8: Celebrating Leosthenes

As we celebrate Leosthenes with wonder, do not you think that we should have before our eyes those of the so-called demi-gods who waged war against Troy? He may have delivered exploits akin to theirs, but indeed he surpassed them in so much as they seized but one city having the whole of Greece at their side, while he brought down the power ruling over Europe and Asia with the forces of his fatherland alone. They stood up for but one woman who had been outraged, while he prevented outrage from coming upon all the women of Greece, assisted by these men who are now being buried with him. And the men who lived after those heroes, who rivalled them in the bravery of their deeds, I mean the followers of Miltiades and Themistocles, who brought honour to their fatherland and glory to their lives by setting Greece free, Leosthenes so far rose above them in bravery and wisdom that whereas they fought back the might of the barbarians as they advanced, he even prevented them from advancing. They saw their enemy set off a struggle in their own land, while Leosthenes defeated his opponents in his enemy's territory.

Notes

1. What do we mean by *polis*?

1 Hom. *Od.* 9.114–15.
2 Hom., *Il.* 9.63.
3 Stentor was the herald of the Greek army fighting at Troy, his brazen voice was 'as the voice of fifty other men' (Hom. *Il.* 5.785–6).

2. The birth of Athens and the roots of democracy

1 Melanthus was a mythical king of Messenia. He was expelled from his country by the descendants of Heracles, and sought refuge in Athens.

3. Two lawgivers: Draco and Solon

1 Solon, fragment 28.
2 Solon, fragment 28.
3 Solon, fragment 28.
4 That is, of grain, wine and oil.

4. Pisistratus: Tyranny as a pathway to democracy

1 566 or 565.
2 534/543.
3 509.

6. Democracy, empire and the Persian Wars

1   February/March.
2   See M&L 15.

13. Democracy and the decline of the *polis*

1   See B. Meritt, 'Greek inscriptions', *Hesperia* (1952), 340–80, pp. 355–9.

Further Reading

General studies

Barrow, R. (1999), *Athenian Democracy*, 2nd edn, London: Bristol Classial Press.

Boedeker, D. and K. A. Raaflaub (eds) (1998), *Democracy, Empire, and the Arts in Fifth-Century Athens*, Cambridge, MA and London: Harvard University Press.

Buckley, T. (1996), *Aspects of Greek History, 750–323 B.C.: A Source-Based Approach*, London: Routledge.

Cartledge, P. (2002), *The Greeks: A Portrait of Self and Others*, 2nd edn Oxford: Oxford University Press.

—ed. (1998), *The Cambridge Illustrated History of Greece*, Cambridge: Cambridge University Press.

Davies, J. K. (1993), *Democracy and Classical Greece*, 2nd edn, Cambridge, MA: Harvard University Press.

Hansen, M. H. (1991), *The Athenian Democracy in the Age of Demosthenes: Structure, Principles, and Ideology*, Oxford: Blackwell.

Morgan, K. A., ed. (2003), *Popular Tyranny: Sovereignty and Its Discontents in Ancient Greece*, Austin: University of Texas Press.

Ober, J. (1996), *The Athenian Revolution: Essays on Ancient Greek Democracy and Political Theory*, Princeton: Princeton University Press.

Osborne, R. (2004), *Greek History*, London: Routledge.

Philips, D. D. (2013), *The Law of Ancient Athens*, Ann Arbor: University of Michigan Press.

Rhodes, P. J., ed. (2004), *Athenian Democracy*, Edinburgh: University of Edinburgh Press.

Saxonhouse, A. W. (2006), *Free Speech and Democracy in Ancient Athens*, Cambridge: Cambridge University Press.

1. What Do We Mean By *Polis*?

Aristotle and the definition of *polis*

Coldstream, J. N. (1984), *The Formation of the Greek polis: Aristotle and Archaeology*, Opladen: Westdeutscher Verlag.

Deslauriers, M. and P. Destrée, eds (2013), *The Cambridge Companion to Aristotle's Politics*, Cambridge: Cambidge University Press.

Develin, R. (1973), 'The good man and the good citizen in Aristotle's "Politics"', *Phronesis* 18, No. 1, 71–9.

Ehrenberg, V. (1937), 'When did the polis rise?', *JHS* 57, 147–59.

Johnson, C. N. (1984), 'Who is Aristotle's citizen?', *Phronesis* 29, No. 1, 73–90.

—(1990), *Aristotle's Theory of State*, Basingstoke: Macmillan.

Keyt, D. and F. D. Miller, Jr, eds (1991), *A Companion to Aristotle's Politics*, Oxford: Blackwell.

Kraut, R. (2002), *Aristotle: Political Philosophy*, Oxford: Oxford University Press.

—ed. (2005), *Aristotle's Politics: Critical Essays*, Lanham and Oxford: Rowman and Littlefield.

Meiksins Wood, E. and N. Wood (1978), *Class Ideology and Ancient Political Theory: Socrates, Plato and Aristotle in Social Context*, Oxford: Oxford University Press.

Miller, F. D. (1997), *Nature, Justice, and Rights in Aristotle's Politics*, Oxford: Oxford University Press.

Mulgan, R. G. (1977), *Aristotle's Political Theory: An Introduction for Students of Political Theory*, Oxford: Oxford University Press.

Murray, O. (1993), 'Polis and politeia in Aristotle', in M. H. Hansen, ed., *The Ancient Greek City-State: Symposium on the Occasion of the 250th Anniversary of the Royal Danish Academy of Sciences and Letters*, 1–4 July 1992, Copenhagen: Royal Danish Academy of Science and Letters, 197–210.

Nagle D. B. (2006), *The Household as the Foundation of Aristotle's Polis*, Cambridge: Cambridge University Press.

Nichols, M. P. (1992), *Citizens and Statesmen: A Study of Aristotle's 'Politics'*, Savage, MD: Rowan and Littlefield.

Roberts, J. (2009), *Routledge Philosophy Guidebook to Aristotle and the* Politics, London and New York: Routledge.

Samaras, T. (2007), 'Aristotle's politics: the city of Book Seven and the question of ideology', *CQ* 57, No. 1, 77–89.

Swanson, J. A. and C. D. Corbin (2009), *Aristotle's Politics: A Reader's Guide*, London: Continuum.

Homer and the development of *polis*

Bobbit, P. (2002), *The Shield of Achilles: War, Peace and the Course of History*, New York: Alfred A. Knopf.

Bowden, H. (1993), 'Hoplites and Homer: warfare, hero cult, and the ideology of the polis', in J. Rich and G. Shipley (eds), *War and Society in the Greek World*, London and New York: Routledge, 45–63.

Edwards, A. T. (1993), 'Homer's ethical geography: country and City in the *Odyssey*, *TAPhA* 123, 27–78.

Finley, M. I. (1979), *The World of Odysseus*, 2nd edn, Harmondsworth: Penguin.

Hammer, D. (2002), *The Iliad as Politics: the Performance of Political Thought*, Norman, OK: University of Oklahoma Press.

Hurwit, J. M, (1993), 'Art, Poetry, and the Polis in the Age of Homer', in S. Langdon, ed., *From Pasture to Polis: Art in the Age of Homer*, Columbia, MO and London: Museum of Art and Archaeology, University of Missouri-Columbia, 14–42.

Langdon, S., ed. (1997), *New Light on a Dark Age: Exploring the Culture of Geometric Greece*, Columbia, MO and London: University of Missouri Press.

Luce, J. V. (1978), 'The polis in Homer and Hesiod', *PRIA* 78, 1–15.

Osborne, R. (2004), 'Homer's society', in R. Fowler, *The Cambridge Companion to Homer*, Cambridge: Cambridge University Press, 206–19.

Powell, B. (2004), *Homer*, Malden, MA and London: Blackwell

Sale, W. M. (1994), 'The government of Troy: politics in the *Iliad*', *GRBS* 35, 5–102.

Scully, S. (1990), 'The polis in Homer. A definition and interpretation', *Ramus* 10, 1–34.

—(1990), *Homer and the Sacred City*, Ithaca: Cornell University Press.

—(2003), 'Reading the shield of Achilles' terror, anger and delight', *HSCP* 101, 29–47.

Silvermintz, D. (2004), *Unravelling the Shroud for Laertes and Waving the Fabric of the City: Kingship and Politics in Homer's Odyssey*, Exeter: Imprint Academic.

Taplin, O. (1980), 'The shield of Achilles within the *Iliad*', *G&R* 27 no. 1, 1–21.

The earliest documents of the *polis*

Brown, B. (2003), 'Homer, funeral contests and the origins of the Greek city, in D. J. Phillips and D. M. Pritchard (eds), *Sport and Festival in the Ancient Greek World*, Swansea: The Classical Press of Wales, 123–62.

Burkert, W. (1992), *The Orientalizing Revolution: Near Eastern Influence on Greek Culture in the Early Archaic Age*, English trans., Cambridge, MA and London: Harvard University Press.

Ehrenberg, V. (1943), 'An early source of polis-constitution', *CQ* 37, Nos. 1/2, 14–18.

Fisher, N. and H. van Wees (eds) (1998), *Archaic Greece: New Approaches and New Evidence*, Oakville, CT: D. Brown Book Co.

Jeffery, L. H, (1961), 'The pact of the first settlers at Cyrene', *Historia* 10, No. 2, 139–47.

Lewis, S. (1976), *Archaic Greece: the City-States, c.700–500 B.C.*, London and Tonbridge: Ernest Benn.

—(2006), *Ancient Tyranny*, Edinburgh: University of Edinburgh Press.

Mitchell, L. G. and P. J. Rhodes (eds) (1997), *The Development of the Polis in Archaic Greece*, New York and London: Routledge.

Morris, I. (1997), 'The art of citizenship', in S. Langdon, ed., *New Light on a Dark Age: Exploring the Culture of Geometric Greece*, Columbia, MO: University of Missouri Press, 9–43.

Osborne, R. (2009), *Greece in the Making, 1200–479 BC*, 2nd edn, London and New York: Routledge.

Raaflaub, K. (1993), 'Homer to Solon: the rise of the polis: the written sources', *The Ancient Greek City-State: Symposium on the Occasion of the 250th Anniversary of the Royal Danish Academy of Sciences and Letters*, 1–4 July 1992, Copenhagen: Royal Danish Academy of Science and Letters, 41–105.

Shapiro, H. A. ed. (2007), *The Cambridge Companion to Archaic Greece*, New York and Cambridge: Cambridge University Press.

Snodgrass, A. (1980), *Archaic Greece: The Age of Experiment*, London: Dent.

2. The Birth of Athens and the Roots of Democracy

Aristotle and democracy

Chambers, M. (1961), 'Aristotle's "Forms of Democracy"', *TAPhA* 92, 20–36.

Creed, J. (1990), 'Aristotle and democracy', in A. Loizou, and H. Lesser (eds), *Polis and Politics, Essays in Greek Moral and Political Philosophy*, Brookfiled, VT: Gower Press, 23–34.

Day, J. and M. Chambers (1962), *Aristotle's History of Athenian Democracy*, Berkeley: University of California Press.

Levêque, P. and P. Vidal-Naquet (1996), *Cleisthenes the Athenian: An Essay on the Representation of Space and Time in Greek Political Thought from the End of the Sixth Century to the Death of Plato*, English trans., New Jersey: Humanities Press.

Lintott, A. (1992), 'Aristotle and democracy', *CQ* 42, No. 1, 114–28.

Vlassopoulos, K. (2007), 'Free spaces: identity, experience and democracy in classical Athens', *CQ* 57, No. 1, 33–52.

Early Athens

Bundgaard, J. A. (1976), *Parthenon and the Mycenaean City on the Heights*, Copenhagen: Publications of the National Museum of Denmark.

Christopoulos, M. (1994), 'Poseidon Erechtheus and EREKHTHEIS THALASSA', in R. Hägg, ed., *Ancient Greek Cult Practice from the Epigraphical Evidence*, Jonsered: Paul Astrom, 123–30.

Hopper, R. J. (1961), '"Plain", "Shore", and "Hill" in early Athens', *ABSA* 56, 189–219.

Roebuck, C. (1974), 'Three classes (?) in early Attica', *Hesperia* 43, 485–93.

Simms, R. M. (1983), 'Eumolpus and the wars of Athens', *GRBS* 24, 197–208.

Stahl, M. and Walter, U. (2008), 'Athens', in Raaflaub, K. and van Wees, H. (eds), *A Companion to Archaic Greece*, Malden, MA and Oxford: Blackwell, 138–61.

Whitley, J. (1994), 'The monuments that stood before Marathon: tomb cult and hero cult in archaic Attica', *AJA* 98, No. 2, 213–30.

Theseus and the synoecism

Agard, W. R. (1928), 'Theseus. A national hero', *CJ* 24, 84–91.

Davie, J. N. (1982), 'Theseus the King in fifth-century Athens', *G&R* 29, 25–34.

Den Boer, W. (1969), 'Theseus: the growth of a myth in history', *G&R* 16, No. 1, 1–13.

Diamant, S. (1982), 'Theseus and the unification of Attica', *Hesperia Supplements* 19, 38–47.

Goušchin, V. (1999), 'Athenian synoikism of the fifth century B.C., or two stories of Theseus', *G&R* 46, No. 2, 168–87.

Mills, S. (1997), *Theseus, Tragedy, and the Athenian Empire*, Oxford: Oxford University Press.

Neils, J. (1987), The *Youthful Deeds of Theseus*, Rome: Bretschneider.

Shapiro, A. H. (1993), 'Theseus: aspects of the hero in Archaic Greece', in D. Buitron-Oliver, ed., *New Perspectives in Early Greek Art*, Washington, DC and Hanover: Yale University Press, 123–39.

—(1992), 'Theseus in Kimonian Athens: the iconography of Empire', *MHR* 7, 29–49.

Simon, E. (1996), 'Theseus and Athenian festivals', in J. Neils, ed., *Worshipping Athena: Panathenaia and Parthenon*, Madison, Wisc.: University of Wisconsin Press, 3–26.

Thomas, C. G. (1982), 'Theseus and synoicism', *SMEA* 23, 337–49.

Van Gelder, K. (1991), 'The Iron hiatus in Attica and the synoikismos of Theseus', *MedArch* 4, 55–64.

Walker, H. J. (1995), *Theseus and Athens*, Oxford: Oxford University Press.

Ward, A. G., ed. (1970), *The Quest for Theseus*, London: Praeger.

3. Two Lawgivers: Draco and Solon

Laws and lawgivers of archaic Greece

Davis Lewis, J. (2007), *Early Greek Lawgivers*, London: Bristol Classical Press.

Gagarin, M. (1989), *Early Greek Law*, Berkeley, Los Angeles: University of California Press.

—(2005), 'Early Greek law', in ibid., ed., *The Cambridge Companion to Ancient Greek Law*, Cambridge: Cambridge University Press, 82–94.

—(2008), *Writing Greek Law*, Cambridge and New York: Cambridge University Press.

Hölkeskamp, K.-J. (1992), 'Written law in archaic Greece', *PCPhS* 38, 87–117.

—(1992), 'Arbitrators, lawgivers and the "codification of law" in archaic Greece: problems and perspectives', *Métis* 7, 49–81.

Humphreys, S. C. (1988), 'The discourse of law in archaic and Classical Greece', *Law and History Review* 6, 465–93.

Papakonstantinou, Z. (2008), *Lawmaking and Adjudication in Archaic Greece*, London: Duckworth.

Szegedy-Maszak, A. (1978), 'Legends of the Greek lawgivers', *GRBS* 19, 199–209.

Stroud, S. (1979), *The Axones and Kyrbeis of Drakon and Solon*, Berkeley: University of California Press.

Hoplitism

Brouwers, J. (2007), 'From horsemen to hoplites: some remarks on archaic Greek warfare', *Babesch* 82, 305–19.

Dayton, J. C. (2006), 'The Athletes of War: An Evaluation of the Agonistic Elements in Greek Warfare', Campellville, ON: Edgar Kent.

Hall, J. M. (2007), 'Warfare and Hoplites', H. A. Shapiro, ed., *The Cambridge Companion to Archaic Greece*, Cambridge: Cambridge University Press, 155–77.

Hanson, V. D. (1991), 'The ideology of hoplite battle, ancient and modern', in ibid., ed., *Hoplites: The Classical Greek Battle Experience*, London: Routledge, 3–11.

Krentz, P. M. (2002), 'Fighting by the rules: the invention of the hoplite agon', *Hesperia* 71, no. 1, 23–39.

Raaflaub, K. (1997), 'Soldiers, citizens and the evolution of the early Greek polis', in L. Mitchell, P. J. Rhodes (eds), *The Development of the Polis Archaic in Greece*, London: Routledge, 49–59.

Salmon, J. (1977), 'Political hoplites?', *JHS* 97, 84–101.

Schwartz, A. (2002), 'The early hoplite phalanx : order or disarray?', *C&M* 53, 31–64.

—(2009), *Reinstating the Hoplite: Arms, Armour and Phalanx Fighting in Archaic and Classical Greece*, Stuttgart: Franz Steiner Verlag.

Snodgrass, A. M. (1965), 'The hoplite reform and history', *JHS* 85, 110–22.

—'The "hoplite reform" revisited', *DHA* 19, no. 1, 47–61.

van Wees, H. (1998), 'Greeks bearing arms: the state, the leisure class and the display of weapons in archaic Greece', in N. Fisher and H. van Wees (eds) *Archaic Greece: New Approach and New Evidence*, London: Duckworth and Classical Press of Wales, 333–78.

—(2000) 'The development of the hoplite phalanx: iconography and reality in the seventh century', in ibid., ed., *War and Violence in Ancient Greece*, Swansea: Classical Press of Wales, 125–66.

—(2002) 'Tyrants, oligarchs, and citizen militias', in A. Chaniotis and P. Ducrey (eds) *Army and Power in the Ancient World*, Stuttgart: Franz Steiner Verlag, 61–82.

Draco and Solon

Almeida, J. A. (2003), *Justice as an Aspect of the Polis Idea in Solon's Political Poems: A Reading of the Fragments in Light of the Researches of New Classical Archaeology*, Leiden and Boston: Brill.

Anhalt, E. K. (1993), *Solon the Singer: Politics and Poetics*, Lanham, MD: Rowman and Littlefield.

Blok, J. H. and A. P. M. H. Lardinois (eds) (2006), *Solon of Athens: New Historical and Philological Approaches*, Leiden and Boston: Brill.

Carawan, E. (1998), *Rhetoric and the Law of Draco*, Cambridge: Cambridge University Press.

Develin, R. (1984), 'The constitution of Drakon', *Athenaeum* 62, 295–307.

Fales, C. De (1972), 'The two steles of Draco's laws on murder', *AJA* 76, LXXVI, 210.

Freeman, K. (1926), *The Work and Life of Solon: with a Translation of his Poems*, New York: Arno Press.

Gallia, A. B. (2004), 'The republication of Draco's law on homicide', *CQ* 54, No. 2, 451–60.

Goldstein, J. A. (1972), 'Solon's law for an activist citizenry', *Historia* 21, 538–45.

Harrison, A. R. W. (1961), 'Drakon's πρῶτος ἄξων', *CQ* 11, 3–5.

Hölkeskamp, K.-J. (2005), 'What's in a code?: Solon's laws between complexity, compilation and contingency', *Hermes* 133, 280–93.

Irwin, E. (2005), *Solon and Early Greek Poetry: The Politics of Exhortation*, Cambridge and New York: Cambridge University Press.

Lape, S. (2002–3), 'Solon and the institution of the "democratic" family form', *CJ* 98, No. 2, 117–39.

Lewis, J. (2006), *Solon the Thinker: Political Thought in Archaic Athens*, London: Duckworth.

Manville, B. (1980), 'Solon's law of stasis and atimia in Archaic Athens', *TAPhA* 110, 213–21.

Owens, R. (2010), *Solon of Athens: Poet, Philosopher, Soldier, Statesman*, Brighton: Sussex Academic Press.

Podlecki, A. J. (2002), 'Solon's vision', *Ktèma* 27, 163–72.

Rexine, J. E. (1958), *Solon and His Political Theory. The Contemporary Significance of a Basic Contribution to Political Theory by One of the Seven Wise Men*, New York: William-Frederick Press.

Rihll, T. E. (1989), 'Lawgivers and tyrants (Solon, Frr. 9–11 West)', *CQ*, New Series, 39, No. 2, 277–86.

Schils, G. (1991), 'Solon and the hectemoroi', *AncSoc* 22, 75–90.

Schlesinger, A. C. (1924), 'Draco in the hearts of his countrymen', *CPh*, 370–73.

Stanley, P. V. (1999), *The Economic Reforms of Solon*, St Katharinen: Scripta Mercaturae Verlag.

Stroud, S. (1968), *Drakon's Law on Homicide*, Berkeley: University of California Press.

Vlastos, G. (1946), 'Solonian justice', *CP* 41, 65–83.

4. Pisistratus: Tyranny as a Pathway to Democracy

Greek tyrannies

Anderson, G. (2005), 'Before "turannoi" were tyrants: rethinking a chapter of early Greek history', *ClAnt* 24, 173–222.

Andrewes, A. (1956), *The Greek Tyrants*, London: Hutchinson.

Boesche, R. (1993), 'Aristotle's "science" of tyranny', *HPTh* 14, 1–25.

Cawkwell, G. L. (1995), 'Early Greek tyranny and the people', *CQ*, New Series, 45, No. 1, 73–86.

Farenga, V. (1981), 'The paradigmatic tyrant. Greek tyranny and the ideology of the proper', *Helios* 8, 1–31.

Ferrill, A. (1978), 'Herodotus on tyranny', *Historia* 28, 385–98.

Lewis, S. (2006), *Ancient Tyranny*, Edinburgh: University of Edinburgh Press.

—(2009), *Greek Tyranny*, Exeter: University of Exeter Press.

Nilsson, M. P. (1936), *The Age of the Early Greek Tyrants*, Belfast: Queen's University Press.

Ober, J. (2003), 'Tyrant Killing as Therapeutic "Stasis": a Political Debate in Images and texts', in A. Morgan, ed., *Popular Tyranny: Sovereignty and Its Discontents in Ancient Greece*, Austin: University of Texas Press, 215–50.

Russell, H. L. (1944), 'Tyranny and democracy', *The Classical Weekly* 37, No. 11, 128–30.

Pisistratus, the Pisistratids and Athenian politics

Arnush, M. F. (1995), 'The career of Peisistratos son of Hippias', *Hesperia* 64, 135–62.

Arrowsmith, S. P. (1988), *The Tyranny in Athens in the Sixth Century B.C.*, Manchester: University of Manchester Press.

Bicknell, P. J. (1970), 'The exile of the Alkmeonidai during the Peisistratid tyranny', *Historia* 19, 129–31.

French, A. (1959), 'The party of Peisistratos', *G&R* 6, 46–57.

Frost, F. J. (1985), 'Toward a History of Peisistratid Athens', in J. W. Eadie and J. Ober (eds) *The Craft of the Ancient Historian. Essays in Honor of Chester G. Starr*, Lanham, Md: University Press of America, 57–78.

—(1990), 'Peisistratos, the cults and the unification of Attica', *AncW* 21, 3–9.

Gouschin, V. (1999), 'Pisistratus' leadership in A.P. 13.3 and the establishment of the tyranny of 561/60', *B.C. CQ*, New Series 49, 14–23.

Hind, J. G. F. (1974), 'The "Tyrannis" and the exiles of Pisistratus', *CQ*, New Series, 24, No. 1, 1–18.

Holladay, J. (1977), 'The followers of Peisistratos', *G&R* 24, 40–56.

Lavelle, B. M. (2000), 'Herodotos and the "parties" of Attika: political realities in Archaic Athens/political pressures in Classical Athens', *C&M* 51, 51–102.

—(2005), *Fame, Money, and Power: The Rise of Peisistratos and "Democratic" Tyranny at Athens*, Ann Arbor: University of Michigan Press.

McGlew, J. F. (1993), *Tyranny and Political Culture in Ancient Greece*, Ithaca, NY: Cornell University Press.

Meyer, E. A. (2008), 'Thucydides on Harmodius and Aristogeiton, tyranny, and history', *CQ*, New Series 58, 13–34.

Ruebel, J. R. (1973), 'The tyrannies of Peisistratos', *GRBS* 14, 125–36.

Sancisi-Weerdenburg, H. (2000), *Peisistratos and the Tyranny: A Reappraisal of the Evidence*, Amsterdam: Gieben.

Shapiro, H. A. (1995), *Art and Cult under the Tyrants in Athens*, Mainz: Philipp von Zabern.

5. Cleisthenes and the Birth of Democracy

Bradeen, D. W. (1955), 'The trittyes in Cleisthenes' reforms', *TAPhA* 86, 22–30.
Ehrenberg, V. (1950), 'Origins of democracy', *Historia* 1, 515–48.
Hamilton, C. D. (1993), 'Cleisthenes and the Demos', in W. J. Cherf, ed., *Alpha to Omega: Studies in Honor of George John Szemler on His Sixty-Fifth Birthday*, Chicago: Ares, 69–93.
Hansen, M. H. (1994), 'The 2500th anniversary of Cleisthenes' Reforms and the Tradition of Athenian Democracy', in R. Osborne and S. Hornblower (eds) *Ritual, Finance, Politics: Athenian Democratic Accounts Presented to David Lewis*, Oxford: Oxford University Press, 25–37.
Lewis, D. M. (1963), 'Cleisthenes and Attica', *Historia* 12, 22–40.
Munro, J. A. R. (1939), 'The ancestral laws of Cleisthenes', *CQ* 33, 84–97.
Oliver, J. H. (1960), 'Reforms of Cleisthenes', *Historia* 9, 503–7.
Ostwald, M. (2000), 'Popular sovereignty and the problem of equality', *SCI* 19, 1–13.
Robinson, C. A., jr (1952), 'Cleisthenes and ostracism', *AJA* 56, 23–6.
Sealey, R. (1960), 'Regionalism in archaic Athens', *Historia* 9, 155–80.

6. Democracy, empire and the Persian Wars

Ostracism and isegoria

Doenges, M. A. (1996), 'Ostracism and the "boulai" of Kleisthenes', *Historia* 45, 387–404.
Forsdyke, S. L. (2005), *Exile, Ostracism, and Democracy: The Politics of Expulsion in Ancient Greece*, Princeton: Princeton University Press.
Kagan, D. (1961), 'The origin and purposes of ostracism', *Hesperia* 30, 393–401.
Lewis, J. D. (1971), 'Isegoria at Athens: when did it begin?', *Historia* 20, 129–40.
Marr, J. and N. Worswick (1994), 'The institution of ostracism at Athens', *Ostraka* 3, 285–90.
Mion, M. (1986), 'Athenian democracy: politicization and constitutional restraints', *JPTh* 7, 219–38.
Nakategawa, Y. (1988), 'Isegoria in Herodotus', *Historia* 37, 257–75.
Raubitschek, A. E. (1951), 'The origin of ostracism', *AJA* 55, 221–9.
Stanton, G. R. (1970), 'The introduction of ostracism and Alcmeonid propaganda', *JHS* 90, 180–83.
Thomsen, R. (1972), *The Origin of Ostracism. A Synthesis*, Copenhagen: Gyldendal.

Woodhead, A. G. (1967), 'ΙΣΗΓΟΡΙΑ and the Council of 500', *Historia* 16, 129–40.

Herodotus' dialogue on constitutions

Brannan, P. T. (1963), 'Herodotus and history. The constitutional debate preceeding Darius' accession', *Traditio* 19, 427–38.

Evans, J. A. S. (1981), 'Notes on the debate of the Persian grandees in Herodotus 3, 80–82', *QUCC* 36, 69–84.

Forsdyke, S. (2006), 'Herodotus, political history and political thought', in C. Dewald and J. Marincola, *The Cambridge Companion to Herodotus*, Cambridge: Cambridge University Press, 224–41.

Gammie, J. G. (1986), 'Herodotus on kings and tyrants. Objective historiography or conventional portraiture?', *JNES* 45, 171–95.

Themistocles and the naval growth of Athens

Chambers, M. H. (1984), 'Themistocles and the Piraeus', in J. K. K. Rigsby, ed., *Studies Presented to Sterling Dow on His Eightieth Birthday*, Durham, NC: Duke University Press, 43–50.

Haas, C. J. (1985), 'Athenian naval power before Themistocles', *Historia* 34, 29–46.

Konstan, D. (1987), 'Persuasion, Greeks and empire', *Arethusa* 20, 59–73.

Lewis, D. M. (1961), 'Notes on the decree of Themistocles', *CQ*, New Series, Vol. 11, No. 1, 61–6.

Podlecki, A. J. (1975), *The Life of Themistocles: A Critical Survey of the Literary and Archaeological Evidence*, Montreal and London: McGill-Queen's University Press.

Robertson, N. (1982), 'The decree of Themistocles in its contemporary setting', *Phoenix* 36, 1–44.

Schreiner, J. H. (2002), 'The naval policy of Themistokles', in K. Ascani, ed., *Ancient History Matters: Studies Presented to Jens Erik Skydsgaard on His Seventieh Birthday*, Rome: L'Erma di Bretschneider, 199–202.

Usher, S. (1967), 'Architects of the Athenian empire: I: Themistocles; II: Pericles', *HT* XVII: 285–92; 402–8.

7. Democracy Accomplished

Ephialtes

Ann, J. L. (1987), 'The role of Ephialtes in the rise of Athenian democracy', *ClAnt* 6, 53–76.

Cawkwell, G. L. (1988), 'ΝΟΜΟΦΥΛΑΚΙΑ and the Areopagus', *JHS* 108, 1–12.

Dover, K. J. (1957), 'The political aspect of Aeschylus' *Eumenides*', *JHS* 77, 230–37.

Finley, J. H. (1966), 'Politics and early Attic tragedy', *HSPh* 71, 1–13.

Fornara, C. W. and L. J. Samons (1991), *Athens from Cleisthenes to Pericles*, Berkeley: University of California Press

Rihll, T. E. (1995), 'Democracy denied: why Ephialtes attacked the Areiopagus', *JHS* 115, 87–98.

Ruschenbusch, E. (1966), 'Ephialtes', *Historia* 15, 369–76.

Sealey, R. (1964), 'Ephialtes', *CPh* 59, 11–22.

Wallace, R. W. (1974), 'Ephialtes and the Areopagus', *GRBS* 15, 259–69.

Aeschylus and democracy

Bowie, A. M. (1993), 'Religion and politics in Aeschylus' *Oresteia*', *CQ*, New Series, 43, 10–31.

Dover, K. J. (1957), 'The political aspect of Aeschylus, Eumenides', *JHS* 77, 230–37.

Finley, J. H. (1966), 'Politics and early Attic tragedy', *HSCP* 71, 1–13.

Rhodes, P. J. (2003), 'Nothing to do with democracy: Athenian drama and the polis', *JHS* 123, 104–19.

Saxonhouse, A. W. (2009), 'Foundings vs. Constitutions: Ancient Tragedy and the Origins Of Political Community', in S. Salkever, ed., *The Cambridge Companion to Ancient Greek Political Thought*, Cambridge: Cambridge University Press, 42–64.

Sewell, R. (2007), *In the Theatre of Dionysos: Democracy and Tragedy in Ancient Athens*, Jefferson, NC and London: McFarland & Co.

Sidwell, K. (1996), 'The politics of Aeschylus' "Eumenides"', *Classics Ireland* 3, 182–203.

Stoessl, F. (1952), 'Aeschylus as a political thinker', *AJPh* 73, 113–39.

Zak, W. F. (1995), *The Polis and the Divine Order: The Oresteia, Sophocles, and the Defense of Democracy*, Lewisburg, PA: Bucknell University Press.

8. Building a Unique Community

Pericles and the funeral speech

Bosworth, A. B. (2000), 'The historical context of Thucydides' funeral oration', *JHS* 120, 1–16.

Harris, E. M. (1992), 'Pericles' praise of Athenian democracy: Thucydides 2, 37, 1', *HSPh* 94, 157–67.

Jacoby, F. (1944), '*Patrios nomos*: state burial in Athens and the public cemetery in the kerameikos', *JHS* 64, 37–66.

Kagan, D. (1990), *Pericles of Athens and the Birth of Democracy*, London: Secker and Warburg.

Podlecki, A. J. (1998), *Perikles and His Circle*, London: Routledge.

Pritchard, D. (1996), 'Thucydides and the tradition of the Athenian funeral oration', *AH* 26, 137–50.

Sicking, C. M. J. (1995), 'The general purport of Pericles' funeral oration and last speech', *Hermes* 123, 404–25.

Waggaman, C. (2000), 'The Problem of Pericles', in M. Gustafson, ed., *Thucydides' Theory of International Relations: A Lasting Possession*, 197–220.

Walcot, P. (1973), 'The funeral speech. A study of values', *G&R* 20, 111–21.

Ziolkowski, J. E. (1981), *Thucydides and the Tradition of Funeral Speeches at Athens*, Salem: Ayer.

Pericles and Athenian citizenship

Boegehold, A. L. and A. C. Scafuro, eds (1993), *Athenian Identity and Civic Ideology*, Baltimore, Md: Johns Hopkins University Press.

Braund, D. (1994), 'The luxuries of Athenian democracy', *G&R* 41, 41–8.

Carawan, E. (2007–8), 'Pericles the Younger and the citizenship law', *CJ* 103, 383–406.

Davies, J. K. (1978), 'Athenian citizenship. The descent group and the alternatives', *CJ* 73, 105–21.

Farenga, V. (2006), *Citizen and Self in Ancient Greece: Individuals Performing Justice and the Law*, Cambridge and New York: Cambridge University Press.

French, A. (1994), 'Pericles' citizenship law', *AHB* 8, 71–5.

Lape, S. (2010), *Race and Citizen Identity in the Classical Athenian Democracy*, Cambridge: Cambridge University Press.

Patterson, C. (1981), *Pericles' Citizenship Law of 451–50 B.C.*, New York: Arno Press.

Vartsos, I. A. (2008), 'Fifth-century Athens: citizens and citizenship', *Parnassos* 50, 65–74.

Walter, K. R. (1983), 'Perikles' citizenship law', *ClAnt* 2, 314–36.

Liturgies and benefactors

Christ, M. R. (1990), 'Liturgy avoidance and antidosis in classical Athens', *TAPAh* 120, 147–69.

—(2007), 'The evolution of the eisphora in classical Athens', *CQ* 57, No. 1, 53–69.

Christesen, P. (2003), 'Economic rationalism in fourth-century BCE Athens', *G&R*, 50, No. 1, 31–56.

Davies, J. K. (1967), 'Demosthenes on liturgies: A note', *JHS* 87, 33–40.

Hunter, V. (2000), 'Policing public debtors in classical Athens', *Phoenix* 54, No. 1/2, 21–38.

Millett, P. (1998) 'The rhetoric of reciprocity in classical Athens', in C. Gill and N. Postlethwaite (eds) *Reciprocity in Ancient Greece*, Oxford: Oxford University Press, 227–53.

Shipton, K. M. W. (1997), 'The private banks in fourth-century B.C. Athens: a reappraisal', *CQ*, New Series, 47, No. 2, 396–422.

Steiner, A. (2002), 'Private and public: links between symposion and syssition in fifth-century Athens', *ClAnt* 21, No. 2, 347–79.

Aristocratic citizenship and ephebia

Conomis, N. C. (1959), 'On the oath of the Athenian epheboi', *Athena* 63, 119–31.
Palagia, O. and D. Lewis (1989), 'The ephebes of Erechtheis, 333/2 B.C. and their dedication', *BSA* 84, 333–44.
Reinmuth, O. W. (1948), 'The ephebate and citizenship in Attica', *TAPhA* 79, 211–31.
—(1952), 'The genesis of the Athenian Ephebia', *TAPhA* 83, 34–50.
—(1961), 'Ephebic texts from Athens', *Hesperia* 30, No. 1, 8–22.
Roberts, J. T. (1986), 'Aristocratic democracy. The perseverance of timocratic principles in Athenian government', *Athenaeum* 64, 355–69.
Siewert, P. (1977), 'The Ephebic Oath in fifth-century Athens', *JHS* 97, 102–11.
Steinbock, B. (2011), 'A lesson in patriotism: Lycurgus' *Against Leocrates*, the ideology of the ephebeia, and Athenian social memory', *ClAnt* 30, 279–317.
Welsh, D. (1977), 'The age of majority in Athens', *EMC* 21, 77–85.

Women in democratic Athens

Blundell, S. (1998), *Women in Classical Athens*, London: Bristol Classical Press.
Cantarella, E. (1987), *Pandora's Daughters: The Role and Status of Women in Greek and Roman Antiquity*, English trans., Baltimore and London: Johns Hopkins University Press.
Foley, H. P. (1982), 'The "female intruder" reconsidered: women in Aristophanes' *Lysistrata* and *Ecclesiazusae*', *CPh* 77, No. 1, 1–21.
Gould, J. (1980), 'Law, custom and myth: aspects of the social position of women in classical Athens', *JHS* 100, 38–59.
Just, R. (1989), *Women in Athenian Law and Life*, London: Routledge.
Lewis, S. (2002), *The Athenian Woman: An Iconographic Handbook*, London and New York: Routledge.
Loraux, N. (1993), *The Children of Athena: Athenian Ideas about Citizenship and the Division between the Sexes*, Princeton: Princeton University Press.
Pomeroy, S. (1995), *Goddesses, Whores, Wives, and Slaves: Women in Classical Antiquity*, 2nd edn, New York: Schocken.
Richter, D. C. (1971), 'The position of women in classical Athens', *CJ* 67, No. 1, 1–8.
Seltman, C. (1955), 'The status of women in Athens', *G&R* 2, No. 3, 119–24.
Westlake, H. D. (1980), 'The "Lysistrata" and the war', *Phoenix* 34, No. 1, 38–54.

Metics

Arnaoutoglou, I. (1994), 'Associations and patronage in ancient Athens', *AncSoc* 25, 5–17.

Baba, K. (1984), 'On Kerameikos Inv. I 388 (Seg XXII, 79): a note on the formation of the Athenian metic-status', *BSA* 79, 1–5.

Bakewell, G. (1999), 'εὔνους καὶ πόλει σωτήριος / μέτοικος : metics, tragedy, and civic ideology', *SyllClass* 10, 43–64.

Duncan-Jones, R. P. (1980), 'Metic numbers in Periclean Athens', *Chiron* 10, 101–9.

Epstein, S. (2008), 'Why did Attic building projects employ free laborers rather than slaves?', *ZPE* 166, 108–12.

Németh, G. (2001), 'Metics in Athens', *AAntHung* 41, 331–48.

Whitehead, D. (1977), *The Ideology of the Athenian Metic*, Cambridge: Cambridge University Press.

Winton, R. (2007), 'Thucydides 2.13.6–7: oldest, youngest, hoplites, metics', *CQ* 57, No. 1, 298–301.

9. Democracy and the Problem of Individual Leadership

Pericles

Andrews, J. A. (2004), 'Pericles on the Athenian constitution (Thuc. 2.37)', *AJPh* 125, 539–61.

Balot, R. K. (2001), 'Pericles' anatomy of democratic courage', *AJPh* 122, 505–26.

— (2004), 'Courage in the democratic polis', *CQ*, New Series, 54, 406–23.

Chambers, M. H. (1957), 'Thucydides and Pericles', *HSPH* 62, 79–92.

Frost, F. J. (1964), 'Pericles, Thucydides, son of Melesias, and Athenian politics before the war', *Historia* 13, No. 4, 385–99.

Harvey, Y. (1991), 'How do the people decide?: Thucydides on Periclean rhetoric and civic instruction', *AJPh* 112, 179–200.

Kagan, D. (1990), *Pericles of Athens and the Birth of Democracy*, London: Secker and Warburg.

Samons II, L. J., ed. (2007), *The Cambridge Companion to the Age of Pericles*, Cambridge: Cambridge University Press.

Sealey, R. (1956), 'The entry of Pericles into history', *Hermes* 84, 234–47.

Alcibiades

Bloedow, E. F. (1973), *Alcibiades Reexamined*, Wiesbaden: Franz Steiner Verlag.

Ellis, W. (1989), *Alcibiades*, London: Routledge.

Farenga, V. (2006), *Citizen and Self in Ancient Greece: Individuals Performing Justice and the Law*, Cambridge and New York: Cambridge University Press.

Faulkner, R. (2007), *The Case for Greatness: Honorable Ambition and Its Critics*, New Haven, Conn.: Yale University Press.

Forde, S. (1989), *The Ambition to Rule: Alcibiades and the Politics of Imperialism in Thucydides*, Ithaca: Cornell University Press.

Gribble, D. (1999), *Alcibiades and Athens: A Study in Literary Presentation*, Oxford: Oxford University Press.

Rosivach, V. J. (1988), 'The tyrant in Athenian Democracy', *QUCC* 30, No. 3, 43–57.

Seager, R. (1967), 'Alcibiades and the charge of aiming at tyranny', *Historia* 16, 6–18.

—(2001), 'Xenophon and Athenian democratic ideology', *CQ*, New Series, 51, 385–97.

Stahl, H. P. (1973), 'Speeches and Course of Events in Books Six and Seven of Thucydides', in P. A. Stadter, ed., *The Speeches in Thucydides. A Collection of Original Studies with a Bibliography*, Chapel Hill: University of North Carolina Press, 60–77.

10. Athens, the Democratic Empire

Thucydides, Athenian imperialism and democracy

Andrewes, A. (1959), 'Thucydides on the causes of the war', *CQ*, New Series, 9, No. 2, 223–39.

Forde, S. (1986), 'Thucydides on the causes of Athenian imperialism', *APRS*, 80, No. 2, 433–48.

Huxley, G. L. (1983), 'Thucydides on the growth of Athenian power', *PRIA* 83C, 191–204.

Orwin, C. (1986), 'Justifying empire: the speech of the Athenians at Sparta and the problem of justice in Thucydides', *JP* 48, No. 1, 72–85.

Pope, M. (1988), 'Thucydides and democracy', *Historia* 37, No. 3, 276–96.

Wick, T. E. (1975), 'A note on Thucydides I,23,6 and ἡ ἀληθεστάτη πρόφασις', *AC* 44, 176–83.

Zumbrunnen, J. G. (2008), *Silence and Democracy: Athenian Politics in Thucydides' History*, University Park, PA: Pennsylvania State University Press.

Pericles' strategy

Bloedow, E. F. (1987), 'Pericles' powers in the counter-strategy of 431', *Historia* 36, 9–27.

Cawkwell, G. (1975), 'Thucydides' judgment of Periclean strategy', *YClS* 24, 53–70.

Knight, D. W. (1970), 'Thucydides and the war strategy of Perikles', *Mnemosyne* 23, 150–61.

Krentz, P. M. (1997), 'The strategic culture of Periclean Athens', in C. D. Hamilton and P. M. Krentz, eds, *Polis and Polemos: Essays on Politics, War, and History in Ancient Greece, in Honor of Donald Kagan*, Claremont, Calif.: Regina, 55–72.

Ober, J. (1996), 'Thucydides, Pericles and the strategy of defense', in id., *The Athenian Revolution. Essays on Ancient Greek Democracy and Political Theory*, Princeton: Princeton University Press, 72–85.

Wet, X. de (1969), 'The so-called defensive policy of Pericles', *AClass* 12, 103–19.

The Melian dialogue

Alker, Jr., H. R. (1988), 'The dialectical logic of Thucydides' Melian dialogue', *APRS* 82, No. 3, 805–20.

Amit, M. (1968), 'The Melian dialogue and history', *Athenaeum* 46, 216–35.

Bosworth, A. B. (1993), 'The humanitarian aspect of the Melian dialogue', *JHS* 113, 30–44.

Low, P. (2005), 'Looking for the language of Athenian imperialism', *JHS* 125, 92–111.

Morrison, J. W. (2000), 'Historical lessons in the Melian episode', *TAPhA* 130, 119–48.

Seaman, M. G. (1997), 'The Athenian expedition to Melos in 416 B.C.', *Historia* 46, 385–41.

11. Democracy and the Effects of the Peloponnesian War: Crisis and Reconstruction

The Sicilian disaster

Buck, R. (1988), 'The Sicilian expedition', *AHB* 2, 73–9.

Dover, K. J. (1981), 'Thucydides' historical judgement. Athens and Sicily', *PRIA* 81, 232–8.

Frank, D. H. (1984), 'The power of truth. Political foresight in Thucydides' account of the Sicilian expedition (6.32–42)', *Prudentia* 16, 99–107.

Harrison, T. (2000), 'Sicily in the Athenian imagination: Thucydides and the Persian Wars', in C. Smith, J. Serrati, eds, *Sicily from Aeneas to Augustus: New Approaches in Archaeology and History*, Edinburgh: University of Edinburgh Press, 84–96.

Jordan, B. (2000), 'The Sicilian expedition was a Potemkin fleet', *CQ*, New Series, 50, 63–79.

Powell, C. A. (1979), 'Religion and the Sicilian expedition', *Historia* 28, 15–31.

Smith, D. G. (2004), 'Thucydides' ignorant Athenians and the drama of the Sicilian expedition', *SyllClass* 15, 33–70.

The Old Oligarch

Fuks, A. (1954), 'The Old Oligarch', *Scripta Hierosolymitana* 1, 21–35.

Hornblower, S. (2000), 'The "Old Oligarch" (Pseudo-Xenophon's "Athenaion Politeia") and Thucydides: a fourth-century date for the "Old Oligarch"?', in P. Flensted-Jensen, T. Heine Nielsen and L. Rubinstein (eds) *Polis & Politics: Studies in Ancient Greek History Presented to Mogens Herman Hansen on his Sixtieth Birthday*, 20 August 2000, Copenhagen: Museum Tusculanum Press, 363–84.

Nakategawa, Y. (1995), 'Athenian democracy and the concept of justice in Pseudo-Xenophon's *Athenaion Politeia*', *Hermes* 123, No. 1, 123, 28–46.

Starr, C. G. (1978), 'Thucydides on sea power', *Mnemosyne* 31, 343–50.

The Four Hundred

Taylor, M. C. (2002), 'Implicating the demos: a reading of Thucydides on the rise of the Four Hundred', *JHS* 122, 91–108.

Walters, K. R. (1973), *Ancestral Laws and the Ancestral Constitution in the Oligarchic Movements of the Late Fifth-Century Athens*, Princeton: Princeton University Press.

—(1976), 'The "ancestral constitution" and fourth-century historiography in Athens', *AJAH* 1, 129–44.

The Arginusae

Andrewes, A. (1974), 'The Arginusai trial', *Phoenix* 28, 112–22.

Asmonti, L. (2006), 'The Arginusae trial, the changing role of strategoi and the relationship between demos and military leadership in late fifth-century Athens', *BICS* 49, 1–22.

Graham, W. (1990), 'The battle of the Arginusae: a reappraisal', *CCC* 11, 234–49.

Hunt, P. (2001), 'The slaves and the generals of Arginusae', *AJPh* 122, No. 3, 359–80.

Aristophanes' *Frogs*

Aristophanes (1996), *Frogs*, edited with translation and notes by Alan H. Sommerstein, Warminster: Aris and Phillips.

Arnott, W. G. (1991), 'A lesson from the Frogs', *G&R* 38, 18–23.

Dover, K. J. (1993), 'The contest in Aristophanes' Frogs: the points at issue', in A. H. Sommerstein, ed., *Tragedy, Comedy and the Polis: Papers from the Greek Drama Conference. Nottingham, 18–20 July 1990*, Bari: Levante, 445–60.

Moorton, R. F. (1988), 'Aristophanes on Alcibiades', *GRBS* 29, 345–59.

The Thirty tyrants and amnesty

Carawan, E. (2006), 'Amnesty and accountings for the Thirty', *CQ*, New Series, 56, No. 1, 57–76.

Joyce, C. (2008), 'The Athenian amnesty and scrutiny of 403', *CQ*, New Series 58, No. 2, 507–18.

Loraux, N. (2002), *The Divided City: On Memory and Forgetting in Ancient Athens*, English trans., New York: Zone Books.

Quillin, J. M. (2002), 'Achieving amnesty: the role of events, institutions, and ideas', *TAPhA* 132, 71–107.

Stern, R. (2003), 'The Thirty at Athens in the summer of 404', *Phoenix* 57, 18–34.

Whitehead, D. (1982–3), 'Sparta and the Thirty Tyrants', *AncSoc* 13–14, 105–30.

Wolpert, A. (2002), *Remembering Defeat: Civil War and Civic Memory in Ancient Athens*, Baltimore: Johns Hopkins University Press.

The death of Socrates, public oratory and democracy

Calvert, B. (1984), 'The politicians of Athens in the Gorgias and Meno', *HPTh* 5, 1–15.

Colaiaco, J. A. (2001), *Socrates against Athens: Philosophy on Trial*, New York and London: Routledge.

Danzig, G. (2010), *Apologizing for Socrates: How Plato and Xenophon Created our Socrates*, Lanham, MD. and Plymouth: Lexington Books.

Green, R. K. (2001), *Democratic Virtue in the Trial and Death of Socrates: Resistance to Imperialism in Classical Athens*, New York and Oxford: Peter Lang.

Mara, G. M. (1997), *Socrates' Discursive Democracy: Logos and Ergon in Platonic Political Philosophy*, Albany: SUNY Press.

Raditsa, L. (1979), 'The collapse of democracy at Athens and the trial of Socrates', *RSA* 9, 11–28.

Schofield, M. (2006), *Plato: Political Philosophy*, Oxford and New York: Oxford University Press.

Sharples, R. W. (1994), 'Plato on democracy and expertise', *G&R* 41, 49–56.

Svoboda, M. (2007), 'Athens, the unjust student of rhetoric: a dramatic historical interpretation of Plato's "Gorgias"', *RSQ* 37, No. 3, 275–305.

Tarnopolsky, C. H. (2010), *Prudes, Perverts, and Tyrants: Plato's Gorgias and the Politics of Shame*, Princeton and Oxford: Princeton University Press.

Wallach, J. R. (1988), 'Socratic citizenship', *HPTh* 9, 393–413.

The second Athenian League

Baron, C. A. (2006), 'The Aristoteles decree and the expansion of the second Athenian League', *Hesperia* 75, 379–95.

Cargill, J. (1981), *The Second Athenian League: Empire or Free Alliance?*, Berkeley and London: University of California Press.

—(1982), 'Hegemony, not empire. The Second Athenian league', *AncW* 5, 91–102.

—(1996), 'The decree of Aristoteles: some epigraphical details', *AncW* 27, No. 1, 39–51.

Horsley, G. H. R. (1982), 'The second Athenian confederacy', in ibid., ed., *Hellenika. Essays on Greek History and Politics North Ryde*, NSW, 131–50.

Kallet-Marx, R. M. (1985), 'Athens, Thebes and the foundation of the second Athenian League', *ClAnt* 4, 127–51.

13. Athenian Democracy in the Fourth Century

Democracy and the Social War

Cawkwell, G. L. (1981), 'Notes on the failure of the second Athenian confederacy', *JHS* 101, 40–55.

Leopold, J. W. (1981), 'Demosthenes on distrust of tyrants', *GRBS* 22, XXI, 227–46.

Michelini, A. M. (1998), 'Isocrates' civic invective: *Acharnians* and *On the Peace*', *TAPhA* 128, 115–33.

Sealey, R. (1955), 'Athens after the social war', *JHS* 75, 74–81.

Demosthenes, Philip and democracy

Cawkwell, G. (1978), *Philip of Macedon*, London: Faber and Faber.

Ellis, J. R. and R. D. Milns, *The Spectre of Philip. Demosthenes' First Philippic, Olynthiacs and Speech On the Peace: A Study in Historical Evidence*, Sydney: Sydney University Press.

Hammond, N. G. L. (1994), *Philip of Macedon*, London: Duckworth.

MacDowell, D. M. (2009), *Demosthenes the Orator*, Oxford: Oxford University Press.

Miller, J. (2002), 'Warning the *démos*: political communication with a democratic audience in Demosthenes', *HPTh* 23, No. 3, 401–17.

Perlman, S. (1973), *Philip and Athens*, Cambridge and New York: Cambridge University Press.

Sealey, R. (1993), *Demosthenes and His Time: A Study in Defeat*, New York and Oxford: Oxford University Press.

Worthington, I., ed. (2000), *Demosthenes: Statesman and Orator*, London: Routledge.

Athens and Alexander

Ashton, N. G. (1983), 'The Lamian War. A false start?', *Antichthon* 17, 47–63.

Habicht, C. (1996), 'Athens, Samos, and Alexander the Great', *PAPhS* 140, No. 3, 397–415.

—(1997), *Athens from Alexander to Antony*, Eng. trans., Cambridge, MA: Harvard
    University Press.
Mitchel, F. (1965), 'Athens in the age of Alexander', *G&R* 12, 189–204.
Schwenk, C. J. (1987), *Athens in the Age of Alexander*, Chicago: Ares.

Index of Passages

Index of Names

95929556R00147

Made in the USA
Lexington, KY
15 August 2018